The Railways of Southern England: The Main Lines

The Railways of Southern England: The Main Lines

Edwin Course

B. T. Batsford Ltd
London

© Edwin Course 1973
First published 1973

ISBN 0 7134 0490 6

Printed and bound in Great Britain
by Cox & Wyman Ltd, London and Fakenham
for the Publishers
B. T. Batsford Ltd
4 Fitzhardinge Street, London W1H 0AH

Contents

The Illustrations

Diagrams and Maps

Acknowledgments

The author and publishers would like to thank the
following for permission to reproduce the illustrations:
A W Burges for nos 7, 44; H C Casserley for 13, 27, 32;
Alan A Jackson for 8, 9, 11, 12, 15, 18, 22, 31, 34, 40, 41,
46; The Mansell Collection for 4, 35, 20; the Ken Nunn
Collection for 6; H J Patterson Rutherford for 17;
Portsmouth City Record Office for 39, 47, 48; Southampton Record Office for 43; the Trustees of the British
Museum for 1, 10, 25, 28, 38. Nos 5, 16, 19, 30 are from
the Publishers' collection, 14, 36, 37, 42 were photographed by the Author, and 2, 3, 21, 23, 24, 26, 29, 33,
45 are from the Author's collection.

Preface

This book gives a description of the railways of Southern
England as they appeared to the interested traveller in 1971. It
concentrates on the railways, and any contributions it may make
to the knowledge of the economic and social history of Southern
England are accidental. It cannot be claimed to be a Domesday
Survey for 1971 for, although the maps cover every mile of railway in standard form, the text accentuates the features which
have given most pleasure to the author. For instance, station
buildings of special interest receive careful attention, but there is
no attempt to reveal the colour of the bricks of every station in
Southern England. The descriptions are intended for the general
reader who is interested in looking at railways, and for the type
of railway enthusiast who reads the itineraries so carefully prepared for the rail tours of the established societies. Although
essential historical background is provided, this is unimpeded by
references or footnotes. However, the author hopes that his work
may fall into the hands of the occasional academic who has an
interest in such things, and would ask anybody who would like
to know about the evidence used, either in general or on particular points, to write to him so that this information may be
made available. But a good indication of the 'credentials' for the
text is given in Sources and Acknowledgments.

Every public railway and most private lines which have
operated in the South, east of the London to Southampton main
line (which is included) and outside the old London Transport
area, are described: the main lines in Volume One, the secondary
lines in Volume Two and the independent railways in Volume

Three. Some minimal knowledge of railway equipment and railway geography and history will prove an aid to appreciation of the text. A full list of the companies involved is given in Appendix 1, but the dominant roles are played by the London & South Western (LSWR), the London, Brighton & South Coast (LBSCR), the London, Chatham & Dover (LCDR) and the South Eastern (SER). In 1899, the management and operations of the last two companies were unified in the South Eastern & Chatham Managing Committee (SECR), and in 1923 all the companies were absorbed into the Southern Railway (SR). In 1948, the Southern Railway was replaced by the Southern Region of British Railways who now operate nearly all the public railways in the South of England.

The railway mileage has risen and declined. The first public railway was opened between Canterbury and Whitstable in 1830; the last to be constructed was the Southern's new route to New Romney in 1937. The peak period for construction was the 1840s, and for closures, the 1960s. (At the end of 1969 the route mileage had dropped to the level reached in 1880.) Apart from closures, the outward signs of both decline and development are mentioned for each of the lines. For instance, the decline of the traditional signal box and semaphore signal is compared to the increase in power signal boxes and colour light signals. While the book is about railways rather than steam locomotives, relics associated with them, such as the sites of engine sheds or the inexplicably surviving water column, are recorded.

Finally, although this is essentially a book about railways, it would be foolish to suggest that they operate in a social and economic vacuum. Traffic is vital and, in the South, passengers have always been the main source of revenue. For many years there has been a strong orientation to London, and the decline in day-excursion traffic to south coast resorts has been amply compensated by the increase in long-distance season-ticket holders. While the passenger is dominant, there are such things as coal trains from the Kent coalfield, and gypsum is carried from the mine at Mountfield. But the electric train running up from Brighton with its load of commuters and day visitors is far more characteristic. Many Southerners have never lost the habit of going 'up to town' by train.

This book is intended as a traveller's companion for those who enjoy looking at railways and appreciate the way they show their past story, their present function and, in some degree, their future. It can be read at home, but the ideal reader will also wish to see at first hand the objects of interest described even though, in some cases, he can travel by train no longer.

Sources and Acknowledgments

Although this book has one author, it has many contributors. It relies partly on the people and institutions whose help is acknowledged below, and partly on numerous people who, in times past, produced the documents which have provided the source material.

Documentary source material falls into two main categories—the primary material, arising from the operation of the railways, and the secondary material consisting of things that have been written about them. Each of the main categories may be subdivided. For instance, primary material was produced by the railways themselves, by government departments with a responsibility for the railways, and by publishers, such as Bradshaw, who produced railway timetables and shareholder's guides. In addition to material which concentrates on railways, local papers, Ordnance Survey maps, local guide books, personal diaries and other writings all provide information. In fact, the problem for the writer may well be not to discover primary sources but rather to decide when he has enough, and may stop searching. The same problem applies to some extent with secondary sources, but in this case it is usually possible to read everything relevant which has been published. In this connection, George Ottley's monumental *Bibliography of British Railway History* is invaluable.

It is not intended to give an exhaustive list of everything consulted, but readers who are interested in the evidence for a particular statement are invited to write to the author for details of his source of information. However, the acknowledgments that follow will give a sufficient indication of the 'pedigree' of the book, and also provide an indication of where information is to be found. First, the most valuable thing an author can have is well-informed criticism, and two people in particular have contributed greatly in this way. Professor M. J. Wise supervised the writing of the thesis on which this book is based, and Alan A. Jackson has read and criticised both the thesis and the book. Other people have read all, or parts of, either the thesis or the book: in particular, Mr L. C. Johnson, former Archivist, British Transport Commission, and Mr Charles E. Lee. With apologies for names omitted, I retain correspondence with the following:

G. Barlow (RHDR); H. V. Borley (dates); Rixon Bucknall (Channel ports); C. R. Clinker (dates and Acts of Parliament); W. Dray (traffic statistics); Professor H. J. Dyos (railways and housing); C. Hadfield (canals); H. W. Hart (Southern Railway); the late P. Hollands (worked on railway construction); R. Job (Kent coalfield); the late R. Kirkland (commuter traffic); C. Maguire (Southern electrification); G. T. Moody (Southern Railway); B. N. Nunns (dating of pictures); F. O. Randall (Hundred of Hoo); R. C. Riley (LBSCR); H. J. P. Rutherford (pictorial records); Dr K. R. Sealy (railways and airports); J. G. Spence (Southern Railway); R. H. G. Thomas (local lines); R. Townsend (railway plans); J. Howard Turner (Southern Railway); A. G. Wells (East Kent) and the late C. Wright (ganger, SECR and BR).

Companies who have provided information include: United Glass Bottles, Pilkingtons, Cellactite and British Uralite, APCM and NCB. The following public libraries were visited: Brighton, Dover, Gravesend, Hastings, Maidstone, Portsmouth, Tonbridge and Southampton. Record offices providing information were as follows: East Sussex (Lewes), Hampshire (Winchester), Kent (Maidstone), London, Portsmouth, Southampton, Surrey (Kingston) and West Sussex (Chichester). Considerable material was made available in the House of Lords Record Office and in the libraries of the Institution of Civil Engineers and the Chartered

Institute of Transport. Finally, this book could not have been written in its present form without the co-operation of the British Transport Record Office with its three successive Archivists, Messrs Johnson, Atkinson and Foulkes. Acknowledgment is made to the staff at all these places who have helped me at some point during the last fifteen years. With regard to secondary sources, the relevant publications are listed in George Ottley's *Bibliography*. However, publications which have been especially useful or have appeared since the *Bibliography* are mentioned in the text. Numerous railway periodicals have been consulted but perhaps the *Railway Magazine* more than any other.

While those mentioned above have provided information, other people have helped in different ways. Typing, including the interpretation of unusually obscure handwriting, has been undertaken by Miss C. Morgan and Mrs Irene Candy; most of the diagrams were drawn by Miss Jane Holdsworth. Two people who have provided not only material help but also encouragement are Mr Peter Kemmis Betty of B. T. Batsford and my wife, who has also developed an unerring instinct for abandoned lines.

In conclusion, acknowledgment is due to the staff of the Southern Region. The author would hesitate to assess the number of hours spent in conversation with them during the last fifteen years and earlier, and in the course of which all kinds of information has come to light. And as will be appreciated from the text, in addition to verbal and documentary evidence, this book relies heavily on what might be called archaeological evidence. For instance, the remains of an abandoned station may be more informative than pages of a vaguely written book. But the men who built the railways and worked on them provide the essential element in the railway system which this book describes.

Abbreviations

BR	British Railways
DNSR	Didcot, Newbury & Southampton Railway
DPLR	Direct Portsmouth & London Railway
GCPFR	Guildford, Chichester, Portsmouth & Fareham Railway
GWR	Great Western Railway
LBSCR	London, Brighton & South Coast Railway
LCDR	London, Chatham & Dover Railway
LSWR	London & South Western Railway
MSWJR	Midland & South Western Junction Railway
RGRR	Reading, Guildford & Reigate Railway
SDR	Southampton & Dorchester Railway
SECR	South Eastern & Chatham Managing Committee
SER	South Eastern Railway
SR	Southern Railway

1

The South Eastern
Railway to Dover

The line to Dover was the first main line to be built through
Kent and has always been one of the most important. But
although it served Kent, this was not the main aim of the promoters. For instance the South Eastern prospectus of October
1835 refers to the eastern terminus at Dover as 'the great commercial and political outlet to the continent', and there is plenty
of evidence to confirm the view that this line was regarded as not
so much a route to Dover as a route to Europe and beyond. Kent
in itself was not very favourable for railway development, having
neither the easy relief to permit low construction costs, nor the
major cities and industrial undertakings to produce a high
revenue. Moreover the principal towns and industrial undertakings of North Kent were well served by water transport.

Partly for this reason, early horse railways or tramroads were
almost non-existent. In *The Times* of 21 December 1829, a
prospectus appeared for a line through North Kent with Thomas
Telford as engineer. The following year plans were deposited for
another railway down to Ramsgate designed by Henry Palmer.
He was responsible for a number of proposals, including a line to
Brighton with cars suspended like panniers on either side of an
elevated central rail, motion being achieved by means of sails.[1]
In 1832, Palmer produced a plan for a line from a point near the
Regents Canal and the West India Docks in London to Canter-
bury. The Thames and the Medway were to be crossed by train
ferries, and beyond Canterbury the rolling stock was to pass

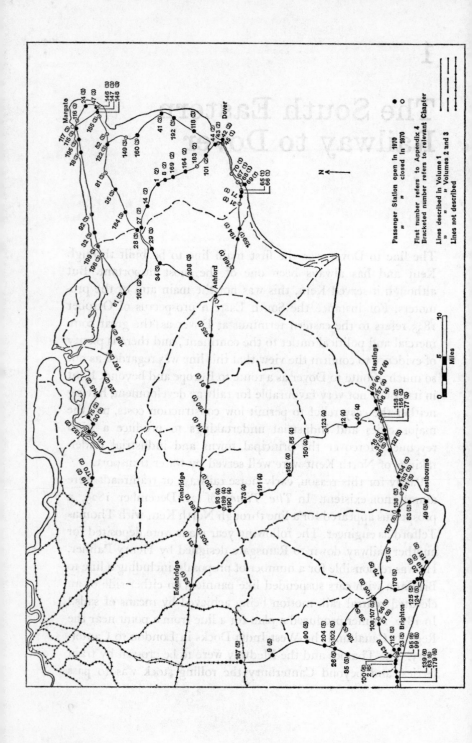

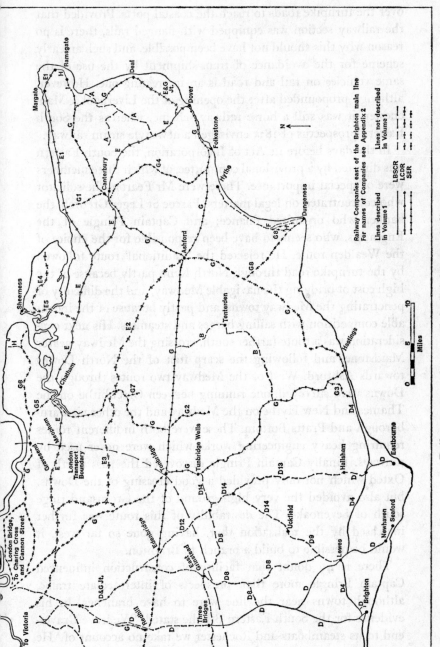

Railway companies east of the Brighton main line

over the turnpike roads to reach the coastal ports. Provided that the railway section was equipped with flanged rails, there is no reason why this should not have been possible, and such an early scheme for the avoidance of trans-shipment by the use of the same vehicles on rail and road is an interesting one. However, although propounded after the opening of the Liverpool & Manchester, it was still a horse railway scheme, whereas the South Eastern prospectus of 1835 envisaged a new-style steam railway.

In the days before its Act of Incorporation, the South Eastern was directed by a provisional committee, of which three members were of special importance. These were Mr Fearon, the solicitor who concentrated on legal matters; Pascoe St Leger Grenfell, the banker who organised finance; and Captain Pringle of the Engineers, who seems to have been responsible for the choice of the Wealden route. He rejected the 'traditional' route followed by the turnpike road through North Kent, partly because of the high cost of bridging the navigable Medway, and the difficulty of penetrating the Medway towns, and partly because of the inevitable competition with sailing barges and steamers. His next consideration was a route farther south, crossing the Medway nearer Maidstone, and following the scarp foot of the North Downs towards Ashford. West of the Medway two routes through the Downs were surveyed, one running between Greenhithe on the Thames and New Hythe on the Medway and the other via Farnborough and Pratts Bottom. These were both indifferent routes requiring heavy engineering works which were never used by railways. Finally Captain Pringle discovered the pass north of Oxted which not only provided a good crossing of the Downs, but also avoided the very high ground of the Greensand ridge south of Sevenoaks. The desirability of this route was further increased by the realisation that, having gone so far west, it would be possible to build a branch to Brighton.

There is no doubt that facility of construction influenced Captain Pringle more than prospects of intermediate traffic, although towns near the line were to have branches. In his evidence for the South Eastern Bill, he stated: 'We leave Gravesend to its steamboats and Rochester we take no account of.' He

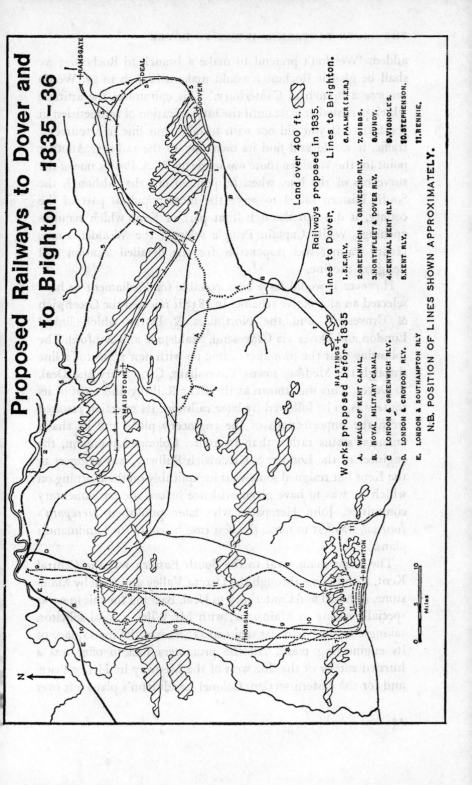

Proposed Railways to Dover and to Brighton 1835–36

Land over 400 ft.

Railways proposed in 1835.

Lines to Brighton.

6. PALMER (S.E.R.)
7. GIBBS.
8. CUNDY.
9. VIGNOLES.
10. STEPHENSON.
11. RENNIE,

Lines to Dover.

1. S.E. RLY.
2. GREENWICH & GRAVESEND RLY.
3. NORTHFLEET & DOVER RLY.
4. CENTRAL KENT RLY
5. KENT RLY.

Works proposed before 1835

A. WEALD OF KENT CANAL.
B. ROYAL MILITARY CANAL.
C. LONDON & GREENWICH RLY.
D. LONDON & CROYDON RLY.
E. LONDON & SOUTHAMPTON RLY

N.B. POSITION OF LINES SHOWN APPROXIMATELY.

N

0 5 10

Miles

added: 'We don't pretend to make a branch to Rochester; we shall be glad if Rochester would make a branch to us. We do propose a branch to Canterbury.' This epitomises the attitude which persisted at least until the intensification of competition in the fifties—if you did not wish to take your line to a source of traffic, it would still find its own way to the railway. Another point for the Wealden route was made by W. A. Provis, one of the surveyors of the line, when he pointed out that although the South Eastern failed to serve the most populous part of the county, it did run through 'that part of Kent which requires opening'. While Captain Pringle selected the Wealden route, Henry Palmer was responsible for the detailed location and design of the line.

However it would have been possible for Parliament to have selected an alternative scheme. In 1835 it rejected the Greenwich & Gravesend, and the Northfleet & Dover which linked London and Dover via Gravesend, Maidstone and Ashford. The following year the promoters came up with new plans for a line through the Medway towns, Faversham, Canterbury and Deal, to Dover. This was known as the Kent Railway and most of its route was to be followed by later railways. Its rejection resulted from the imperfections of the engineer's plans and its shaky financial status rather than its route. Colonel Landmann, the engineer of the London & Greenwich Railway, was engineer to the Kent but resigned somewhat inexplicably on the morning on which he was to have given evidence before the parliamentary committee. John Herepath, who later published *Herepath's Journal*, was left to make the best case he could for Landmann's plans.

The other main rival to the South Eastern was the Central Kent, with its line through the Darent Valley and then by Maidstone, Ashford and Canterbury to Deal. Backing for this line was specially strong in Maidstone, with Mr Wiles, a local solicitor, taking a leading part. Its main weakness was the inadequacy of its engineering plans. All the promoters had to offer was a hurried survey of the line west of the Medway by Henry Price, and for the eastern section, Colonel Landmann's plans left over from the rejected Northfleet & Dover Railway. Price himself discovered errors in the levels, and this brought the Central Kent's plans into disrepute. Later they were revised and improved, and were deposited regularly each year from 1836 until 1842. After that the Central Kent faded away. All three concerns —the Central Kent, the Kent and the South Eastern—were seeking continental traffic, but each had subsidiary objectives. The Central Kent was especially concerned with the interests of Maidstone, the Kent was intended to feed traffic on to the London & Greenwich, and the South Eastern attached great importance to its branch line to Brighton.

Rejecting the Kent and the Central Kent in no way obliged the parliamentary committee to authorise the roundabout Wealden route of the South Eastern, and the South Eastern Committee did not rely exclusively on the force of their arguments. For instance, the committee of investigation on the North Kent Bill of 1846 noted that they had supplied Mr Bonham, who was a member of the parliamentary committee, with scrip at par, which he was able to re-sell at a premium. However there is no evidence that this influenced the committee's decision. One of the arguments against the South Eastern was that it missed the main centres of population. The Kent Railway claimed to have 278,580 persons within five miles of its line compared to the South Eastern's 115,313. Mr Yeats, the South Eastern secretary, undertook a similar calculation and produced figures of 273,082 for the Kent against 223,642 for the South Eastern. But there could be no serious suggestion that there were more people in the Weald than in North Kent, and in order to make its case, the South Eastern had to invoke the branch lines they intended to construct including those to Maidstone, to Hastings, and to Canterbury and Thanet. (In fact, with the exception of Hastings, these places were all served by 1846.)

Another more forceful argument was that whereas North Kent was already well served by water transport, especially since the Weald of Kent Canal had failed to materialise, the Wealden area was badly served. Among the numerous witnesses for the South Eastern Bill was Mr Neve, a farmer and surveyor from

Benenden, near Cranbrook. He described the way in which hops, corn and timber in his locality went by road to Maidstone, and on to London by the rivers Medway and Thames. For their heavy soil, and for hop-growing in particular, they needed good supplies of manure. Mainly for the hops, rags came from London by water and road, Seaweed was brought from Folkestone; the cost of carrying chalk was prohibitive, but some lime was used. Neve kept sheep which grazed during much of the year on Romney Marsh. They were driven to Smithfield Market, spending about a week on the road, and losing on average about four pounds of their weight. He felt that quite apart from the direct benefit of railway transport, it could also be used to bring in shingle and gravel to improve the dirt roads of the Weald.

Mr Stedley of Ashford was a timber merchant, buying mainly oak, ash and elm, and shipping most of it from Faversham, with smaller quantities from Rye and Maidstone. He mentioned in particular the parish roads of Smarden which in winter were impassable for heavy traffic, and the fact that some of the turn-pike trusts charged double tolls after 1 November. He was particularly interested in developing a trade in chalk, which was not only useful as a manure and for making lime, but also for cement manufacture.[2]

Mr Turner was the proprietor of a paper mill at Chafford near Penshurst, using rags from London as his raw material. He had ceased relying on water power by installing a steam engine, which consumed about 500 tons of coal per annum. He purchased coal at Rochester and paid 8s (40p) per ton for conveyance up the Medway to Tonbridge and 2s (10p) per ton for the road haul on to Chafford. The South Eastern would bring his coal to Penshurst and also handle most of the paper output of about 50 hundred-weights per week.

Mr Delves, a house agent from the residential area of Tun-bridge Wells was confident that the railway would encourage people to move into the area, rather than away from it.

Most of the witnesses were concerned with the benefits which only the South Eastern would bring, but the fish interests of London and the Kent coasts could have been served by any one of the three proposed railways. Mr Tapley, a fish salesman from Billingsgate Market, stated that fish delivered by road took about twenty-one hours, and by sea from eight hours to five days depending on wind and tide. (Presumably the steamers did not carry fish.) Mr Brown, the honorary secretary of the Committee for Promoting Fisheries of the South Eastern Counties, was particularly concerned with the advantage which would be enjoyed by the fishermen of the southern and western counties once the railway from Southampton was completed. Not only would the South Eastern Railway counteract this advantage; it would also open up new markets for fish in the Wealden district.

Many other witnesses appeared, combining to give a very fair picture of economic activity in the Weald of Kent before the coming of the railway. Their evidence indicated the weight of traffic the railway hoped to carry; passenger traffic was forecast by means of population statistics and traffic surveys. For instance, Mr Storey, a coal merchant, who carried out a traffic census from the Angel at Strood in August and September 1834. In the following year he made similar counts at Godstone and at Bromley. Evidence was also taken from clerks at the steamer and stage-coach offices. In common with most of the companies at this time, the South Eastern expected to get more revenue from passengers than from freight, but unlike other companies, in this respect its forecast was correct.

From a national point of view, the roundabout route through the Weald was undoubtedly desirable, but whether in the long run it was a good thing for the South Eastern is doubtful. It was an accepted principle that it was unwise to attempt to create a new line of traffic flow where one was already established. This was exactly what the South Eastern did, with a line which, especially between Tonbridge and Ashford, ran across the 'grain' of the established road and water network. Even building the Wealden route first would have been less important if the South Eastern had not somewhat complacently left the North Kent route between the Medway towns and Faversham unoccupied, to form a breeding ground for the most unwelcome competition that developed into the London, Chatham & Dover Railway. Even making full allowance for the influence of Tunbridge Wells and the attractions of Brighton, it is still surprising that the first main line should have been built through the Weald.

Authorisation by Parliament was one essential; the raising of sufficient capital was the other. Three vital statistics determined the viability of a railway company: the capital expended on land, construction costs and equipment; the cost of operating; and the revenue. The Liverpool & Manchester had paid 10 per cent and, like many companies at the time, the South Eastern forecast a similar dividend for its shareholders. Estimates of revenue were based on existing traffic, with some allowance for the inevitable expansion which would follow the opening of the line. Operating costs were obtained by adapting the costs of the Liverpool & Manchester Railway. Construction costs depended on the value of the land taken, and the extent of the engineering works.

It was decided that the line could be built and equipped for £1,400,000, and in addition Parliament authorised the company to raise £450,000 by mortgage loan. The money was raised in £50 shares, most of it provided by London investors. Although the shareholders from Liverpool and from Manchester always exercised a strong influence on policy, in fact each place only provided about a tenth of the capital, which was only slightly more than the amount from Tunbridge Wells. Money also came from the 'retirement and half-pay' towns such as Bath and Cheltenham, and from industrial centres, including Birmingham, Leicester and Rochdale. Many of the places on or near the line of railway provided money, especially Dover. It is not surprising that nothing at all came from Maidstone or the towns of North Kent. Much of the capital came from merchants and bankers; smaller quantities were supplied by tradesmen, service officers, and people covering the whole social range, including Lord De L'Isle and Dudley, and the gardener at Earl's Court, near Tunbridge Wells. The groom at Earl's Court put his name down for three £50 shares. It is not known if all the scrip holders paid up on their shares, but companies were expected to check up on their reliability, and at this time personal servants were sometimes able to accumulate wealth. However the subscription contract is perhaps better regarded as an indication rather than a definitive statement on the provenance of capital.

Reference has already been made to Henry Robinson Palmer, the engineer to the provisional committee. He had the misfortune to be too soon to benefit from the great wave of railway construction. He designed the original alignment of the South Eastern, and after their Act received the Royal Assent on 21 June 1836, he was offered the coveted post of engineer-in-chief to the newly incorporated company. The offer came too late, for Palmer was already a sick man, and he regretfully declined the appointment. However, in his letter to the board of 6 July, he reminded the directors of his responsibility for designing the railway, including the imaginative cliff section at Dover to 'which the success of the Bill is mainly attributable'. He hoped that the company would show their appreciation of his services by employing him as a consultant. On 15 July it was announced that William Cubitt had accepted the post of engineer-in-chief, and the possibility of consultation vanished.

Cubitt was born in Norfolk in 1785, and after apprenticeship to a cabinet-maker became a millwright. By 1826 he had become a partner in the famous engineering works of Ransomes of Ipswich, but in the thirties he moved from mechanical work to the more 'respectable' profession of civil engineering. He was engineer to the London and Croydon Railway, but the South Eastern was his first major responsibility. He was paid £1,200 per annum plus seven guineas a day to cover the cost of some of his assistants. At other times Cubitt worked on the Paris–Lyons Railway, and the Berlin water works, but apart from the South Eastern his main railway engagement was to the Great Northern Railway. In 1850 he was honoured with the Presidency of the Institution of Civil Engineers. He died in 1861 at the age of 76, which may indicate that he abstained from the notorious overwork to which most of his contemporaries subjected themselves.

Strengthened with the compulsory purchasing powers of the 1836 Act, Cubitt re-surveyed the authorised line. Palmer had designed an end-on junction with the London and Croydon at their terminus, now West Croydon station. From there the line was to pass to the west of the town and follow a natural valley through the North Downs by Riddlesdown to penetrate the scarp by a tunnel, emerging near Oxted. In order to shorten the tunnel to about one and a half miles, an inclined plane of 1 in 100, to be worked either by a stationary engine or an assistant locomotive, was included. The line passed north of Edenbridge and then maintained an undulating but remarkably direct line by Tonbridge and Staplehurst to Ashford. East of Ashford difficulty arose, not from the country, but from Mr Deedes of Sandling Park. The best alignment ran through his estate, but his opposition could not be overcome, so a deviation by Beachborough, which included another inclined plane, was unavoidable.

The imaginative cliff section, referred to above, carried the line between Folkestone and Dover. Instead of taking a roundabout route through the Alkham Valley, Palmer niched his line into the face of the chalk cliffs. Alternating between tunnels and galleries it terminated 100 feet above the town of Dover. To bring it lower would have increased the gradient to the west. At the same time, this somewhat inaccessible station could hardly have given adequate service to the port of Dover, and after the opening of the rival London, Chatham & Dover route would have placed the South Eastern at a very considerable disadvantage. As built, the South Eastern followed Palmer's plans from Bough Beach near Penshurst through Tonbridge and Ashford to a point west of Westenhanger. Palmer's line was rejoined just west of Folkestone Warren.

Cubitt realised that the end-on junction with the London and Croydon left a 'trough' in the profile where the line passed west of the town. He avoided this with a plan to keep up on higher ground, east of Croydon, and make a junction farther north on a site near the present Norwood junction. This deviation, combined with an increase in the ruling gradient to 1 in 264 and a lengthening of Oxted tunnel by three quarters of a mile, enabled Palmer's inclined plane to be dispensed with. In the same session Rennie's Brighton line was under consideration, and from Norwood almost to Purley this was parallel and adjacent to Cubitt's deviation. As the two lines both converged on the Croydon Railway at Norwood it was obvious that this was a case of wasteful duplication. Section 135 of the London and Brighton Act of 1837 stated that if the Brighton and South Eastern companies shared a line 'such expenditure of money and much intersection of country might be very advantageously avoided'. It went on to specify that within two years the South Eastern might obtain powers to alter their line so as to join the Brighton 'at any point upon or to northward of Earlswood Common'. If this were done, then the Brighton were to convey to the South Eastern at cost price all the railway north of the junction.

In addition to the important deviation at the Croydon end, there were a number of minor deviations from Palmer's line through the North Downs, but their significance is minimal as this part of the line was never constructed. In any case the deviations near Caterham and near Godstone were dropped because of landowners' opposition. At Ramhurst, just west of Tonbridge, a Cubitt deviation would have given the gunpowder mills at Ramhurst a wider berth, but would have necessitated a greater encroachment on the property of Lord De L'Isle and Dudley, so this also was dropped. In fact, only one of the deviations authorised by the 1837 Act materialised, and this was of great importance. Cubitt decided to go nearer to Folkestone to avoid leaving it on a branch, and to lower the terminus at Dover to the level of the harbour.

Constructional work had been started at Riddlesdown in the North Downs in 1837 but, in view of Section 135 of the Brighton company's Act, was suspended in 1838. In June of that year, Cubitt reported on the three alternative routes under consideration between Bough Beech and the junction with the London & Croydon Railway at Norwood. First the authorised line of 18 miles 11 chains via Oxted was estimated to cost £603,043. A line keeping south of the Downs and joining the Brighton line at Merstham would be 24 miles 32 chains in length, of which the South Eastern would construct 13 miles 60 chains for £303,634, sharing the balance of 10 miles 52 chains with the Brighton company. Finally joining the Brighton line farther south at Redhill would give a line of 26 miles 64 chains with 13 miles 53 chains for the South Eastern to construct for £229,144, and 13 miles 11 chains to be shared with the Brighton.

At this time, the South Eastern were having difficulty in persuading the scrip holders to pay the calls on their shares, and it was clear that either of the routes south of the Downs would enable them to get some return on their capital more quickly. The Merstham route was more convenient, but the land values were higher and the opposition of the landowners more intense. Cubitt reported on an interview with Mr Turner of Rooks Nest House who was insistent that the line should be kept away to the south. Opposition went to the extent of the arrest and detention of Cubitt's son Joseph for taking levels on some roads near Godstone. Nevertheless plans for the Merstham route had been deposited in February and March 1838, and the southerly Redhill route was not finally selected until November 1838.

The problem remained of arranging to purchase at cost the relevant part of the Brighton line, and this was not settled until February 1839 when leave was given to bring in a late Bill. It was agreed that the South Eastern would purchase only the southern half of the line between Redhill and Norwood, and that each of the companies would run toll free over the other company's section. The price was to be based on construction costs plus maintenance until the public opening plus the accumulated interest at 5 per cent, and after much altercation the line between Redhill and Stoats Nest near Coulsdon was conveyed to the South Eastern for £240,000. A special committee appointed to report to the general meeting of 1839 regretted that lack of available capital had led to the taking up of inferior alignments and this is almost certainly the main reason for providing Dover with such a very indirect route.

It will be seen that the actual cost of the line from Redhill to Stoats Nest near Coulsdon, plus the estimated cost of Bough Beech to Redhill, was almost as much as the estimate for the Oxted line, but it is very probable that the latter estimate was inadequate. The new route did give a lower summit level, and

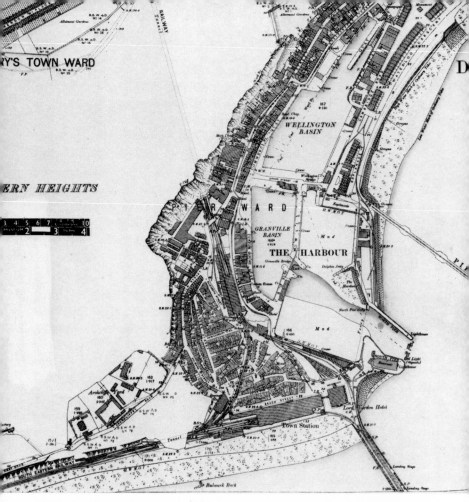

Dover. Ordnance Survey Map 1898 Edition. On the South Eastern Railway this shows
the following features which have been demolished: Archcliffe Tunnel and Dover
Town Station with the engine shed in Bulwark Street and the Goods Depot on the up
side. The Lord Warden Hotel is now in use as an office

On the London, Chatham and Dover Railway, the Harbour Station, most of which has
been demolished, and the single line connection to the Admiralty Pier are shown. On
the marine side, the enclosed Granville and Wellington Basins are marked while the yet
unnamed Prince of Wales Pier is under construction. The electric street tramway of
1897 is shown; when the railway to the Pier was opened in 1904 it crossed the tramway
on the level at the end of Strond Street. Among the later developments not shown are the
railway to the Pier, later extended along Waterloo Crescent to the Eastern Arm, the
Marine Station to the east of the Admiralty Pier and the Train Ferry Dock to the south
of the Harbour Entrance. (Scale 25 ins. to 1 mile: Scale of inches shown on left)

2 Folkestone Warren Halt after the slip of December 1915

3 Foord Viaduct from the street below. SE&C D class 4–4–0 locomotive crossing with an up express about 1906

the tunnel at Merstham was shorter than the Oxted tunnel would have been. This had commercial implications at a time when public prejudice against tunnels was sufficiently strong to induce the Brighton company to whitewash its tunnels and provide them with gas lighting. (There were, of course, no lights in the coaches.) As far as the Merstham tunnel was concerned, this practice ended when the impecunious South Eastern took it over in 1842. As for revenue-earning potential, although the new route missed Oxted by more than three miles, Redhill was only two miles from the market town of Reigate. Both routes served lime works. Although the greater distance would obviously increase operating costs, this would be more than offset in the days of virtual railway monopoly, by greater fares.

While the decision to share the crossing of the North Downs with the Brighton was expedient, in the long run it added to the disadvantage the South Eastern suffered from its choice of the Wealden route. As soon as it was faced with the competition of the London, Chatham & Dover Railway it was forced to reduce its deviousness by constructing, at great expense, its cut-off line through Sevenoaks joining its original line at Tonbridge. The immediate effects were the termination of any hopes the South Eastern might have retained of obtaining any revenue from Brighton traffic, and at the same time, a close relationship with the Brighton company that led to the most bitter quarrels.

The two final changes in the alignment of the South Eastern were authorised by the Acts of 1840 and 1843. First, Mr Deedes of Sandling Park near Hythe changed his mind, and allowed the railway to go through his estate, thus avoiding Beachborough incline. The 1843 Act was even more important. Under the authority of the 1837 Act, the line at Dover was to emerge from Shakespeare Cliff tunnel to run along the top of the beach on a wooden trestle viaduct to terminate against a projecting cliff surmounted by Archcliffe Fort. Prolonged negotiation with the Board of Ordnance and the Lord Warden of the Cinque Ports finally ended in agreement, and powers were granted to extend the line in a tunnel under the Archcliffe Fort to a terminus near the harbour. The admission of the railway to the precincts of the

c

fort was accompanied by many conditions, including the need for the approval of the Lord Warden's surveyor for all buildings, and the banning of coke ovens. (These were constructed at Folkestone instead.)

At this time, the financial position of the South Eastern was not conducive to the provision of architect-designed stations, but Dover was exceptional and Lewis Cubitt produced a striking design embellished with a tower. In the event this was never completed, the company being permitted to save on the station provided that the money was put into the Lord Warden Hotel.

Quite apart from the difficulties over capital, Cubitt had other problems which combined to delay the opening of the line through to Dover until 1844. Frequently there were delays in obtaining land. Sometimes this was due to difficulty in finding the owners; occasionally no agreement could be reached on price and a case had to be presented for arbitration. Cubitt mentioned a field at Brenchley in which forty-seven people had an interest, of whom two were in Cornwall, some in Ireland, and others gone abroad. The railway did not of course resort to arbitration by the local Justices unless it felt it had a very good case, and even then it was not always successful. For instance, J. Harvey of the Mulberry Tree public house at Dover was awarded £28 4s (£28·20) above the company's offer. More typical however was the case of the landowner on the Margate branch who asked £18,023 and was awarded £5,265.

Another type of problem arose at Bletchingley tunnel on the Bough Beech to Redhill section, where bricklayers had to be employed on Sundays as the excavations made in the day on Saturdays had to be supported as soon as possible. Complaints from the local clergy reached board level. The navvies made their usual impact on the countryside, but perhaps less dramatically than on some of the lines where major engineering works in sparsely inhabited districts produced temporary settlements. On the South Eastern, a greater proportion of the navvies were lodged with local inhabitants, and although this did not prevent an increase in the number of cases of poaching, illegitimacy, assault and the like, it did moderate it. The longest continuous

4 Bletchingley Tunnel on the original main line to Dover between Redhill and Tonbridge. The engraver did more than justice to the scale of the earthworks by diminishing the entrance to the tunnel and the train. This was probably inserted from memory, as the shadows indicate an up train running on the down line. A guard is shown seated on the roof of the leading coach, virtually in stage-coach style. (*Illustrated London News*, 1 July 1843)

'navvy' occupation was between Folkestone and Dover where work began on 2 November 1837, and the line was not opened until 7 February 1844.

Opening in sections is uneconomic, as the gaps have to be filled by road transport and the flow of through traffic is impeded. Unfortunately, the South Eastern exacerbated its financial difficulties in this way, opening from Redhill to Tonbridge on 26 May 1842, on to Headcorn on 31 August 1842, to Ashford on 1 December 1842, and on to a temporary station west of the Foord viaduct at Folkestone on 28 June 1843. After the completion of the viaduct, the trains were extended to Folkestone junction on 18 December 1843, and finally reached Dover on 7 February 1844.

Although the South Eastern was essentially a post-Liverpool & Manchester railway, some of the clauses in its Act of Incorporation reflected its horse tramroad antecedents. For instance the 'toll road' concept was reflected in the regulations for people using their own locomotives and coaches, and in a stipulation that the railway was not to be used as a drove road for horses or cattle. The clauses concerning mineral rights and the granting of power to ascertain whether or not mining was taking place under the line of railway were a reminder of the early railways of the mining districts. Other general requirements were designed to protect the country penetrated by the railway. The width of land on level ground to which the powers of compulsory purchase were applicable was 25 yards, but where banks or cuttings were necessary, it depended on their depth and the nature of the underlying strata. (For instance, because of the need for gentler slopes, a cutting in clay would be wider and take more land than a cutting of the same depth in chalk.) Comparable widths for the single-track Canterbury & Whitstable were 15 yards, and for the double-track Brighton main line, 22 yards. Some of the clauses of the South Eastern Railway Act were later confirmed or amended by general legislation. For instance, Section 72 of the South Eastern Act required level-crossing gates to be set normally for road traffic, but the Railway Clauses Consolidation Act of 1845 stipulated that they should be set for rail traffic.

Special clauses covered the effect of banks and cuttings on drainage and water supply. Normally with banks it was only necessary to provide culverts or underbridges sufficient to maintain the normal flow of water, but in some cases, especially where water was required for power, specific requirements were mentioned. For instance, the bridges over the Medway west of Tonbridge were not to interfere with the water supply for the 'mills of William Ford Buxton', i.e. Ramhurst gunpowder mills. Cuttings presented greater problems for they could not only interrupt drainage patterns, but also reduce water levels in wells. Drainage of the cuttings themselves was facilitated by the fact that they were usually on gradients; where it was necessary to preserve the line of a natural stream this was done by means of an aqueduct or pipe, or sometimes taking the water down one side and up the other with a siphon.

Other clauses protected the pattern of communications. Unless otherwise specified, all crossings with turnpike roads or public highways had to be provided with bridges. Underbridges were to have a span of at least 25 feet and a height of 16 feet. These were constructed when the railway was elevated on an embankment; if it was on the level or in a cutting, an overbridge was provided. In the case of the cutting being shallow, or the railway being level with the road, the approach ramps to the bridge were not to exceed 1 in 30. The South Eastern main line did not cross any navigable waterways and it had no movable bridges. Agricultural interests were protected in several ways. First, livestock was to be kept off the railway by a rail and post fence supplemented by a quick hedge. Where farms were severed, occupiers were given a right of way across the line by an occupation level-crossing, or if the line was much above or below ground level, by an occupation bridge. In cases where a parcel of land of less than half an acre was intersected, the owner having no adjacent ground, the South Eastern was required to buy the whole parcel. As the railway usually re-sold the land it did not need, this led to minor changes in land ownership. Later Acts of Parliament often stated that the original owners should be given a first refusal of requisitioned land in the event of re-sale.

Whereas visits to such minor lines as the Canterbury & Whit-stable are now of archaeological interest, some of the main lines also have very little left from their early days, in their case owing to replacement rather than demolition. East of Tonbridge, where the cut-off line of 1868 comes in, the South Eastern has been electrified and modernised, and only such outstanding features as the Foord viaduct have survived almost unchanged. But the line from Redhill to Tonbridge, from a passenger point of view, has become almost a local line, served by diesel trains, most of which run through to Reading.

As mentioned above, the South Eastern opened their line between Redhill and Tonbridge in 1842, and exercised their right to purchase the section of the Brighton company's line between Redhill and Coulsdon. (This had been opened in July 1841.) The Brighton company had opened its Reigate station about half a mile south of the junction, while the South Eastern opened a temporary station east of the junction. The South Eastern station was temporary because they favoured a single station north of the junction whereas the Brighton preferred two separate stations. It was content to leave passengers changing from one line to the other to find their own way over the distance between the two stations, and for goods to be exchanged at the first station to the north, at Merstham. The South Eastern estimated that a single station could be provided for £1,000 per annum whereas the total cost of the two stations would be about £1,800 per annum. Finally, in September 1843, agreement was reached on Redhill station, even though the wrangle over the price to be paid by the South Eastern for the section of the Brighton line to which it was entitled was not resolved until the following year.

The South Eastern board approved the construction of the new station in November 1843. It was ready by March 1844, and the Brighton services transferred to it in April 1844. The site was selected for convenience of railway operation and a special approach road had to be constructed to enable passengers to reach it. Plenty of reasonably priced land suitable for building development was available, and here the first considerable resi-dential settlement, south of Croydon, developed rapidly. In 1849 the importance of the junction station was increased when the line from Reading and Guildford came in at its south end. The South Eastern provided it with four tracks, on a similar style to Tonbridge and Ashford, the two centre tracks having no platforms and therefore being usable only for non-stop trains. A bay was added on the down side and the up platform became an island, reached by means of a subway. After the opening of the alternative Quarry line in 1900, and the subsequent diversion of many of the Brighton company's expresses, Redhill lost some of its through traffic, but it has remained one of the main junctions on the South Eastern system.

South of the station, the South Eastern curved sharply to the east to take up a direction from which there was no significant diversion until it reached Ashford. The Redhill steam locomotive sheds, on the up side, were maintained successively by the South Eastern, the South Eastern & Chatham, the Southern, and by British Railways. The station at Nutfield was opened in 1883, complete with signal box and goods facilities. Over the nineteen and a half miles from Redhill to Tonbridge the maximum gradient was 1 in 250, and to achieve this the line included a tunnel at Bletchingley of 1,327 yards and substantial earthworks east of Penshurst. It is in a way contradictory that such a roundabout route to Dover as the South Eastern provided should be for much of its length so very straight. For most of the way the slight relief of the Wealden clay country posed few problems for the engineer; only near Tonbridge was the more difficult country of the High Weald approached.

The station at Godstone was built mainly to serve the village about two and three quarter miles away to the north. Although the company was content to leave passengers to find their own way to the stations, it usually did enter into agreements with local road transport operators. Frequently access to the station premises was granted to the owners of horse buses or hackney carriages in return for a guarantee to meet trains, and an arrangement of this kind was made for Godstone. Like all the original South Eastern stations, its platforms, instead of being opposite each other, were staggered so that passengers always crossed the tracks behind the train they had left. Now a footbridge has been provided and extensions have led to some overlapping between the two platforms.

Although it was the usual practice for the South Eastern to provide both passenger and freight facilities at its stations, exceptionally it did provide for passengers only or freight only. Just over a mile beyond Godstone, a siding for general use was opened at Crowhurst, Lane End, and was served by the pick-up goods trains which called at each place along the line. In 1884 the new line from South Croydon to East Grinstead was opened, passing underneath the South Eastern. The section from South Croydon to Crowhurst was jointly owned by the South Eastern and the London, Brighton & South Coast, and for much of its length came close to the alignment proposed for the South Eastern main line of 1836. This line ran through what had been designated by an agreement of 1848 as South Eastern territory, and because of this the London, Brighton & South Coast Railway invited the South Eastern's participation in a spur at Crowhurst giving a connection to Tonbridge.

A second London, Brighton & South Coast line, the Oxted and Groombridge of 1888, was opened to improve their routes to Eastbourne and to Tunbridge Wells. It passed under the South Eastern about a mile and a half east of Crowhurst, but in this case the South Eastern expressed no interest in part ownership, and there is no connection between the two lines. As the London, Brighton & South Coast is in a short tunnel at this point, mutual visibility is difficult.

Edenbridge is the second of the three original stations between Redhill and Tonbridge, and is situated about one mile north of the town. The relationship between station and town is typical of the South Eastern between Redhill and Ashford, as it cuts across the grain of the road system, with stations built to serve the places on either side of the line. Hamlets grew up near many of the stations, but in the case of Edenbridge development was more substantial, and the railway had a significant influence on the pattern of growth of the town. Between Edenbridge and Penshurst is Bough Beech, at which point we take up the original

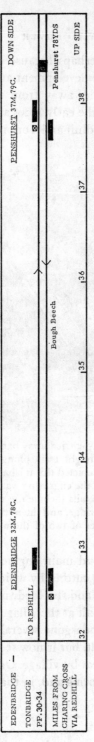
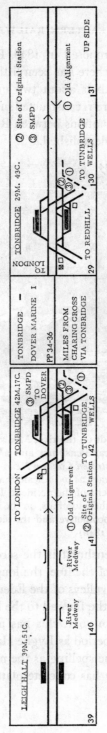
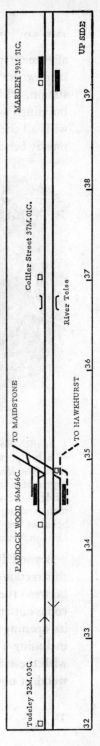

KEY TO DIAGRAMS

Running Lines in Use in 1971	———
Site of Running Lines Out of Use by 1971	·········
Bridge or Viaduct	] [
Tunnel	)(

Signal Boxes in Use in 1971 ⊠
Signal Boxes Disused or Demolished by 1971 ▢
(Note : The same symbol is used for mechanical boxes operating block sections, electric boxes and crossing boxes.)

Train Depot in Use in 1971   TD
(Note : Diesel and Electric Locomotives are based on certain train depots.)

Site of Motive Power Depot for Steam Locomotives ⊠
Passenger Platform in Use in 1971 ▮
Passenger Platform Disused or Demolished by 1971 ▯
(Note : Stations open in 1971 have names underlined.)

Level Crossings with Public Roads in Use in 1971 ✕ ✕
Level Crossings with Lifting Barriers instead of Gates in 1971 ✕ LB
Level Crossing Out of Use by 1971 ⋉⋊

DOWN SIDE

UP SIDE

EDENBRIDGE 32M.78C.

EDENBRIDGE —
TONBRIDGE
PP. 30-34

MILES FROM CHARING CROSS VIA REDHILL

TO REDHILL

PENSHURST 37M.79C.

Penshurst 78YDS

Bough Beech

UP SIDE

TONBRIDGE 29M. 43C.

② Site of Original Station
③ SMPD
① Old Alignment

TO TUNBRIDGE WELLS

TO REDHILL

TO LONDON

TONBRIDGE —
DOVER MARINE I
PP. 34-36

MILES FROM CHARING CROSS VIA TONBRIDGE

TONBRIDGE 42M.17C.

③ SMPD
TO DOVER
②
① Old Alignment
② Site of Original Station
TO TUNBRIDGE WELLS

TO LONDON

River Medway

River Medway

LEIGH HALT 39M.51C.

MARDEN 39M 51C.

UP SIDE

Collier Street 37M.01C.

River Teise

TO MAINDSTONE

TO HAWKHURST

PADDOCK WOOD 36M.66C.

UP SIDE

Tudeley 32M.03C.

alignment proposed in 1836. Perhaps because of the policy of landowners, there has been little development around Penshurst station, which is about two miles away from the village. The buildings were reconstructed in the early 1920s after a fire, but as with all the stations between Redhill and Tonbridge, these have mostly been demolished.

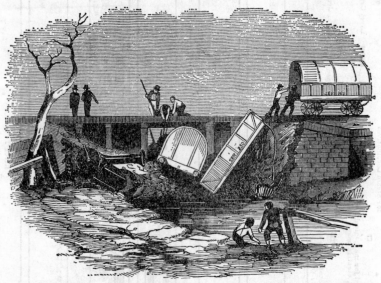

5 In 1846, floods on the river Medway carried away part of the abutments of a bridge near Penshurst and a freight train plunged down into the river. The *Illustrated London News* depicted this mishap with such a high degree of accuracy as to indicate that the engraving was based on a sketch made at the scene of the accident. Details include the two railway police-men, wearing their top hats, on the bridge, and the numbers on the buffer beam of the locomotive and the sides of two of the wagons. (*Illustrated London News*, 1846)

Beyond Penshurst is the second main engineering feature of this section of the line, the long cutting by which the interfluve between the valleys of the Eden and the Medway is crossed. We come out at the far end to the halt at the village of Leigh. Since its opening in 1911, this has undergone several name changes, including a period as Lyghe Halt, but it now seems to be settled with the same spelling as the near-by village. Originally built of wood, it now has concrete platforms and, in that passengers are handled but not freight, makes a contrast with Crowhurst siding. We cross the Medway near the site of the Ramhurst powder mills to run into Tonbridge.

Once the direct line to Tonbridge was opened, the Redhill to Tonbridge section was in danger of becoming a backwater. However, it did form part of the route from the North, Midlands, and West to Dover via Reading which avoided London, and this has brought it a significant freight traffic. The first through passenger service began in the summer of 1897, when the Great Western and South Eastern combined to work through coaches between Birkenhead, Birmingham and Folkestone Harbour. After winter withdrawal, the service appeared in the summer timetables for 1898, with its northern terminal extended from Birkenhead to Liverpool Central via the Mersey Railway. Through coaches were missing from 1900 to 1903, but then reappeared as a complete train, running from Birkenhead to Dover and Deal. There were breaks resulting from the First and Second World Wars, but the service continued until finally, in accordance with the general policy of routing passengers via London, it was suspended.

Until the First World War the South Eastern continued to run at least one express train a day via Redhill; for instance, in 1910 it was the 7.40 a.m. from Cannon Street. From 1884 it provided a service down the Oxted line to Edenbridge and Tonbridge, but suspended it in 1917. After the end of hostilities in 1919 it was very partially restored in the form of one train per day each way between Oxted and Tonbridge. There was a second suspension from 1939 to 1946, and services over the Crowhurst spur finally ended in 1955. At present the passenger service between Redhill and Tonbridge is provided by multiple-unit diesel trains running at roughly hourly intervals and calling at all stations.

Redhill, Tonbridge and Ashford all became important junction stations, but if London, Brighton and South Coast trains are left out of the count, then after the completion of the cut-off line through Sevenoaks in 1868, Tonbridge was probably the busiest junction on the South Eastern outside the London area. It first became a junction in 1845 when the branch line to Tunbridge Wells was opened.[3] The direct line of 1868 approached Tonbridge almost but not quite as awkwardly as the Tunbridge Wells branch. Here the problems arose from the need to give a wide berth to Ramhurst powder mills, to secure a convenient crossing of the River Medway, and to use the existing Tonbridge station. The alignment selected involved a sharp curve which for many years carried a 25 miles per hour speed limit. However, in December 1933 work began on easing the curve, reconstructing the junction, and largely rebuilding Tonbridge station. The side of the cutting, consisting of hard sandstone on the north side of the curve, was scooped out, the use of explosives being precluded by the proximity of houses and of the running lines. This allowed the curve to be re-aligned and the speed limit raised to 40 miles per hour. The spoil was divided between Folkestone Harbour and Southampton where it was needed in connection with harbour works.

The station had the typical South Eastern arrangement of two platform roads with two through lines in the centre, and terminal bays on the outside of each of the two platforms. The up bay was extended at its eastern end to join the main line, and thus became a loop-road accessible from both the Dover and the Hastings lines. Both platforms were extended and given new buildings and new roofs. (It was recorded that the name 'Tonbridge' had been written in large white letters on the old roof on the up side, presumably to assist airmen who were lost.) New signal boxes were constructed both east (in 1935) and west (in 1934) of the station. Electrification and coloured light signals came in as part of phase two of the Kent Coast modernisation scheme, and after a period of disuse, both the 'new' signal boxes were demolished in 1962. The steam motive power depot was situated in the fork between the Dover and Hastings lines and this too has gone. Also east of the roadbridge was the first Tonbridge station—replaced by that on the present site in 1864.

Whereas the line from Redhill to Tonbridge lost much of its importance when it was 'by-passed' in 1868, between Tonbridge and Dover the South Eastern is still very much a main line. In common with other main lines, such as the London & North Western, it has been electrified and equipped with colour light signals, but differs from many in that only two of its intermediate stations have been closed. This however, is not to say that many South Eastern buildings remain. Perhaps the most striking survival was at the first station east of Tonbridge, named somewhat euphemistically Maidstone Road, but re-named Paddock Wood when the branch line to Maidstone was opened in 1844. Maidstone had, of course, supported the Central Kent Railway, but nevertheless at Maidstone Road the South Eastern constructed the best intermediate station building on its original line. In view of the fact that it served the county town for only two years, its construction was a slightly inexplicable flourish. Like all the principal South Eastern stations of the 1840s, it had a classical flavour with pediments not only on both sides but also at the ends. It was demolished as part of the modernisation scheme of the 1960s.

From an operating point of view, Paddock Wood was a small-scale Tonbridge, with the same arrangement of two platform roads, two through roads and terminal bays on the outside of each platform. As with Tonbridge, lines went off in two directions, but whereas in the former case, the junctions were at opposite ends of the station, the lines for Paddock Wood and Hawkhurst both diverged to the east of the station.[4] The Hawkhurst branch was opened as far as Goudhurst in 1892 and on to its terminal in 1893. Trains for either Maidstone to the north of the line or Hawkhurst to the south, leaving from the bays on the down side or the up side respectively, were provided with independent tracks and did not run on to the main line. The signal box at the east end, like Tonbridge East Yard box, was built on stilts over a track and was demolished in 1962. (The signal box at the west end had gone by 1934.) Paddock Wood was always associated with hops, a link now indicated by the extensive premises of the Hop Marketing Board which adjoin the station. The author has a photograph bearing the caption 'Hop-Pickers Homeward Bound' taken outside Paddock Wood station, probably about 1900. This was almost the peak period for the annual migration, mainly from East and South East London, to the hop-fields, where primitive temporary accommodation was provided.

35

Hop-picking was essentially a family occupation and the photograph shows as many children as adults. As railway passengers, the hop-pickers and the friends who went to visit them by day-excursion trains, were regarded with some misgivings by railwaymen, rather like present-day football fans. At Paddock Wood a stretcher was available to convey to the police station any of them who the ticket collector deemed too drunk to travel. Special trains of vintage coaches were provided for them, often running at unpopular times. (A print showing hop-pickers starting from London Bridge station at midnight in the late summer of 1891 was reproduced in the present author's book *London Railways*.) The problem of providing for them has solved itself by their virtual replacement with hop-picking machinery; the few who still travel down to the hop-fields now use normal services.[5]

Between Tonbridge and Ashford no passenger stations have been added since 1842 and none have been closed, although they have nearly all lost their goods facilities. Marden, Staplehurst, Headcorn and Pluckley were provided with staggered platforms, similar to those described at Godstone. In every case platform extensions have obscured the 'stagger' which in any case, following the provision of footbridges, loses its point. Buildings were provided on either the up or the down side depending on the position of the main access road—for instance, at Marden on the up side and at Pluckley on the down side. Marden and Headcorn both adjoined the villages they served, but at Staplehurst and Pluckley small hamlets, including the inevitable inn, sprang up around the station. When signal boxes were at their most prolific, in addition to those at the stations, there were boxes at Tudeley 2½ miles east of Tonbridge, Collier Street 2 miles east of Paddock Wood, Swift's Green 2½ miles east of Headcorn, and Chart 3½ miles east of Pluckley. In 1935 Tudeley was closed and its signals worked from the new box at Tonbridge East.

Now, in 1971, only Staplehurst box is retained, mainly for the small coal depot, and most of the others have been demolished. All the stations have undergone changes but Staplehurst and Headcorn may serve as examples. The original buildings at Staplehurst, on the up side, were damaged beyond repair by a

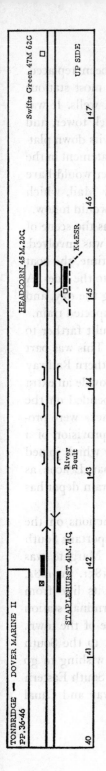
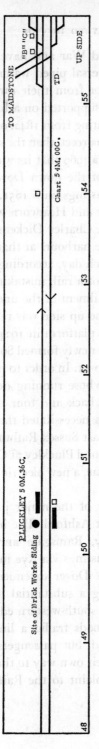
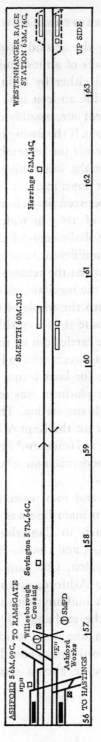
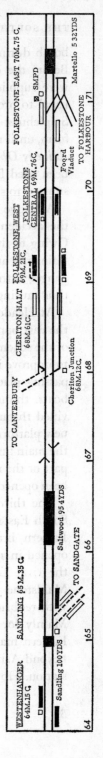

TONBRIDGE — DOVER MARINE II
PP.36-46

Swifts Green 47M.20C   UP SIDE

HEADCORN 45M.20C

STAPLEHURST 41M.71C

River Beult

"B" "C"

TO MAIDSTONE

TD

UP SIDE

K&ESR

Chart 5 4M.00C.

PLUCKLEY 5 0M.36C.
Site of Brick Works Siding

SMEETH 60M.31C.

Herrings 62M.14C.

WESTENHANGER RACE STATION 63M.74C.

UP SIDE

ASHFORD 5 6M.09C. TO RAMSGATE

"D"   "E"

Ashford Works

SMPD

Willesborough Crossing

TO CANTERBURY

Sevington 5 7M.64C.

CHERITON HALT 68M.61C.

Cheriton Junction 68M.12C.

FOLKESTONE EAST 70M.75 C.

SMPD

FOLKESTONE WEST 69M.21C.

FOLKESTONE CENTRAL 69M.76C.

Ford Viaduct

TO FOLKESTONE HARBOUR

Martello 5 32YDS

56 TO HASTINGS

WESTENHANGER 64M.15 G

Sandling 100YDS

SANDLING 65M.35 G

Saltwood 95 4YDS

TO SANDGATE

bomb during the Second World War and have been replaced. Before the days of almost universal piped water, most stations were supplied either by train or from their own wells. It was usual to provide an iron tank, supported on a brick tower, and Staplehurst had one, possibly dating from 1842, on its down platform, until 1969. If the dating is correct, then the statement in the *Railway Observer* for September 1969 that its water would have been used for the locomotive of the down Dover Mail, which stopped to set down mail for Hastings until 1851, would follow.

A bridge between Staplehurst and Headcorn was the scene of the accident of 1865 in which Charles Dickens was involved. Owing to the shallowness of the harbours at that time, the boat trains ran at a different hour each day, according to the tides. A ganger authorised the removal of a rail, mistaking the day, and thus causing the inevitable derailment of the unexpected train.

At Headcorn the whole of the up side was rebuilt farther to the east opposite the down side platform in 1924. This was part of the scheme carried out by the newly formed Southern Railway to improve its three routes to Dover. In order to provide an extra passing place for boat trains, whose running depended on the boats, the up platform was set back and four tracks were provided through the station. This necessitated the provision of a new platform for the Kent & East Sussex Railway which joined the main line at Headcorn.[6] Beyond Pluckley at Chart Leacon, as part of the modernisation scheme, a new electric train depot has been opened.

The third and most easterly of the major junctions on the South Eastern main line was at Ashford. The important South Eastern branch to Canterbury, Ramsgate and Margate was opened in 1846, and that to Hastings via Rye in 1851.[7] In 1884, the rival London, Chatham & Dover extended its line from Maidstone to Ashford, opening a substantial terminal station with redbrick buildings on the south-western edge of the town. Mainly for the exchange of goods traffic, a link to the South Eastern main line was provided, but passengers wishing to go beyond Ashford had to find their own way to the South Eastern station. However, after a complaint to the Railway and Canal

6 Down 'Golden Arrow' emerging from Shakespeare Cliff Tunnel on 16 September 1950 hauled by West Country class No. 34103 'Calstock' built at Brighton Works in 1950

7 Up Boat express crossing the viaduct over Folkestone Harbour headed as far as Folkestone Junction by three SE&C P class 0–6–0 tank locomotives in the summer of 1955

8 Ashford Motor Power Depot after transfer to the Ashford Steam Centre. This view shows SE&C H class 0–4–4 tank locomotive No. 263 built at Ashford in 1905, SE O1 class 0–6–0 No. 65 built at Ashford in 1896 and Pullman Cars 'Phylis' and 'Lucille' in March 1970

9 Trains passing on the curve of the viaduct at Strood. A view from the 13.15 Cannon Street to Ramsgate express hauled by a rebuilt light Pacific class locomotive on the last day of steam operation, 13 June 1959

Commission in 1891, London, Chatham & Dover trains began to run through to the South Eastern station, and in 1898, only fourteen years after it had been opened, the London, Chatham & Dover's Ashford station was closed. The South Eastern establishment was an enlarged version of Paddock Wood, with two platform roads, two through roads and two terminal bays on the outside of the platforms. As at Paddock Wood, the main buildings were on the down side. Until the opening of the present signal box, Ashford was the most extensively 'signal boxed' junction on the line, with boxes lettered 'B', 'C', 'D' and 'E' at intervals of about a quarter of a mile.

The rebuilding of the station as part of the modernisation scheme was unusually slow, work being spread over the five years from 1961 to 1965. It included provision of new buildings, a new overbridge at the west end of the station and the conversion of the bay roads into loops. When the railway first came to Ashford, it was a market town with the usual associated industries such as milling, brewing and tanning. In 1845 the South Eastern decided to leave the works at New Cross, London, and to build on a new site to the south east of Ashford where cheap, flat land was available. The works were opened in 1847 and, to ensure a suitable labour supply, the company built Alfred Town. (It was named after Alfred, Duke of Connaught, who had a residence near Ashford.)

Alfred Town was built alongside the works on a most enlightened plan, with the houses surrounding a pleasant green. A central feature was the bath-house, surmounted by an enormous water tank, and flanked by a store and a public house. Later a school was added, to be extended in 1912, and taken over by Kent Education Committee in 1921. The first housing was perhaps not as progressive as the general plan, consisting of back-to-back dwellings, divided into ground-floor and first-floor flats. Housing of a considerably better type, ornamented with Dutch gables, was added in the 1860s. A mansion was provided for the locomotive superintendent. Rents were based, not on the costs of the houses, but on the means of the tenants. For instance, a South Eastern board minute records a request to Mr Cudworth, the locomotive superintendent, to discover if 3s. 6d. (17½p) was a suitable rental for the workpeople. The name Alfred Town for some reason did not stick, and the railway settlement became known as Ashford New Town. The works expanded during the second half of the century, but the additional dwellings required were provided by private builders beyond the boundary of the railway land in South Ashford and in Beaver. However when the SECR closed down the former LCDR's Longhedge works, 126 new dwellings were provided by the company for the workpeople moved down from Battersea. The new houses almost surrounded the original Alfred Town, forming an 'outer skin' which reflected the change in building styles between the early Victorian and the period just before the First World War. The original works were constructed in the fork between the Dover and Hastings lines, but successive extensions led to the erection of new premises for the carriage and wagon department on the opposite side of the Hastings line. The period of rapid change suffered by the railways in the 1960s has not left Ashford works unscathed, but at the moment there is enough work, mainly on wagon construction, to sustain a reduced labour force. However a number of the older houses in the New Town are empty and their future seems doubtful. The steam motive power depot was on the down side of the main line, opposite the railway works. Considerable but not complete demolition has taken place, and in 1971 two steam locomotives and two Pullman cars were preserved there.[9]

The next section of line from Ashford to Folkestone was opened in 1843. At Willesborough on the eastern outskirts of Ashford the only public level-crossing between London and Dover is still in use. The station at Smeeth was opened in 1852 and closed in 1954. A photograph taken on the last day of 1953 shows a conventional South Eastern station with no footbridge and the platforms fully staggered. The buildings are on the up side and oil lamps are placed at either end of the foot level-crossing by which passengers crossed the line. The signal box, which adjoins the level-crossing, is of a typical SER design, weatherboarded, with sash windows and a low-pitched slate roof. This box was replaced by the new installation at Ashford although freight traffic continued at Smeeth until 1964. Westenhanger was opened in 1844 and, as it was the station for Hythe, was provided with a building approaching the one at Paddock Wood in scale and style. In 1969 it was proposed for closure, but was reprieved by the Minister of Transport. Just west of the station, the SECR provided special race platforms served by loop lines, at which trains could stand without interrupting main line traffic. The platforms adjoined the racecourse and carried a heavy traffic for the few days of the year on which they were used. Needless to say, such spasmodic traffic could hardly justify the facilities provided, and although remains of the platforms survive they have not been used for many years.

The railway history of Folkestone is complex and the train of events has left very clear marks on the railway landscape as far west as Sandling Junction. For twenty years after 1843, the only passenger stations in the district were Folkestone Junction, and from 1849, Folkestone Harbour. Between them these served the boat train traffic, the residential and holiday traffic, the military traffic and the freight, which included quantities of fish. The great military camp at Shorncliffe had been established in 1794, and in 1863 it was provided with its own station on the SER main line. However, in 1864 powers were obtained to build a branch from a junction near Sandling Bridge to a point on the coast about a quarter of a mile from Shorncliffe Camp. There was little co-operation from the War Office. In fact a request for the loan of military labour, for which the railway were ready to pay, although authorised by the War Office, was refused by the colonel at Shorncliffe. It was 1874 before the line was opened and although its terminal was at Seabrook it was named Sandgate after the seaside resort about a mile away to the east. The branch was built to main line standards, with double track, and the reason for this became clear when powers were sought to extend it along the top of the beach to the harbour, in a manner not dissimilar to that adopted by the Great Western Railway at Dawlish.

Needless to say, this project was not well received by the people of Folkestone, and Sir Edward Watkin, the SER chairman, referred to 'anonymous slanderers' who 'degrade the walls of Folkestone by personal attacks on me'. (Sir Edward was the Liberal MP for Hythe, and Folkestone was part of his constituency.) In February 1876, he went down to address a public meeting at the town hall. One speaker suggested that the line was intended to syphon off potential Folkestone visitors to Seabrook for the benefit of the estate company at that place. The beauty of the cliffs and beach was extolled, but one speaker rather spoiled this by pointing out that 'the foreshore, spoken of as a sublime retreat for visitors, is seriously interrupted by that enormous cesspool of General Hankey's and the three stinking drains that run on the beach'.

Although the SER attempted to establish good relations with the townspeople, in fact the last word lay with the principal landowner, the Earl of Radnor. He required a deviation of line away from the beach and into a tunnel, and in that form it was authorised. In view of the expense it is not surprising that it was never constructed. One further alternative to the steeply inclined branch from the Junction to the Harbour was authorised in 1885, when powers were obtained for a spur leaving the main line just east of Folkestone Central station and joining the Harbour branch south of Radnor Street. Again, no further action was taken and at the present time trains continue to go up and down the 1 in 30 gradient of the original Harbour branch.

Apart from the problem of improved access to the Harbour, the SER was always irked by the fact that the receipts from Folkestone traffic had to be paid into the 'continental' pool, which since 1865 had been shared by the SER and the LCDR. In 1881 the SER replaced its modest establishment at Shorncliffe Camp with a fine new station, complete with refreshment rooms and other amenities, designed to attract Folkestone traffic away from the Junction station. (This was a counter move to the LCDR which had instituted a steamer service from Queenborough to Flushing which the SER considered an evasion of the 'continental' agreement.) In 1883 the LCDR countered Shorncliffe station by promoting a branch line from its main line at Kearsney through the

Alkham Valley to Folkestone. This was rejected by Parliament but it spurred the SER to make two further moves. First, in 1884, it opened another new station west of Foord viaduct, and near the proposed LCDR terminus, which it called Cheriton Arch. Its distance from Cheriton led to confusion and about two years later it was re-named Radnor Park. The second move was to associate itself with the Elham Valley Light Railway, which had been authorised in 1881, and linked Canterbury to Folkestone. (This had been the main traffic claimed for the LCDR branch from Kearnsey.) Litigation was inevitable, and by 1888 the House of Lords had ruled that the Queensborough service did not invalidate the continental agreement. The SER suffered a second blow when the Lords decided that Shorncliffe was handling Folkestone traffic, and its receipts should be paid into the pool. There followed a third series of cases as to how much the SER owed the LCDR, final judgement being delivered by the House of Lords in 1893. The companies had spent about £250,000 on litigation which might have better been used to reward their shareholders or improve their services.

In 1888 a third station was added to the main line at the junction of the Hythe and Sandgate branch. Sandling Junction was provided with independent platforms on the branch so that Sandgate trains no longer had to saunter up and down the main line between Westenhanger and the junction. At a period when the SER showed a predilection for wooden station buildings, Sandling was made of brick, with a separate but ample residence for the station master. A footbridge spanned the main line so that passengers leaving down trains to join the local to Sandgate did not have to cross the tracks on the level. The inhabitants of Sandgate showed an understandable tendency to patronise the stations on the main line, and so in 1931 their branch was downgraded. With all intentions of extension to the Harbour line long forgotten, it was reduced from two tracks to one, only as far as Hythe, and beyond that it was closed and the track removed. After a wartime closure from 1943 until 1945 the line was finally closed in 1951. A replacement bus service was instituted and 'Sandling Junction' became 'Sandling for Hythe'.[10]

While the deviation through Sandling Park avoided the Beachborough incline, there was still high ground to be penetrated, and the gradient of 1 in 266 was achieved by means of the very wet Saltwood tunnel. It gave rise to considerable constructional problems but later its leakiness was turned to good account by using the water for quenching at the coke ovens at Folkestone Junction and for other purposes. At Cheriton Junction, about one and a half miles beyond the tunnel, the Elham Valley line from Canterbury came in on the down side. It was opened throughout by 1889 and closed to passengers north of Lyminge in 1940. The section from Cheriton Junction to Lyminge followed in 1943 but had its passenger service restored in 1946. It was finally withdrawn in 1947.[11] At one time, most Elham Valley trains terminated at Shorncliffe, and to keep them clear of the main line, a third track was provided on the down side between Shorncliffe and Cheriton Junction, together with a bay platform at the station. As part of the electrification scheme, this was extended to Folkestone Central and at the same time another track was added on the up side. But the actual site of Cheriton Junction is marked by an empty cutting curving away on the down side. Three quarters of a mile beyond the junction, Cheriton Halt was opened in 1908. It was served mainly by the Elham Valley trains and after temporary closures in both wars it was finally closed in 1947. It consisted of wooden platforms alongside the up line and the down relief line, with modest wooden shelters, and no trace of it is visible from passing trains.

In contrast Shorncliffe, now named Folkestone West, even if it does not survive in all its glory, is still virtually intact and provides an interesting memorial to the days of SER and LCDR strife. Only three quarters of a mile to the east is the passenger station named successively Cheriton Arch, Radnor Park and now Folkestone Central. Until its rebuilding, completed in 1962, this was a rather modest establishment with up and down platforms and an up bay. Its signal box, with its characteristic sash windows, weatherboarding and low-pitched roof, stood at the London end of the down platform. The site, on an embankment, was easily accessible from Folkestone but made reconstruction expensive. Basically the new station consists of a circulating area at ground level on the down side, with subway and steps giving access to the two island platforms. Because of its elevated site and also the proximity to Shorncliffe, Folkestone Central has never handled freight. As mentioned above, there was a temporary station on the site, opened in 1843 while Foord viaduct was being completed.

This is undoubtedly the most impressive work on the main line to Dover. Contemporary writers draw attention to its 'extraordinary compactness and stability' and to the lightness of construction which made the pressure at the foundations of the piers as low as 1,200 pounds per square foot. While none of the SER stations, even if Dover had been built as planned, would have ranked with the great stations of the North, Foord viaduct stands comparison with any of the viaducts of England. It is perhaps unfortunate that the people who see the least of it are the railway passengers who use it. Viewed from below, with its nineteen arches and height of 100 feet, it continues to dominate the east end of Folkestone. Inevitably parts of the brickwork have been renewed and a few tie plates attached, but no great changes have been required over the last 120 years. Beyond was Folkestone Junction station which, like the viaduct but perhaps less appropriately, for many years changed but little.

Before the opening of the Shorncliffe and Folkestone Central stations, the Harbour station, despite being at the end of a precipitous branch, was regarded as the main passenger station for the town. A correspondent writing to the *Railway Magazine* in 1920 stated: 'I had old relations who had lived in Folkestone and they regarded the Junction as being quite outside the town "in the Folly Fields" as they called it.' Folkestone Junction retains the arrangement which once existed at Tonbridge, where a steeply graded line, instead of joining the main line directly, terminates in a siding. This unusual type of junction survives at Folkestone, partly because of the prohibitive cost of the alternative approaches to the harbour, described above. Because the branch consisted mainly of a 1 in 30 incline, with no opportunity for trains to acquire momentum before they reached it, special locomotive power was necessary. A small stud of tank locomotives was kept at the motive power depot on the down side of the station which was finally closed when electric traction was introduced in 1961.

For many years the locomotive type best represented was James Stirling's R class, latterly in rebuilt form as the R 1 class. However in 1959 they were replaced by 0–6–0 Pannier tanks transferred from the Western Region. To tackle the gradient, double heading was general, treble heading not uncommon and occasionally if locomotives were needed up at the Junction, boat trains departed with three locomotives at the head and one at the rear. Main line locomotives backed on to the trains in the reversing siding for the run up to London. At the present time with multiple-unit electric stock, the procedure is greatly simplified. Until the Harbour branch was opened to passengers in 1849, Folkestone Junction handled all the passenger traffic for both town and harbour. It then lost all the harbour and much of the town traffic, and most of the remaining town traffic went to Shorncliffe and Folkestone Central. It was re-named Folkestone East in 1962 and was closed to passengers in 1965. However, it remains open for freight. The platforms have been demolished except for a short section outside the new signal box, retained for the use of staff.

In many ways the last section of the SER main line, not completed until 1844, is the most dramatic. Reference has already been made to the way in which Dover Harbour was reached by following the line of the cliffs. However, before the comparative stability of the 'white cliffs of Dover' was reached, the line had to cross the treacherous and unstable Folkestone Warren. For about two miles, roughly from the eastern portal of Martello Tunnel to the western end of Abbotscliffe Tunnel, the line ran over fallen chalk resting on clay which sloped very slightly towards the sea. Slips had been recorded in 1765 and 1800 but Cubitt evidently decided that the Warren was sufficiently stable to bear a railway. He must have known the risk involved as there was another slip in 1836, and in his report to the SER Board in January 1837, he advised the purchase of 'slipped land'. It would

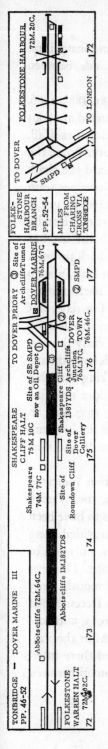

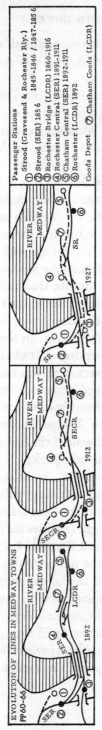

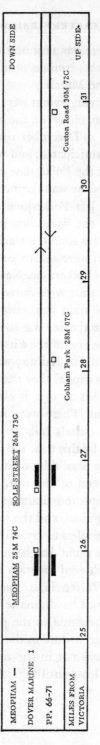

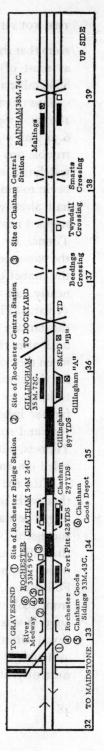

TONBRIDGE — DOVER MARINE III
PP. 46-52

FOLKESTONE WARREN HALT 72M 02C.

Abbotscliffe 1M 182YDS

74 74M 77C Shakespeare
Shakespeare Cliff 75 M 10C
SHAKESPEARE CLIFF HALT

Site of Roundown Cliff
Site of Dover Colliery

Abbotscliffe 72M 64C.

Abbotscliffe 1387YDS Shakespeare Cliff

Site of SE SMPD now an Oil Depot ①

TO DOVER PRIORY ③ Site of Archcliffe Tunnel
76 76M 37C. Archcliffe Junction 76M 46C. DOVER TOWN
DOVER MARINE 76M 67C. 77 ② SMPD

FOLKE-STONE HARBOUR BRANCH PP. 52-54
MILLS FROM CHARING CROSS VIA TONBRIDGE

FOLKESTONE HARBOUR 72M 20C.
TO DOVER TO LONDON 71

EVOLUTION OF LINES IN MEDWAY TOWNS
PP 60-66

Passenger Stations
① Strood (Gravesend & Rochester Rly.) 1845-1846 / 1847-1856 6
② Strood (SER) 1856
③ Rochester Bridge (LCDR) 1860-1916
④ Rochester Central (SER) 1891-1911
⑤ Chatham Central (SER) 1892-1911
⑥ Rochester (LCDR) 1892

Goods Depot ⑦ Chatham Goods (LCDR)

1892   LCDR   SECR   SECR   SR   SR
RIVER MEDWAY

1892 / 1912 / 1927

MEOPHAM — DOVER MARINE I
PP. 66-71

MILES FROM VICTORIA

DOWN SIDE

UP SIDE

MEOPHAM 25 M 74C   SOLE STREET 26M 73C
Cobham Park 28M 07C
Cuxton Road 30M 72C
Site of Rochester Bridge Station

TO GRAVESEND
TO MAIDSTONE
River Medway
ROCHESTER 33M 5 9C
Rochester Goods
Chatham Goods Sidings 33M 43C.
CHATHAM 34M 24C
Fort Pitt 428YDS
Chatham 297YDS
Chatham Goods Depot
Site of Rochester Central Station ② Site of Chatham Central Station ③
GILLINGHAM 35 M 72C.
TO DOCKYARD
Gillingham 897 YDS
Gillingham "A"   "B"   TD   SMPD
RAINHAM 38M 74C.
Maltings
Beedings Crossing
Twyndall Crossing
Smarts Crossing

UP SIDE

32   33   34   35   36   37   38   39

25   26   27   28   29   30   31

seem that there was a connection between rainfall and instability, as most of the trouble occurred during wet periods between September and March.

Slips of varying extent were recorded in 1877, 1881, 1885, 1886, 1892 and 1896. However, the worst of the slips occurred at about 6.50 p.m. on 19 December 1915. Because of exceptional rainfall, trouble was anticipated, and watchmen were on duty. When the watchman at the Folkestone end of the Warren heard the chalk begin to move, he was alarmed by the fact that a passenger train had already left Folkestone Junction, but managed to get it stopped near the signal box in the cutting just east of Martello Tunnel. By this time the track was moving towards the sea, but the passengers were able to leave the train and walk back through the tunnel to Folkestone. Near Folkestone Warren Halt, a strip nearly half a mile wide moved seawards, the Halt itself moving 53 yards. The train was retrieved within the next few days, but the damage to the line was so severe that restoration was delayed until after the end of the First World War. In the early thirties, when the Southern Railway was seeking worthwhile investments for the cheap capital that the government was making available to it, by its Act of 1934 it obtained powers to build a new line farther inland. There were further slips in 1936, 1937 and, in 1939 and 1940, chalk falls between Abbotscliffe and Shakespeare Tunnels, but by this time the outbreak of the Second World War ruled out any possibility of major new works.

After the end of the war, geological investigation indicated that with improved drainage and retaining walls, the Warren might be stabilised, and the work carried out seems to have been successful. Needless to say, no freight facilities are provided along the cliffs, but traffic has been handled at two halts, only one of which has achieved mention in the public timetables. This was Folkestone Warren Halt, opened in the summer months only from 1908 until its dramatic displacement in the December of 1915. It was restored to the public timetables in 1923, and conveyed summer visitors to the Warren until 1939. After the war, although it was not in the timetables, trains called there intermittently, at least until 1951. At present it is still sometimes used for staff working on the line, as there is no convenient road access.

Shakespeare Cliff Halt, situated at the western end of Shakespeare Cliff tunnel, is even more obscure than Folkestone Warren. It has never appeared in the public timetable, probably for the very good reason that any members of the public leaving trains at this point would find themselves stranded on a wedge of flat land niched into the chalk cliff. This became important in the 1870s when work began on the first Channel Tunnel, and workmen reached this isolated spot by train. As related in the account of the East Kent Railways, subsequently it became the site of the Dover colliery.[12] For some years, a watchman resided here, and a zig-zag footpath up the side of the cliff provided an alternative access to the railway halt. Now that the plans for a Channel Tunnel have been revived, it may well be that the S.E. main line will enter on a new lease of life.

Between Folkestone Warren and Dover two major tunnels were constructed, but the need for a third through Roundown Cliff was obviated by blowing away the face of the cliff. Cubitt felt that his alignment brought the line too close to the cliff face for satisfactory tunnelling and that to carve out a niche by normal excavation would take a year and cost £10,000. His decision was to blow out the base of the cliff with 18,500 pounds of gunpowder, thus allowing the rest to collapse on to the beach. While the plan was executed by Cubitt, it is worth noting that, when he was giving evidence for the SER Bill in 1836, Palmer had talked of using gunpowder in a similar way. The operation attracted a great deal of attention and was fully reported in the *Illustrated London News* of 4 February 1843. The article describes how 'the work of packing the powder and inserting the fusing wires was completed in three hours on Tuesday afternoon by Mr Hodges, the assistant engineer, and Corporal Rae of Her Majesty's Sappers and Miners'. There follows a description of the battery shed and firing arrangements, with which the reporter seems not to have been very conversant, followed by an account of the 'commodious pavilion erected for the reception of a multitude of distinguished visitors' which he describes with great aplomb. He continues: 'Punctual to their arrangements the Miners communicated the electric spark to the gunpowder by their connecting wires; on the signal being given the earth trembled under our feet . . . and a stifled report—not loud but deep—was heard. The base of the cliff, extending on either hand to upwards of 500 feet, was shot as from a cannon from under the superincumbent mass of chalk, and in a few seconds 1,000,000 tons of chalk were dislodged by the shock and settled gently down into the sea below. Tremendous cheers followed the blast and a royal salute was fired.'

The two tunnels, Abbotscliff of 1 mile 182 yards and Shakespeare Cliff of 1,387 yards, were both constructed through chalk, but whereas the former consisted of a conventional bore, the latter was built with two separate bores, shaped like Gothic pointed arches, each taking a single line of track. Cubitt felt that in this case the chalk was so hard that by using this special design, a brick lining could be dispensed with, and although in the light of experience, bricking was carried out, the unique cross-section was retained. Another feature of interest was that, in addition to the conventional vertical shafts for the inter-mediate working faces, shafts were driven in from the cliff face, enabling the excavated chalk to be dropped directly on to the beach. The gradients were so arranged that the east end of Shakespeare Cliff Tunnel led out on to the top of the beach, which the railway followed on a wooden trestle viaduct. In 1927, as part of the Southern Railway's improvements for continental traffic, this was replaced by an embankment supported on the seaward side by a concrete retaining wall.

It will be remembered that, under the 1836 Act, the line was to terminate short of the promontory surmounted by Archcliffe Fort, but an Act of 1843 authorised an extension through a short tunnel to a terminal station. The Admiralty Pier was not brought into use for cross-channel steamers until 1851, although its construction had been envisaged for some years. The SER station was built on a site near the docks, and also the, as yet, unconstructed Admiralty Pier. Reference has already been made to the impressive station designed by Lewis Cubitt that was never completed, and to the Lord Warden Hotel of 1851 into which the unspent capital was diverted. The station as built consisted of a plain three-storey building with a rather steeply pitched roof and unusually prominent chimneys. There was an arrival platform, a departure platform and three spare carriage roads protected by an overall roof. Dover Town was closed in 1914, local passenger traffic being served by the near-by Harbour station. A photograph taken in the summer of 1921 shows it largely as built but with two changes. First a wooden platform has been added on the south side to serve the single track which was brought into use in 1861 as an extension to the Admiralty Pier. Secondly, the overall roof has been removed. The next development, after the extension to the pier, took place in 1881 when a spur was constructed from a point just east of Archcliffe tunnel to the south end of the LCDR Harbour station. The SER constructed new engine sheds on this spur, but after the union these were closed, the locomotives being transferred to the LCDR establishment at Dover Priory. The site of the motive power depot was occupied by Bulwark Street goods depot, which was closed in 1966, and is now used for an oil depot.

The fine new Marine station was built alongside the Admiralty Pier and opened in 1914 for military traffic. Public services commenced in January 1919. Reference has already been made to work done in its early days by the Southern Railway to improve the facilities for continental traffic. At the Dover end of the SER line Archcliffe Tunnel was demolished. The southern platform of the former Town station was removed and the space used to provide a double track on to Marine station. The motive power depot adjoining Priory station was replaced by a new one built partly on reclaimed land south of the Town station. The Harbour station was closed and partly demolished, and new signal boxes were erected at each end of the 1881 spur line, at Archcliffe Junction and at Hawkesbury Street Junction. The LCDR Priory station was rebuilt, and in all, over £325,000 was spent in Dover, most of the new works being ready by 1928. (The scheme was not finally completed until 1932.)

Other developments at Dover, including the train ferry dock

and the lines to the docks and the eastern arm, will be mentioned in connection with the second main line to Dover, that of the LCDR.

Changes at Dover after electrification were less fundamental than, for instance, in the Folkestone district. The steam motive power depot was closed in 1961 but there have been no major changes. The famous Lord Warden, converted into offices during the Second World War, has not been re-opened as an hotel. What was left of the Town station has been demolished, while the platforms of the Marine station have been extended. But Dover retains its position, described in the Dover Harbour Act of 1828 as 'of the utmost importance not only for the safety and shelter of ships and vessels navigating the British Channel, but also the station of His Majesty's Post Offices Packets, and the principal port of communication with the Continent of Europe'. However, an increasing proportion of its traffic no longer uses rail access, but comes by road to cross the Channel by car-carrying vessels. The opening of a Channel Tunnel would have an adverse effect on the volume of traffic using the marine terminals, although it would probably increase the traffic on the sections of the main line inland from the tunnel approaches.

The Folkestone Harbour branch is operated as part of the main line to Dover. The development of Folkestone as a port may well owe something to the fact that the South Eastern purchased the harbour and opened the branch down to it in 1843, before its line had reached Dover. With its 1 in 30 gradient, it had more of the character of a rope-worked incline than a conventional branch, which accounts for the fact that passengers were not carried until 1849. (The parallel thoroughfare is still called the Tram Road.) With this difficult access, the continued use of Folkestone owes much to conditions at Dover. Firstly, the port of Folkestone belonged to the SER, whereas at Dover the Admiralty and the Harbour Commissioners (replaced in 1861 by a Harbour Board) were in charge. From the 1860s at Dover the SER faced competition from the LCDR but was able to maintain its monopoly at Folkestone. However, by 1895 plans for improved rail access had fallen through, there was a need to cater for larger ships, and the traffic agreement with the LCDR foreshadowed imminent union. Under these circumstances, the abandonment of Folkestone was contemplated. Not surprisingly, the towns-people opposed the idea, but the balance may have been tilted in Folkestone's favour by the uncertainty created at Dover by the plans of the Admiralty. So Folkestone's pier was extended still farther out to sea, reaching a length of 1,200 feet by 1902. When the final stone was laid by the French Ambassador in 1904, there were berths for three vessels on the north-east side (normally the lee side) and two on the south-west side (usually the weather side), but the latter have been out of use since 1940. At present Folkestone Harbour retains its share of the conventional cross-channel traffic but, unlike Dover and Newhaven, it has no roll-on, roll-off services.[13] A recent development has been the use of boat trains and conventional steamers to feed coach tours starting from French ports.

The original incline ended at the water's edge on the north side of the harbour. In 1847 it was extended across the harbour by a swing bridge. In 1849 passengers were taken down the incline to a temporary station short of the bridge, but in 1850 a permanent station was opened on the south side of the harbour. Subsequent extensions have coincided with those of the pier, accompanied by longitudinal rather than lateral additions to the platforms. The two original platforms were on opposite sides of the double track, reached almost immediately after crossing the swing bridge; but, because of the linear nature of the extensions out to sea, addi-tional platforms, instead of being alongside the older ones, were constructed end-on so that, at one stage, on the up side, there were three platforms 'in line ahead'. A second, stronger swing bridge was provided in 1893. Finally, considerable improvements were carried out by the Southern Railway between the wars. In 1930 a third swing bridge was installed to carry more powerful locomotives which, in the event, were not used. (As mentioned above, double or treble heading of boat trains up to the reversing siding continued until the end of steam.) The combination of a 1 in 30 gradient and curves of 5 chains radius ensured the survival of tank locomotives working in concert, producing unforgettably dramatic scenes for the steam enthusiast. The reversing siding was an asset rather than a hindrance, as it facilitated the substitution of an appropriate locomotive for the main line. Now electric multiple-unit trains have simplified operation. If the main line motorman does not drive his train up the incline, then no time is lost in 'changing ends' in the reversing siding. Since 1968 only passenger traffic has been carried, and the branch is used exclusively by boat trains. The survival of the Folkestone Harbour branch is almost as remarkable as its unique character.

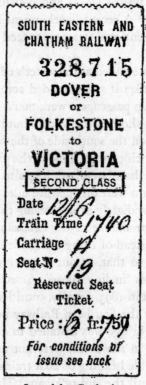

SOUTH EASTERN AND
CHATHAM RAILWAY

328,715

DOVER
or
FOLKESTONE
to
VICTORIA

SECOND CLASS

Date 12/6
Train Time 1740
Carriage A
Seat No 19
Reserved Seat
Ticket

Price: 6 fr. 750

For conditions of
issue see back

Issued by Cooks in
Paris, c. 1920

2

The London, Chatham & Dover Railway

One of the outstanding features of the railway system of the South-East is the duplication of the routes to all the principal towns. Travelling from London there are alternative routes to the Medway Towns, Maidstone, Sevenoaks, Ashford, Canterbury, Dover and Thanet. All these spring from the activities of that redoubtable rival of the South Eastern, the London, Chatham & Dover. (It changed its name from the East Kent Railway to the London, Chatham & Dover Railway in 1859.) Perhaps the most remarkable development of the 1860s was the mushroom growth of the Chatham company's system. Its genesis is attributable to wealthy landowners from East Kent, but its rapid expansion was largely the work of contractors, backed by powerful financial interests. The germ of the system was a secondary line, 28½ miles in length, designed to give railway accommodation to that part of Kent between the Medway Towns and Canterbury which the South Eastern had missed. After the collapse of the South Eastern plans for this district in 1847, Bills for a railway for East Kent appeared almost annually. The attitude of the SER was expressed in a letter written by its chairman, Mr MacGregor, on 17 November 1851 : 'Your profits will be nil ... the South Eastern would not take it at any price, and if you, the gentry, embark on it you will be ruined.' In fact, his advice was not disinterested, as there is evidence that the South Eastern was opposed to the con-struction, by itself or by anybody else, of a line which would inevitably abstract some traffic from its Wealden route. However, when Mr MacGregor's letter was quoted at the Committee stage of the East Kent Bill, the SER claimed that its attitude was entirely dependent on the prevailing state of the capital market.

The landowners, led by Lord Sondes and aided by Sir Charles Fox, the great contractor, finally triumphed in 1853 when a line from the SER at Strood to the SER at Canterbury was authorised. It was to serve Sittingbourne and Faversham, and short branches were included to Faversham quays and to the SER at Chilham near Canterbury. Subsequently it was claimed that the company was promoted merely for the benefit of contractors and financiers. For instance in 1857, when the company was applying for an extension westward from Strood, it was alleged that Sir Charles Fox had taken up shares to the value of £31,000, while his clerk held a further £41,000. Financial interests included Mr Hazlewood, a stockbroker, with £25,000 of shares and Mr Rhodes, a banker, with £21,000.

While there is no doubt that for a time a rapid expansionist policy was fostered by contractors and their financial allies, there seems little doubt that the original East Kent line, from the Medway Towns to Canterbury, sprang from the enterprise of Lord Sondes and other landowners. Apparently coincidentally a similar line, called the Chatham & Canterbury Local Railway, was projected. Initially this was not intended to provide a through route, as although it joined the SER at Chilham, its Chatham terminal was near the Sun Pier on the opposite side of the Medway to the SER terminal at Strood. However, when it became clear that Parliament preferred a through route, it did attempt to 'upgrade' itself. The influence of the SER might be suspected and Sir J. Tylden, giving evidence for the East Kent, suggested that the Chatham & Canterbury was merely a front for the SER. However there is no indisputable evidence to support this view.

The East Kent promoters were aware of the need to feed their line with through traffic, and they were granted running powers into the SER stations at Strood and at Canterbury. More than this, Section 42 of the East Kent Railway Act was the 'Facilitation Clause', governing the South Eastern's transmission of through traffic originating or terminating on the East Kent. There were hopes that through trains would run over the SER North Kent line to London Bridge, but these failed to materialise. Another plan of the East Kent was for a line from Strood to Maidstone, but this was granted to the SER. However, in return for accepting this, the East Kent managed to persuade the SER not to oppose any future East Kent application for an extension to Dover. The necessary powers were obtained in 1855 and it was probably at this point that the future of the East Kent as an independent company was determined. The Preamble of the Act makes it clear that, like the Ashford to Hastings line, the Dover extension found favour for military reasons. It provided direct communication between the strategic bases of Chatham and Dover, and also gave an alternative to the exposed and unstable section of the SER between Folkestone and Dover—the latter advantage was demonstrated during the First World War when the SER route to Dover was closed owing to the slip at Folkestone Warren. The East Kent offered to lease itself to the SER but the latter, as it proved unwisely, refused to have anything to do with a line it considered both unnecessary and parasitic. (It may also have felt that if it waited, financial difficulties might drop the East Kent into its lap.)

This left the company with two problems. First the original contractors, Messrs Fox and Henderson, were suffering from financial difficulties which delayed construction, and second, the problem remained of operating the line when it was completed. Both were solved by the new contract with Messrs Crampton, Morris and Birge, who agreed to accept payment in shares, and to lease the line, paying 5 per cent on the capital when it was completed. However, at the general meeting of February 1858, the chairman announced that, after all, the company had decided to work their own traffic.

A collection of locomotives was acquired from various British manufacturers, including six constructed by Sharp, Stewart and Co. in 1856, which were purchased from the Dutch Rhenish Railway. The quality of the locomotives varied, some of the oddities being based on unconventional designs by Thomas Russell Crampton. When William Martley was appointed locomotive superintendent in 1860 he acquired a remarkable collection of locomotives of varying efficiency and in varying condition. By dint of careful second-hand purchases, and from 1869 constructing its own locomotives, the company managed to move its traffic. However, its efforts did not escape criticism. In his book *The Locomotives of the London, Chatham and Dover Railway*, Mr D. L. Bradley quotes the MP for Whitstable speaking in the Commons in 1877:

> Its trains are formed of unclean cattle trucks propelled at snail-like speeds with frequent stops of great length by Machiavellian locomotives of monstrous antiquity held together by pieces of wire, rusty bolts and occasionally by lengths of string which clanked, groaned, hissed and oozed a scalding conglomeration of oil, steam and water from every pore.

Such a statement might well have precipitated legal proceedings if the speaker had not been protected by Parliamentary privilege, for although this was certainly the popular impression of the Chatham, not everything said about it was justified. For instance, its nickname was the 'Smash 'em and Turnover Railway', but in fact it was one of the first lines to introduce Sykes's lock and block system of signalling and had only two fatal accidents worth mentioning throughout its existence.

The weakness of the LCDR arose from its rickety financial structure and its competition with the SER. For instance, when it became clear that the SER would not provide satisfactory facilities for the forwarding of LCDR traffic from Strood, an independent route to London was acquired. Initially this consisted of the Western Extension from Strood to Bickley, from which point trains reached Victoria by using leased lines and exercising running powers. Later, new expensive railways were constructed to give the LCDR its own routes to the West End at Victoria and the City at Ludgate Hill. Outside London, branches were constructed to Sevenoaks, Maidstone and Ashford, to Gravesend, to Sheerness and to Margate and Ramsgate. The effect of competition on the traffic between London and the Channel ports was mitigated by the Continental Agreement of 1865, which enabled the SER and LCDR to charge standard fares which were paid into a traffic pool. The division began by allotting 68 per cent to the SER and 32 per cent to the LCDR, but moved in the LCDR's favour until a 50–50 division was reached in 1872. The gimcrack nature of LCDR finance was revealed in 1866 by a special inquiry, and it required the LCDR (Arrangement) Act of 1867 to institute something approaching a respectable financial structure.

With the disadvantageous results of competition so clearly demonstrated, it is strange that the companies of Southern England continued to indulge in it. For instance, Captain Tyler of the Board of Trade wrote in a report on amalgamations in 1872:

> Impelled partly by territorial ambition, partly by apprehension of invasion or competition, they damaged themselves, not only by direct expenditure before Parliament . . . but also by too easily grasping at quasi-independent lines constructed for the purpose by ingenious promoters. . . . Thus, rather than by legitimate enterprise, the railway system extended with unhealthy rapidity.

As early as 1854, an anonymous SER shareholder wrote that 'the principal cause of the falling off of dividends in English Railways has been the mania to make unprofitable extensions'.

However, after the financial strains of 1866, the SER, LBSCR and LCDR, all directed by new managements, altered course and deposited a Bill for Amalgamation. It failed because the SER objected to the maximum rates laid down for the new group by Parliament—this would have reduced SER charges to the level of those charged on the LBSCR.

In 1870 there were further negotiations, and in 1874 a measure of agreement. In the following year the SER and the LCDR were on the brink of union but owing to the unwillingness of Mr Forbes, the LCDR chairman, to accept an arbitration on a sum of £11,000, there was further delay. This left the shareholders in a state of near-revolt and in 1877, a Bill for fusion was deposited. However, a landslide on the SER main line at Folkestone Warren upset the balance of prosperity between the two companies sufficiently to lead the Chatham shareholders to reject the Bill at their Wharncliffe meeting on 14 February 1878. In 1885 the LCDR initiated a Bill for union with the LBSCR, but this failed to gain the support of the Brighton company. In 1890, another proposal for LCDR and SER amalgamation failed, but in 1892 the negotiations which led up to the working union commenced.

An important step forward was made in 1895 when standard fares were introduced to all competitive points and the resultant revenues were pooled. Without question the way to the union was made easier by the retirement in 1894 of Sir Edward Watkin, chairman of the SER, followed by that of Mr Forbes of the LCDR. It finally came in 1899, and while the ownership of capital assets remained separate, management and revenue was pooled. Rationalisation of the network was slower than might have been anticipated, but to some extent the apparently extravagant provision of rail routes could be justified by the different intermediate stations which they served. Even in 1971 alternative routes to such places as the Medway Towns, Sevenoaks, Maidstone, Canterbury, Ashford and Dover are still in use for this reason. The successive impacts of the South Eastern & Chatham Managing Committee, the Southern Railway and British Railways have done much to remove the distinctive characteristics of the LCDR from its main line, but a journey from Strood to Dover still reveals something of this aggressive Victorian company.

It is impossible to describe the LCDR route through the Medway Towns without reference to the South Eastern. (See Diagram 6: Evolution of Lines in Medway Towns.) In 1856 the South Eastern North Kent line was extended from its terminus at the side of the terminal basin of the Thames and Medway Canal at Strood, along the left bank of the Medway to Maidstone. Its position had a considerable effect on the geography of the original East Kent line. The East Kent plans were produced by William Mills, but by the time construction was under way the responsibility had passed to Joseph Cubitt. He was the son of Sir William Cubitt, engineer of the South Eastern, who also acted as consultant for the East Kent. The line through the Medway Towns to the junction with the SER at Strood was influenced by the desirability of constructing the railway bridge over the

Medway alongside a new roadbridge under construction at the same time, of avoiding demolition in Rochester and of satisfying the requirements of the Commanding Royal Engineer concerning the penetration of fortifications. His requirements were met by a considerable amount of curvature, up to 18 chains radius, and by three tunnels. The bridge over the Medway was the heaviest work on the line, with foundations reaching down to the chalk and an ingeniously designed movable section at the western end. In practice, it was found that the elevation of the bridge was sufficient to clear river traffic and subsequently powers were obtained to fix the movable span. For many years, the ancient roadbridge had been a navigational limit for sea-going vessels, and cargoes for places farther up the river were transshipped into barges. But for this roadbridge, which by happy chance was being replaced at the same time that the railway bridge was being constructed, it is not improbable that more exacting demands would have been imposed on the railway company.

The three tunnels were all excavated in chalk—Fort Pitt of 428 yards, Chatham of 297 yards and Gillingham of 897 yards. Although initially only one track was laid, all the engineering works were of sufficient width to allow for doubling. Fort Pitt tunnel was extended about 260 yards to the west and 46 yards to the east, as the Commanding Royal Engineer considered that open cuttings in this position weakened the fortifications. A Wesleyan Methodist chapel was able to obtain protection by means of a high wall between its property and the railway, to preserve it from noise and smell.

Between the western end of Fort Pitt tunnel and the bridge, the railway crossed the low ground north of Rochester on an embankment constructed of chalk moved from the tunnels, with underbridges for the roads which led down to the riverside wharves. West of the river the line curved sharply at about 12 chains radius, falling at about 1 in 52 to its junction with the South Eastern. Needless to say this gradient and curve was a considerable obstacle to trains starting up from Strood station. Once, however, the bridge over the Medway was reached, the tunnels were designed to give a ruling gradient of 1 in 132 to a summit near Gillingham station.

When the rest of the line was ready for opening in 1858, unfortunately the marshy ground under the embankment at Strood gave way and for just over two months a horse bus service linked the South Eastern station at Strood to the East Kent at Chatham. It will be remembered that although the East Kent had no parliamentary running powers over the SER line, the Facilitation Clause in its Act required the SER to handle traffic passing to and from the new line. While it is true that its efforts in this direction were somewhat minimal, and it continued to provide its own horse bus service to Chatham, it is only fair to note that the East Kent was seeking powers for an independent route to London even before its trains had reached Strood. Powers to extend from the western end of the bridge over the Medway to a junction with the Mid Kent (Bromley to St Mary's Cray) Railway were obtained in July 1858.

Whereas the SER solved the problem of reaching the Medway valley by using an old canal tunnel, the best the East Kent could do was to turn south, climb obliquely up the valley side nearly to Cuxton and then turn west into a dry valley. It was impossible to avoid a curve of 16 chains radius between the end of the bridge and the alignment along the side of the Medway, the line being carried through Strood on a curved brick viaduct. From the point of view of railway operation, the position of this curve was particularly unfortunate as it came at the foot of a climb of 5 miles at 1 in 100. Because of this, up trains were unable to approach the bank at any speed, while down trains had to use their brakes to destroy the momentum which the gradient gave them. In 1859, the East Kent had anticipated its becoming a main line by changing its name to the London, Chatham & Dover, and in 1860 its new line from Strood towards London was opened.

Any attempt to facilitate the exchange of traffic between the two companies was quickly dropped. The SER continued its horse bus service to Chatham, and the LCDR opened a station in Strood which it gave the slightly misleading name of Rochester Bridge.

The distance between the two stations was only a quarter of a mile, but the timetables were not designed to encourage passengers of either company to change to trains of the other. The connecting line remained in position, but no regular passenger service was provided, and finally in 1876 Mr Toomer, the Mayor of Rochester, together with other influential citizens, lodged a complaint with the Railway Commission. An order was made carrying heavy penalties if a service over the spur was not provided so, with due reluctance, in April 1877, it was restored. Strangely enough the part played by Mr Toomer was not forgotten, and the service between Strood (SER) and Chatham (LCDR) was known locally as Toomer's service, and the spur line as 'Toomer's Loop'.

After the Chatham withdrawal from the proposed union in 1878, relations between the two companies deteriorated and at the SER general meeting of February 1881, Sir Edward Watkin was complaining that the Chatham had 'captured' 70 per cent of the traffic from Canterbury, Thanet and the Medway Towns. (In fact it provided better services to these places.) However, he felt that the situation in the Medway Towns would be improved if instead of leaving passengers to reach the SER by Toomer's service, it constructed its own line to Chatham. This was authorised in 1881, but the recession of the middle eighties delayed the raising of the necessary capital. Perhaps unfortunately for the SER, the powers were revived in 1888 and the new branch was completed with an expensive bridge over the Medway in 1892. Its alignment was virtually parallel to that of the LCDR, and its authorisation by Parliament is somewhat surprising. Mr Forbes, speaking as chairman of the LCDR, in 1887 estimated that the bridge alone would cost £250,000, and that a 'more unwarrantable act of aggression was never perpetrated'.

The South Eastern railway bridge was built alongside that of the LCDR, making, with the roadbridge, a set of three, all with four spans and in order not to impede navigation, with the piers in line and spans of the same length. Beyond the end of the bridge, apart from some brick arches, the LCDR had been carried on chalk excavated from the near-by tunnels but for lack of similar material the SER was built on a wooden trestle viaduct. The first station, opened in 1891 just under a quarter of a mile beyond the end of the bridge, was known at different times as Rochester, Rochester Central and Rochester Common. (This rural appellation had an historical basis, but a truer indication of the character of the district was given by the near-by thoroughfare—Gas House Road.) The line crossed the approaches to the LCDR Chatham goods depot and terminated, still on its wooden viaduct, at a point in the no-man's-land between Rochester and Chatham. Further extension to the victualling yard was authorised, but this involved an expense that even Sir Edward Watkin would have found hard to justify to his shareholders.

The terminal station was opened in 1892 and included a brick-built house for the station master at street level. Its name was as misleading as that of Rochester Common, for it was called Chatham Central, a name that cannot fail to have annoyed any strangers to the district who took it literally. The point was stressed by the LCDR which in the same year opened a station about 250 yards to the west which it called 'Rochester'. In fact within two years Rochester, which had never had its own station (for Rochester Bridge station was in Strood), suddenly found itself with three. However after the union of 1899, there was no possible justification for this unremunerative branch, and the only surprise is that it remained open until 1911.

Almost the whole of the line from a point just east of the bridge was demolished, which must have provided the SECR with a plentiful supply of heavy timber for many years to come. However, space under railway viaducts in towns has usually been let, and the section of viaduct which supported the tracks in Chatham Central station remained in use as a garage, the spaces between the timbers being filled with corrugated iron. From an architectural point of view, the resulting building could have been regarded as a nightmarish version of a timber-framed building. This strange edifice survived at least until 1954, when it was photographed by the author. But most of the line disappeared, almost without a trace, except for the bridge over the Medway. This remained in use, a connection being constructed between the east end of the bridge and the former LCDR main line, thus providing an alternative to Toomer's loop.

In connection with the rationalisation of the lines in the Medway Towns during this period, two of the stations were rebuilt. The original rickety edifice at Rochester Bridge was replaced by a solid three-storey building of red brick in 1908. It had a short working life, being closed in 1917 and demolished in 1968. Partly to replace Chatham Central, the former LCDR Rochester station had its two side platforms replaced by two island platforms and its two tracks replaced by four. The extra land used on the north side became available following the closure of the line to Chatham Central. A fire in June 1919 destroyed the timber decking of the SER bridge, so Toomer's loop was restored and all traffic used the LCDR bridge until January 1922.

The next development followed the formation of the Southern Railway in 1923, when the three routes to Dover were improved to carry heavier trains. At the west end of the Medway bridge, the former LCDR line was slewed and the curve eased to take trains on to the former SER bridge, the original LCDR bridge being abandoned. The tracks were moved away from the already closed Rochester Bridge station, and a new and stronger bridge carried the former LCDR over the SER line to Maidstone. Gillingham station was rebuilt in 1932. The up platform was converted into an island and both platforms were extended as far as the near-by overbridge. Modern buildings at the side of the roadbridge, with steps leading down to both platforms, were constructed in the characteristic Southern Railway style.

The next spate of development was associated with the electrification of both the former LCDR and former SER routes at the end of the 1930s, when two new signal boxes were constructed at Strood. Electric trains first ran to Gillingham in July 1939. Only two months after the inauguration of electric passenger services, the Second World War began. Compared with the other great naval bases at Plymouth and Portsmouth, the railways of the Medway Towns did not suffer badly from aerial bombardment, although they did not escape unscathed. Fears were entertained for the safety of the Medway bridge—its destruction was several times threatened by Joyce (Lord Haw Haw), who was responsible for the English-language broadcasts from Germany. In November 1942 work was completed on reconditioning the LCDR bridge. There were connections for road traffic, and the new floor consisted of girders supporting the rails and longitudinal deck timbers for road traffic. It was never used.

The final phase of development in the Medway Towns was associated with the electrification of the lines to Dover and the Kent Coast completed in 1959. The lines had already been electrified for twenty years, but changes were made in signalling and track layout. At Chatham the platform loop lines were removed, making the island platforms into side platforms and reducing the tracks from four to two. (This was a reversal of the change which had been made at Rochester before the First World War.) A new signal box, named Rochester, was opened alongside Chatham Goods signal box, just west of Rochester station, and in addition to Chatham Goods signal box, the remaining box at Chatham station was closed. Semaphore signals were replaced by coloured lights. Since 1959 there have been no major changes in the railways of the Medway Towns, and modern development has obscured and sometimes removed the evidence of their history. Although the speed of trains through the Medway Towns is restricted, it is difficult to sight features from the line, and it is suggested that the rail journey from Strood to Chatham might be supplemented by a walk along the neighbouring roads.

Details of Strood Dock and the near-by station are given in Volume Two, Chapter 4. The most dramatic visual approach to the Medway Towns is by a train on the LCDR route, coming down the Sole Street bank. The line curves away from the side of the dry valley which it has followed from beyond Sole Street station to emerge above the left bank of the Medway, about two miles upstream from the city of Rochester. From a suitable position by the carriage window on the up side there is a view of the new roadbridge carrying the M2 high over the valley. Farther downstream are the old established bridges over the Medway, dominated by the keep of Rochester Castle. To its right is the distinctive spire of the cathedral. By this time the brakes should have been applied for the 30 m.p.h. speed limit which operates from milepost 32¼ to the country end of Chatham station.

Just before we cross over London Road the embankment ends, and we pass through the older part of Strood on a brick viaduct, curving at a maximum of 16 chains radius. A short length of high embankment leads up to a bridge over the SER Maidstone line, and we follow the new alignment of 1927 to the SER bridge. Until 1968 the buildings of Rochester Bridge station were visible on the up side. On the down side there is a good view of Strood Junction station and of the spur coming in from the North Kent line. Until 1968 it was possible to see the disused LCDR bridge but demolition operations were followed by the construction of a new roadbridge, using the same foundations, which was opened in 1970. The construction of the western approach to this bridge necessitated the demolition of the disused Rochester Bridge station. On the far side of the bridge, reverse curves of 18 chains radius take us from the alignment of the Chatham Central branch back on to the LCDR. A gentle gradient of 1 in 255 leads down to the 'low point' of the section, near the new Rochester signal box; from here we climb at 1 in 132 through Fort Pitt tunnel to a level stretch through Chatham station. On the down side there is a good view of Chatham goods depot. At Rochester station both the platforms rest on an embankment and partly owing to subsidence, the buildings have been renewed since 1968. Shortly beyond the station we cross the High Street on a steel skew bridge, and enter the cutting leading to Fort Pitt tunnel.

As suggested, some features of the line merit a perambulation. Starting from the Strood end, the SER 'territory', as described in Volume Two Chapter 4, first claims attention. As nothing remains of Rochester Bridge station or the approach viaduct to the LCDR bridge, the next feature of interest is the SER bridge of 1891, its piers lining up with the two bridges that pre-dated it. Having reached the right bank and the city of Rochester, we follow Corporation Street; the South Eastern Rochester station was demolished, but the position of its forecourt is indicated by a widening of Gas House Road. Returning to Corporation Street, and having turned into Blue Boar Lane, after passing under the

LCDR main line, a footbridge provides an elevated view of Chatham goods depot. At the end of Corporation Street, Bardell Terrace consists of railway-owned houses enriched by door knockers bearing the letters 'SER'.

The main building of Rochester station is on the up side of the embankment, the two island platforms being reached by a subway. It combines railway offices and residential accommodation in a rather plain building of yellow brick, relieved by the use of darker bricks above the sash windows and stone for the sills. It is symmetrical, with three 'bays' on either side of a central projection surmounted by a low gable containing a round window, above three closely set sash windows. The rather high-pitched roof of slate has its ridge line broken by three chimneys. A wooden canopy supported by four metal columns gave protection at the front of the station until its removal in the 1960s. It is worth looking at, not because it has any special architectural merit but rather as a typical, solid station of 1892.

Continuing along High Street under the skew bridge which carries the main line, only the lower part of the outer wall of the redbrick station master's house of Chatham Central survives. Unfortunately the last section of the wooden viaduct, which served as a garage, has now been demolished. Near-by, on the opposite side of the road, is the Wesleyan Methodist chapel, now in use by Kent Art Printers, with the wall at the back which once protected it from the noise and smoke of the railway. It makes it virtually impossible to obtain a sight of the entrance to Fort Pitt tunnel. The next vantage point may be reached by going along Gundulph Road, across New Road and into Victoria Gardens. From here there is an admirable view of Chatham station squeezed into the valley between Fort Pitt and Chatham tunnels. Two roads—Railway Street and Maidstone Road—cross the line, station buildings being erected behind a small forecourt on Railway Street bridge. The two side platforms, no longer islands, are reached by descending stairways. On both sides the new platform buildings have been erected at the London end. Before this rebuilding Chatham was a decidedly dark station, especially in the days of steam with the propensity to produce railway scenes which it would be hard to forget. I remember standing at the country end of the up platform on a cold moonlit night in November 1938, not long before electrification. We had enjoyed a performance at the old Theatre Royal and were returning to Tilbury Docks via Gravesend. The white walls of chalk round the entrance to Chatham tunnel were clear in the moonlight and on the down road, perhaps waiting to run on to the turntable, a locomotive was standing in the shadow of Maidstone Road bridge. It drew forward, the fireman opened the firehole door and at the same time a plume of steam sprang from the safety valve. Our train could be heard in the tunnel and before long it ran out into the moonlight, with one of Wainwright's graceful D class locomotives at its head. In 1938 it was an everyday scene but I would give a great deal to be able to recapture the atmosphere of Chatham station, with its gaslight and steam, on that particular evening.

While Chatham station may have been modernised, the view from the line has changed little. It emerges from Chatham tunnel on a 28-chain curve to cross another valley crowded with houses. This is followed by the darkness of Gillingham tunnel. The station at Gillingham has had four names—New Brompton (1858–1886), New Brompton and Gillingham (1886–1912), Gillingham (1912–1923) and, to distinguish it from Gillingham in Dorset, Gillingham (Kent) from 1923 until the present day. The original buildings of 1858 were of the type normally provided by the East Kent for their wayside stations, and they have survived near the country end of the down platform. As already mentioned, major rebuilding took place in 1932 with a new entrance on an overbridge, better placed to serve the built-up area which had developed since 1858. From 1939 until 1959, Gillingham was the terminus for electric services, and a four-road train depot, together with a carriage-washing plant, was constructed beyond the steam motive power depot. (This was on the up side at the country end of the station; it was closed in 1960, after the completion of electrification to the Kent Coast and has now been demolished.)

Trailing in on the down side, shortly beyond the station, is the steeply graded branch to the Chatham dockyard. In response to government pressure, in 1874 the LCDR agreed to construct this line in return for a guaranteed annual revenue, and it was opened in 1877. Its main function was the conveyance of naval stores and materials for shipbuilding, and it never had a passenger service. However, the present writer has ridden over the line on two occasions. In 1942 the journey was on a naval special train from Ipswich made up of Great Western coaches. We were hauled from Kensington by an ex-SEC E class locomotive which remained at one end of the train when we reversed down the dockyard branch, with a C class 0–6–0 on the other. My second visit took place in March 1968 by a special train for railway enthusiasts, with 09 class diesel no. 3665 at one end, and 33 class no. 6566 on the other. One feature of interest which still survives is a typical metal LCDR signal post, supporting a distant signal arm about half a mile from the junction and located at the top of the cutting. Before the general adoption of yellow spectacle glasses for distant signals, red was used, but on some lines, including the Chatham, a light in the form of a fish tail appeared at the side of the red light to remind drivers that it was a warning and not a stop signal. The Coligny-Welch lamp, which showed this fish tail, survived on this particular signal at least until 1954, but had gone by March 1968. The line is a reminder of the vital importance of railway communication to any major establishment during the Victorian period.

Between Gillingham and Canterbury, the line traverses a classic fruit-growing area. Towards the end of spring, of all the lineside views in the county this twenty-six miles justifies the description of Kent as 'the garden of England'. The apple and cherry orchards of Teynham have been famed for many years; Richard Harris, fruiterer to Henry VIII established orchards there in the sixteenth century. Before the coming of the railway, most of the fruit for the London market went by water, carried by sailing barges from the wharves which were to be found on most of the numerous creeks. For instance, Teynham was served by Conyer Wharf, Newington by Lower Halstow Wharf and Rainham by Otterham Quay. Some of the large-scale growers

o Rochester. Ordnance Survey May 1909 Edition. This shows the LCD main line and also
e SE Chatham extension. The SE Rochester station is just off the map, but Chatham
entral is shown. The LCD Rochester station appears in its original condition, before the
building which followed the closure of the Chatham Central branch. Other features
ferred to in the text include the Chatham Goods Depôt, Bardell Terrace, the Wesleyan
hapel adjoining the entrance to Fort Pitt Tunnel and Blue Boar Pier. Corporation
reet was not built at this time. (Scale 25 ins. to 1 mile; scale of inches shown at the
ottom)

11 View of Chatham Station taken from Victoria Gardens above the end of Fort Pitt Tunnel on the last day of steam operation. It shows the original buildings on the bridge carrying Railway Street; the Maidstone Road bridge is visible in the background, in front of the entrance to Chatham Tunnel. Reconstruction is in progress; the island platforms have been converted to side platforms and extended towards Fort Pitt Tunnel. The loading bay on the up side has lost its track but Fyffes Depot was still in use on 13 June 1959

12 View of Dover Priory Station taken from a down train in the Priory Tunnel. This shows the rebuilt station of 1932 on its restricted site between the Priory and Harbour Tunnels. The original engine and carriage sheds were on the right and the goods depot on the left. A post-electrification view taken on 20 August 1961

operated their own sailing barges which, during the picking seasons when the demand for transport exceeded the supply, placed them at a considerable advantage. With a fair wind and a favourable tide, London could be reached in twelve hours, but this could not, of course, be relied on. When the railway was constructed, cereal production, including barley of malting quality, was of importance, and maltings were constructed in the station yard at Rainham. But compared with East Anglia, malt production was modest, and the main hop-growing districts were on the SER line. It was fruit which was an important source of revenue to the LCDR, especially at Rainham, Newington, Teynham and Selling.

Much of the LCDR line was above or below ground level but between Gillingham and Sittingbourne there was an unusual concentration of level-crossings. They survive at the country ends of both Gillingham and Rainham stations and also at three points in between.[1] Rainham used to be a typical LCDR wayside station, with platforms with an almost SER degree of stagger but has now been rebuilt. Maltings, contemporary with the station, are to be used as a youth centre. When the electrified service was being planned it was necessary to make provision for fast trains to overtake, and it was decided that the stretch between Rainham and Newington was the best place to provide passing loops. There were no major embankments or cuttings, and although there were twelve underbridges—Nos 178 to 189—they were all of limited span. One of them had been the site of a serious accident on 16 August 1944. A flying bomb on its way to London was shot down and unfortunately struck an underbridge spanning a country lane east of Rainham. A Kent Coast express was approaching and the driver had no time to stop. The locomotive went off the track, dragging the leading coaches after it, killing eight people and injuring others.

The new four-track section was one of the last—perhaps it will be the last—examples of railway widening in England. It necessitated re-siting a platform at Newington, which also lost its signal box. Newington had been opened in 1862, four years after the line, and failed to acquire 'standard' LCDR buildings; it was

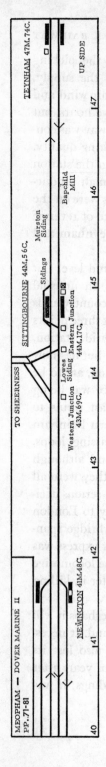
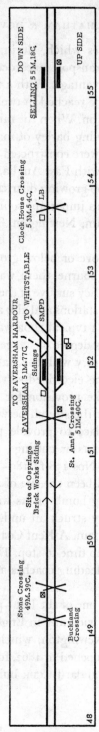
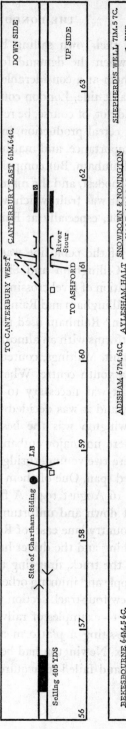
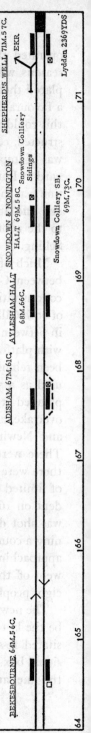

rebuilt by British Rail in 1970. Beyond Newington, Keycol Hill prevented a direct line on to Sittingbourne, and a gradient of 1 in 132 combined with a reverse curve of 45 chains radius takes the line to a summit in a cutting near Bobbing. From Bobbing on to Sittingbourne the average down gradient is 1 in 120. On the outskirts of the town is the triangular junction for the Sheerness branch, opened in 1860.[2]

Sittingbourne has little in common with 'garden of England' Kent, but rather bears the essential flavour of industrial England. Bricks and paper have been the basis of its industrial expansion, and although both industries made considerable use of water transport, they did bring some traffic to the railway. Private sidings are a feature of industrial areas and there are two in the Sittingbourne area. Lowes siding joins the up line about half a mile west of the station, and Murston siding joins the down line about three quarters of a mile to the east. The points leading into them are operated by ground frames released from Sittingbourne signal box. This was perhaps the most interesting of the new signal boxes opened at the time of the electrification, for it exercised remote control over the eight miles of the Sheerness branch. This included the movable bridge over the Swale. After a fair share of teething troubles, the box and its remotely controlled colour light signals and electrically operated points are working satisfactorily. The sidings at Sittingbourne were of sufficient importance to be provided with overhead wires for the supply of electricity to locomotives on tracks where a live rail would have been discontinuous and dangerous.

The passenger station, which consists of a side platform and an island platform, has undergone less change than either Chatham or Gillingham. The main buildings, constructed of the local yellow brick which was used for all the stations on the line, are on the side nearest to the town, in this case the up side. Sittingbourne had one of the overall roofs much favoured by the LCDR, which were notorious for the wind-tunnel effects which they generated. The one at Sittingbourne was removed after the Second World War. The outside face of the island platform is used by the trains for the Sheerness branch. About two miles beyond Sittingbourne there is a reversion from an industrial landscape to the 'garden of England', but here rather more tinged with industry, especially brick-making, than the district west of Sittingbourne. The picturesque water mill at Bapchild, just south of the railway, roughly marks the transition, although the houses around Teynham station were mostly built for workers in near-by brick yards. Until 1968 Teynham retained its signal box, although it was only used to a very limited extent. The LCDR station house remains but other buildings were replaced in 1970. Between Teynham and Faversham is the second 'hump' to be traversed, the summit at Beacon Hill being marked by a cutting, with gradients of 1 in 132 on either side of it. Although much of this section of the line is above or below ground level, there are three level-crossings—Buckland serving a farm, Stone on a very minor road and St Ann's, a street crossing on the outskirts of Faversham. A private siding on the down side served the brick works at Ospringe. Brick works in most parts of the country used to rely on railways to bring in their coal and take away their bricks, but a good proportion of those between Sittingbourne and Faversham were served by sailing barges from London. (In addition to its main line rail connections, Ospringe works had a tramway leading to a wharf at Oare.)

The character of Faversham is markedly different from that of Sittingbourne. It had the old established industries usually associated with an historic market town of which brewing remains of importance. In addition, up to the First World War, it was a centre of the explosives industry. All of North Kent was well served by water transport, and in general the LCDR made no attempt to link the numerous wharves and landing places to its main line. Most of their traffic was to and from London, and they were considered as competitors rather than sources of traffic. The explosives industry continued to make considerable use of water transport after the coming of the railway, but although only a proportion of its raw materials and products were rail-borne, its continued prosperity inevitably brought passenger and other traffic to the railway. The industry declined rapidly after the First World War.

Although the first section of the Kent Coast line was not opened until two years after the railway reached Faversham, it was designed as a junction and therefore was rather more elaborate than, for instance, Canterbury. In its present form, the station consists of two island platforms reached from a subway. Originally there was a level-crossing at the west end of the station, but vehicular traffic was diverted to an underbridge, a short distance to the west, a subway being provided for pedestrians. The Harbour branch, when it was in use, and the Kent Coast line, diverge on the down side about a quarter of a mile east of the station. The Faversham Harbour branch was an exception to the policy of not giving rail connection to wharves. Its construction was authorised by the original East Kent Act of 1853, and its genesis seems to have been political rather than economic—it served to gain local support for the East Kent rather than make money for the railway company. In evidence before a parliamentary committee, it was stated that the line was for 'coals only', intended mainly for the Ashford district via the Chilham spur and the SER line. It was opened in 1860, at the same time as the extensions to Canterbury and to Whitstable.

The main marshalling yards at Faversham are on the down side, between the station and the junction for the Kent Coast, and the Harbour branch was worked as an extension of the sidings. It consisted of a single track making a wide sweep round the east side of the town and then running up the east side of Faversham Creek to serve the principal wharves. On a visit in April 1955, the track was found to include a chair marked 'LC&DR 1876'. Now it has been closed and the track has been lifted. One object of interest which, at least in 1971, still survived in the goods yard, was an old LCDR metal signalpost, bearing two arms facing in opposite directions.

Outside the metropolitan area, Faversham was the principal junction on the LCDR, corresponding closely to Ashford on the SER, and it is not surprising that careful consideration was given to the possibility of selecting it for the location of the company's locomotive, carriage and wagon works. However, in the event, a site in Battersea was chosen instead, Faversham becoming

75

merely a motive power depot. (This was in contrast to the SER which had moved out from New Cross near London to Ashford.) The sheds were located in the fork between the two lines, and closed after electrification. An unusual survival of the days of steam is a memorial to a driver in a churchyard at Faversham, which bears the following inscription:

His last drive is over, death has put on the break,
His soul has been signalled its long journey to take,
When death sounds the whistle, the steam of life falls,
And his mortal clay shunted till the last trumpet calls.

Although the Kent Coast line is now regarded as the main line, this is approached by a 28-chain curve with a 30 m.p.h. speed restriction, whereas the original line to Dover runs straight ahead. However it does not follow the direct line of the Roman Watling Street (now the A2 Dover Road) to Canterbury. The LCDR avoided Boughton Hill by taking lower ground to the south and approaching Canterbury by the Stour valley. An earlier line, proposed by Vignoles in 1845, had taken the direct line but this involved a long tunnel, which the slightly circuitous route of the LCDR avoided. Nevertheless their alignment included a climb, mainly at 1 in 100 up to Selling tunnel (405 yards) and a descent at 1 in 132 down to Canterbury. There were no places of importance on this ten-mile section, and the only wayside station was opened at Selling. Rather surprisingly, despite the SER's having a well-placed station in the village, the LCDR did not open a station at Chartham, but until 1961 maintained a public siding for goods traffic.

Most of the line through this very pleasant undulating country is either above or below ground level, but there are two level-crossings, one at Clock House between Faversham and Selling, and the other at Chartham. They are now both protected by lifting barriers. While this particular form of modernisation has reached the line from Faversham to Dover, it has retained most of its semaphore signals. After the continuous run of coloured light signals from London to Faversham, Selling provides the first example of traditional semaphore signalling. The LCDR had considerable difficulty in finding the money to advance beyond Faversham, and the extension to Canterbury was not opened until 1860.

Buildings at such stations as Rainham were plain but built with bricks; Selling was constructed of wood. (The adjacent station-master's house was added in about 1901 and built of brick.) One very unusual feature of Selling is that when the platforms were raised, this was done by constructing a timber layer above the existing bricks. Although the goods facilities were withdrawn in 1962, a refuge siding is available on the down side which will take forty-six wagons plus locomotive and brake van.

From Chartham the line runs obliquely down the side of the Stour valley at an alignment designed to joint the SER west of its Canterbury station. There were also plans for a spur to Chilham to give a direct run to Ashford, but neither connection materialised. However, in the First World War a loop line was constructed, more or less on the original planned alignment, connecting the LCDR and SER. It was a double line, used mainly for ammunition trains from Faversham to Richborough, opened in 1918 and closed in 1920. The signals were removed in 1924 and the track lifted in 1935. Only six years later, in 1941, the loop was re-laid with a single track, and the signal boxes at each end reconnected. Mr A. G. Wells of Canterbury has made a special study of the loop and states that it was fairly well used from the day of its opening in March 1941 until 1942, mainly for special military traffic, but subsequently traffic declined sharply until its last use on 28 November 1946. It was used as an alternative route during two emergencies, first in 1944 when the flying bomb destroyed the bridge between Rainham and Newington, and again in 1946 when the line was blocked at Strood. Presumably in both cases expresses from Victoria to the Kent Coast were diverted to the SER route at Bickley running via Tonbridge and Ashford to Canterbury West, where they would reverse over the loop to reach Faversham and continue by their scheduled route.

After a decent interval, in October 1951, the signal boxes at each end of the loop were again put out of use, the points clipped

77

and locked and the signals removed. However, somewhat unexpectedly the loop was to have a third life. After the disastrous floods of 1953, the Kent Coast line was severed on both sides of Whitstable and Herne Bay. Initially Ramsgate and Margate trains reached London via the Kearsney loop near Dover and Canterbury, or via Ashford and Tonbridge, but when it was realised that the restoration of the coastal line was a major task it was decided to restore the Canterbury loop. In this way trains would regain their scheduled route at Faversham without going round by the Kearsney loop. Double track was to be provided and on 11 February Mr Wells noted: 'The ballast was laid for the new "up" line and by tonight this line was laid but not connected.' On 16 February, he wrote that the new 'up' line was connected up and finally, on 23 February, 'the loop line was opened for trains from today, and the "fast" ones now run direct from Faversham to Ramsgate via Canterbury West non-stop'. The coast line was not fully restored until the following May and on 13 May, Mr Wells photographed an up Kent Coast express on the loop, hauled by a West Country class locomotive. The last scheduled train used the loop on 20 May 1953. However, it did carry some special traffic, and the present writer rode over it on Sunday 12 September 1954. This was on the Railway Correspondence and Travel Society's 'Invicta Special' which, having left Liverpool Street station in London at 9.47 a.m., was scheduled to pass over the Canterbury loop between 1.28½ and 1.31 p.m. The track was finally lifted in 1955, but as in 1935 and 1951, the signal box buildings remained—they were not demolished until 1969.

Beyond the site of the junction with the loop line, the LCDR curved sharply over the SER, although, despite a curve of 30 chains radius, it still made an oblique crossing, necessitating a skewed bridge. The speed limit of 40 m.p.h. coming at the foot of the long descent from Selling is in an unfortunate position for trains not stopping at Canterbury. After crossing the Stour, the LCDR skirted the south side of the city and its station was slightly better placed than that of its SER rivals. There were side platforms with an overall roof spanning the gap between the walls on either side. The buildings were on the side approached from the city—the down side—and were of yellow brick, rather like Sittingbourne in style. An early edition of an Ordnance Survey map shows that about 1872 there was a small engine shed on the up side, but no trace of it has survived. After the union, the station was named Canterbury East to distinguish it from the SER station. In fact, the stations lie north and south of the city, but the name Canterbury South was already in use for a station on the Elham Valley line.

The need for signalmen to be able to see the lines they controlled produced some unusual locations for signal boxes and the one at Canterbury is elevated on stilts above a siding at the country end of the station. It is flanked by a substantial goods shed of brick with a slate roof. Considering the prestige of Canterbury and its value as a tourist centre, it is a little surprising that the LCDR did not produce something more distinguished, but probably its financial condition ruled this out. There were virtually no changes until after electrification, when, in 1960, the station had a 'facelift'. The overall roof was removed, and the platforms were protected by roofs of the normal veranda type, removed from the station at Lullingstone. (This had been completed in 1939, but owing to the houses it was built to serve failing to materialise, it was never opened.) The gas lamps which had survived the electrification of the trains were replaced by electric lighting, and in the sidings a short passenger loop was constructed.

The LCDR managed to open the line between Canterbury and Dover in 1861, with wayside stations at Bekesbourne, Adisham and Shepherds Well. (Kearsney was opened as Ewell in 1862.) All of the three original stations had brick buildings, and all were provided with goods sheds. The station buildings were of the typical LCDR 'suburban villa' style, the only unusual feature being certain of the chimney pots. However, the cost of the stations was little compared with that of constructing the line through country which, compared with that between Chatham and Faversham, was decidedly difficult. Natural features were of little help until the valley running north-west from Dover was reached at Lydden. Although there is a deviation from the direct line between Canterbury and Dover to avoid the higher ground to the south and west of Adisham, even with the aid of 2,369 yards of tunnel between Shepherds Well and Lydden, much of the line is inclined at 1 in 132. There are two breaks in the climb up to the summit which is reached in the cutting at Shepherds Well, both occurring where the line crosses valleys between Bekesbourne and Adisham. For almost all of the sixteen miles to Dover the line is either raised on embankments or lowered into cuttings. However, one factor which did reduce construction costs was that most of the excavation was in chalk, much of it strong enough to allow very steep sides to the cuttings. In some cases, for instance bridge no. 301 at Shepherds Well, it was possible for the brick arch of an overbridge to rest on the sides of a cutting. While in general the alignment was influenced by natural features, and the final entry to Dover followed the line of the valley of the Dour, in detail the Dover end reflected artificial influences. The bottom of the valley was built over, and so the line followed the west side, cuttings and tunnels being as common as on the London side of Shepherds Well, where the route was running across the grain of the country.

It will be remembered that on the London side of Canterbury, the railway looped round to the south of the Dover Road to avoid high ground; on the Dover side it crosses to the north-east of the road for the same reason. To reach this position reverse curves of 38 chains radius were decided on and at present a speed limit of 60 m.p.h. is imposed at this point. (This compares with the 40 m.p.h. limit over the curves on the other side of the city, the overall limits of 75 m.p.h. for passenger trains composed of multiple-unit stock and 85 m.p.h. for those with coaches hauled by a locomotive.) The gradient at both ends of the section, at Canterbury and at Dover, is steeper than the normal 1 in 132, being 1 in 105 in each case.

There is a noticeable change from the fruit-growing country of the Stour valley to the chalk country beyond Bekesbourne. Between Adisham and Shepherds Well we cross the Kentish coalfield and although its existence is clearly reflected in the scenery, its impact has been far less than might be expected. Firstly, there has been no great development of subsidiary industries and secondly, apart from some small 'model' mining villages, the miners have settled in the adjacent towns, including Canterbury and Dover. But while the scenic effects may have been limited, the coalfield has brought both passenger and coal traffic to the railway. The history of the coalfield is outlined in the chapter on the East Kent Railway.[3] It is explained why production did not become significant until the First World War, and also why almost the entire output of the four collieries that were finally established passed to the main line railway company. Snowdown Colliery adjoined the Canterbury to Dover line, while Tilmanstone was joined to it at Shepherds Well by the East Kent Railway. The pithead and the tip heaps of Snowdown appear on the down side just beyond Snowdon and Nonington Halt. There are extensive sidings, with overhead wires for electric locomotives, access being controlled from Snowdon Colliery signal box. Snow-down & Nonington Halt was opened in 1914, mainly to convey miners from Canterbury and Dover to the pit; Aylesham Halt was opened in 1928, about one mile nearer to Canterbury, to serve the new 'model' village opened for the miners at that point. Until recently both the halts had rather primitive accommodation with the window-panes protected by wire netting against the attacks frequently mounted by vandals on unstaffed premises. In 1968, Aylesham was 'upgraded', with attractive prefabricated buildings. On the other hand Shepherds Well retains its original LCDR buildings. Here public goods traffic ceased in 1963. (Bekesbourne and Kearsney had both closed to goods in 1961 and Adisham in 1962.) However, the exchange sidings with the former East Kent Railway still handle almost the entire output of Tilmanstone colliery, its influence being reflected in the provision of overhead electric wires for locomotives.

All the stations had their platforms extended at the time of the electrification, in the case of Shepherds Well the work being carried out at the Dover end. In most cases, the discontinuity in the platform face has not yet been obliterated by weathering. Although excavated through chalk, the 2,369 yards of Lydden

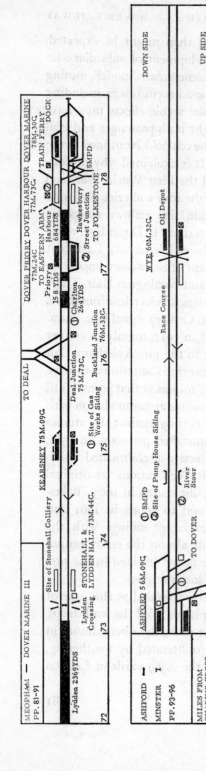
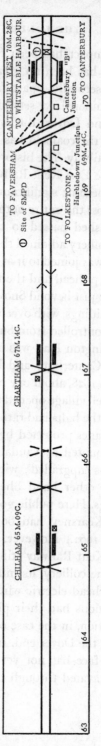
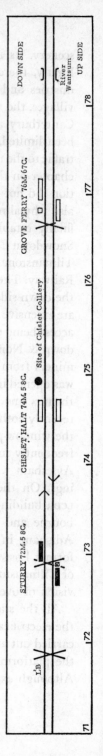

tunnel are bricked throughout; rather plain brick portals were constructed at both ends. A photograph taken from the over-bridge near the south portal in 1921 shows a mound of chalk spoil for which presumably no use could be found, dumped over the line of the tunnel. After a 40-chain curve, there is a short stretch of straight track on which Stonehall & Lydden Halt was opened in 1914. This was the third halt to be opened between Canterbury and Dover and, like the other two, was associated with the coalfield. The broken ground on the east side of the line is all that remains of Stonehall colliery which failed to establish itself. Probably for this reason, although the halt remained open to serve Lydden until 1954, it was never rebuilt but retained its wooden platforms and shelters until they were demolished. The signal box which was on the up side and a private siding on the down side have also been removed. The box, which was called Lydden Crossing, also controlled the road access to the colliery site. At this point the line enters the valley of the Dour and the site of Stonehall colliery is the last sign of the Kentish coalfield.

Kearsney, opened as Ewell in 1862 on the outskirts of Dover, was renamed in 1869 to avoid confusion with Ewell in Surrey. (For the same reason, the place is now officially called Temple Ewell.) Although they are now disused, bay platforms survive on both up and down sides, these being associated with the Dover and Deal line. The LCDR obtained powers to build a branch to Deal in 1862 but these were not used. It was finally built under the Dover and Deal Railway Act of 1874, over which the rival companies acted jointly. The Dover & Deal was the only joint SER and LCDR line to materialise, the end-on junction at Deal joining the SER, and Buckland junction at the Dover end joining the LCDR. As described above, the tendency towards co-operation was reversed after 1878, but by that time, work on the Dover & Deal was well advanced.[4] The main physical obstacle to be sur-mounted was the great chalk ridge bounding the north-east side of the deeply entrenched Dour valley, and it was decided to tunnel at a point bringing the line out on a fairly direct line for Deal. Even with Guston tunnel 1,412 yards long, the ruling gradient down to Deal was 1 in 64. A direct line between the south end of the tunnel and Dover would have been precipitous, so the town was reached by a feature virtually unknown in South East England, namely a horseshoe curve. One 'side' of the horseshoe was already in existence, consisting of part of the LCDR main line; the new limb was reached by a 12-chain curve and climbed obliquely up the side of the valley at 1 in 70, above and parallel to the LCDR main line.

The new railway joined the LCDR stations at Dover to the SER station at Deal, but to give a direct run for down trains on the two main lines, additional spurs were necessary. The one constructed by the SER from Archcliffe Junction on its main line just west of their Dover Town station, to Hawkesbury Street junction on the LCDR just south of Dover Harbour station, has already been mentioned in Chapter 1. As the new connection was slightly less than a quarter of a mile long, both its alignment and profile depended on the lines it connected. Considerable demolition of buildings was unavoidable, and the line was built with curves of 7 chains radius at either end of a short straight line. The gradient was 1 in 96 and as nothing could be done about levels, it had five level-crossings, which must have been a record for a line of this length. (There was one footbridge at Elizabeth Street.) However, shortly after the First World War all the crossings were replaced by a new overbridge, no. 2119A.

At the present time, main line trains use this spur on their way between Folkestone and Dover Priory, but for most of the time in SER days it was served by about four local trains a day from Dover Town to Deal. (It may be that the service was inhibited by the need to run over the LCDR from Hawkesbury Street to Buckland junction.) The trains did not use the platforms of the Town station, but were accommodated at a wooden platform on the spur which passengers reached through the main station. But as far as London traffic was concerned the SER confined itself to a projection of its Deal trains over the new line as far as Walmer.

The LCDR service to Deal connected with main line trains at Kearsney, using a spur line authorised in 1881 and opened in

1882, leaving the main line at Deal junction and reaching the Dover and Deal at Kearsney loop junction. It was 8 chains longer than the spur in Dover and was similar to it, in that it consisted of a straight length with curves of 17 chains radius at one end and 9 chains at the other. It had no level-crossings, but to cross under the Dover Road it dipped at 1 in 130 before climbing at 1 in 70. An unexpected feature of the bay platforms at Kearsney from which the service operated is that the tracks trailed into the up and down main lines so that there was no direct run from the Deal line into the up bay platform. Evidently it was never considered worth while to build a third line, comparable to that used by Elham Valley line trains between Shorncliffe and Cheriton junction, between Kearsney and Deal junction to keep the Deal trains off the main line. In 1913, main line connections were still being made at Kearsney on the former LCDR, and Minster on the former SER. The local trains were starting from either Dover Harbour or Dover Priory, some via Kearsney, and some extended beyond Deal to Minster. (A few, such as the 10.23 from Dover Harbour, reversed at Minster and Ramsgate and finally reached Margate Sands, in this case at 11.43.)

After the First World War some of the Folkestone and Dover expresses were extended to Deal and Sandwich, and from 1927, when the spur at Minster was opened for main line traffic, they went on to Thanet. At present the main line service runs in this way, with most of the trains in summer, and a proportion in the winter, running on to Margate. This of course has led to the disuse of the bay platforms at Kearsney and of the Kearsney loop. It has, however, been retained and after the floods of 1953 until the Canterbury loop was restored, was used to enable trains from Thanet to reach Faversham. Strangely enough, the same enthusiasts' special train which used the Canterbury loop on 12 September 1954, also descended the Kearsney loop. The most recent occasion on which the present writer has traversed it was on another 'Invicta Rail Tour' run by the Locomotive Club of Great Britain on 3 March 1968, climbing instead of descending, and with an electro-diesel locomotive, class 73, no. E 6013 instead of D 1 class 4–4–0, no. 31505.

Beyond Kearsney come first Deal Junction and then Buckland Junction signal boxes. The site of the gas works siding is on the up side and we then penetrate Charlton tunnel (264 yards) and Dover Priory tunnel (158 yards). Here, in a somewhat restricted site in a valley branching off from that of the Dour, the LCDR had a site very similar to that at Chatham. However, while the valley was no wider than the one at Chatham, there was more space to spread and the company managed to find room for goods facilities and an engine shed on opposite sides of the line. It provided a two-platform station with an overall roof similar to those at Sittingbourne and Canterbury. The station was built on a 1 in 106 gradient while the engine shed was on a level with the London end. To enable locomotives to reach it from the harbour, an up loop line was provided so that they could pass the station and then reverse into the engine shed. Until the Harbour station was opened in 1863, Priory was called Dover Town. After this, the new station was Dover Town and Harbour and the original Dover Town took its new name, Dover Priory, from the remains of the near-by St Martin's Priory now occupied by Dover College. In fact it is rather surprising that, since the closure of both the LCDR Harbour and the SER Town stations, Priory has not reverted to its original name, which gives a fair indication of its position. Although one may be accustomed to abbeys and castles that turn out to be eighteenth-century mansions, it is unusual to find a priory that is in fact a railway station.

The major rebuilding that followed the First World War has been referred to in Chapter 1, and it will be remembered that this included the replacement of the Dover Priory engine sheds by a new goods yard. The station itself was rebuilt, the work being finally completed in 1932. The overall roof was removed and new premises, in the characteristic Southern style of the 1930s, replaced the original Victorian buildings on the down side. The signal box on the down side was replaced by a new one on the up, and the up loop line was made a passenger line by opening up what had been the back of the up platform. After seven years came the Second World War and Dover Priory was badly damaged. Although restored since the war, it still gives a very

Up-train running into Canterbury West Station hauled by SE F class 4–4–0 No. A 139 built at Ashford in 1891. The station name board invites passengers to change for the Whitstable and Elham Valley lines, and a train for Whitstable is waiting in the bay platform. The space it occupies has now been filled in and the small engine shed, visible under the signal box, has been demolished. There have been changes in such details as the lamps and the seats, but the main features, such as the signal box and the goods depot, have not altered since this photograph was taken on 3 March 1928

The buildings of the SE terminus at Margate of 1858, closed to railway passengers in 1926 and demolished in 1961. Shown here as it appeared on 26 August 1954

15 The entrance to the tunnel leading down to Ramsgate Harbour Station. The Thanet line of 1926 is at a higher level and diverges to the right. Third rail and new chain link fencing have already been provided but this is a pre-electrification view of 25 July 1958

16 Ramsgate Harbour Station in 1864 shortly after its opening. The view shows the position of the tunnel mouth and also the overall roof, a feature favoured by the LCDR. The houses facing the sea and the bathing machines are characteristic of Victorian seaside resorts. (From *The Illustrated London News*, Vol. 45, p. 88)

fair impression of the modern style introduced by the Southern in its vintage period during the thirties.

The goods depot was closed in 1961, one hundred years after Priory was opened. Six hundred and eighty-four yards of tunnelling brought the LCDR alongside Dover Harbour where it opened a temporary station. After nearly two years, in June 1863, it opened a permanent establishment with yellow brick buildings, an overall roof, and an impressive clock tower. This is a somewhat baffling feature, for although towers have sometimes been added to stations as architectural features, for instance, at Nottingham Victoria, and by London Transport at some of its new stations of the 1930s, at no other point on its system did the Chatham company indulge in this kind of display. One possibility is that the tower contained the necessary head of water for a hydraulic power system. The SER had opened an extension on to the Admiralty Pier in 1861, so that even after the LCDR had reached the Harbour, it was still at a disadvantage. While the SER train was drawn up on the pier, a walk of about 600 yards was necessary to reach the Chatham train, waiting at the Harbour station. However, the tower would at least have given the passengers an indication of the direction they might follow. But by 1862, the difficulties with the Admiralty had been overcome and the extension to the pier was authorised. In 1864, albeit as a single track with tortuous curves, it was opened. Perhaps, after all, the tower was no more than a status symbol, and a counterblast to the tower which Cubitt had designed for the SER station which that company had never constructed. Incidentally, the SER did get a clause inserted in the Act for the LCDR pier extension which prohibited LCDR locomotives from whistling or blowing off steam within 100 yards of their Lord Warden Hotel.

The other extension of the LCDR trailed in at the London end of the Harbour station and ran as a street tramway to the quay wall. As the platforms were extended, the down platform crossed this line and therefore included a section which could be swung to one side when there was a train for the quay. In 1861 the Dover Harbour Board, which included a representative from each of the railway companies, replaced the Commissioners, and pursued

G

a vigorous policy of expansion. While passengers were landed at the Admiralty Pier, for general cargo, docks had been constructed, consisting of the Tidal Harbour, the Inner Harbour which grew to become the Granville Basin and the Pent which developed into the Wellington Basin. By 1879 the Harbour Board's first scheme of improvements was complete and the LCDR, owning the line near the docks, was the main beneficiary.

The next step was a Harbour Board scheme for enclosing forty-six acres of water offshore for a commercial harbour, together with a long pier which could be reached by ocean liners. Their plans were swamped by the Admiralty plans of 1897, for a harbour of refuge of 600 acres. Under conditions of spasmodic international tension, work on the scheme proceeded rapidly and was completed by 1909. It interfered with the Harbour Board's plans, and work on the Prince of Wales Pier ceased in 1902 before it was completed as intended. However, ocean liners did begin to use it, the Hamburg–Amerika line being followed by the Belgian Red Star and other companies. The railway was constructed along the quay wall and the length of the Prince of Wales Pier and a new bridge was constructed over the entrance to Wellington Basin to carry boat trains. In his book *Boat Trains and Channel Packets*, published in 1957, Colonel Rixon Bucknall included some most interesting photographs belonging to J. W. Sutton, Esq., of the Dover Harbour Board. One of them showed the Hamburg–Amerika line *Deutschland* using the Prince of Wales Pier in 1903. Unfortunately in 1906, partly as a result of the Admiralty works, the *Deutschland* suffered a mishap and ceased to call at the pier.

In 1907 the Admiralty took over its north-east side while the Harbour Board took the Admiralty Pier which they leased to the railway company. When facilities for coal exports and also an oil depot were opened on the eastern arm, the railway obtained powers to extend their line from the entrance to the Prince of Wales Pier along Waterloo Crescent, thus giving Dover the distinction of having coal and oil trains steaming slowly along its promenade. At first, reversal at the Prince of Wales Pier was necessary, but later a spur line was inserted. A photograph of

May 1955 shows a B4 class 0–4–0 tank engine steaming along the front with a train of petrol tankers. However, the Eastern Docks is now far busier with vehicular traffic than ever it was with coal or oil, and the track along the promenade has been lifted.

If the port of Dover is thought of in three parts, the rail connections to the eastern arm and to the docks have been abolished, but rail facilities on the western side remain of great importance. As soon as the Harbour Board knew that they were going to acquire the Admiralty Pier, plans for a massive extension of its inadequate facilities were prepared. These consisted of filling in the area on its north-east side to provide space for a new station, while, in collaboration with the Admiralty, it was extended to form part of the protective wall for the harbour of refuge. As mentioned in Chapter 1, the work was virtually completed by 1914, but the new station was not opened to the public until 1919.

The first step was the reclamation of 11¾ acres on the leeward side of the existing pier. This was achieved by constructing a sea-wall with concrete blocks, about 2,300 feet in length, and filling in the space between it and the old pier with chalk. This work was carried out by the Harbour Board at a cost of about £400,000. The railway company built their new station, together with ancillary buildings and carriage sheds, on 1,200 reinforced concrete piles, many of them going down about 75 feet into the chalk bedrock. This cost nearly £300,000. The station is one of the most elaborate of the railway marine terminals, comparing favourably with those at Folkestone, Weymouth, Fishguard, Heysham or any other packet station. Three steamers could be berthed alongside the main station. Inside there were two island platforms about 700 feet long by 60 feet wide, each with three blocks of buildings allocated to a variety of purposes. A photograph of 1921 shows the signs by some of the doors, reflecting the fact that the main steamer services served France and Belgium—'Bookstall, Library, Bibliothèque, Journaux', 'Tea Room, Salon de Thé', 'Dining Room, Salle à Manger'.

Dover Pier can be a very windy place. (Mr Wells of Canterbury photographed parts of a train blown over on its side in March 1951.) The LCDR had experience of overall roofs but Dover Marine not only had an overall roof, but was also walled at both ends with arches over the four running lines—two in the centre and one on the outside of each of the island platforms. With all tracks in use, four trains could be drawn up in the station. Almost invariably this was sufficient, even in the height of the summer season, but between the wars additional berthing was provided on the pier extension alongside the Dover landing platform. At the end of the First World War, it is significant that the SECR erected their main war memorial to the 556 of their people who had been killed, not at any of their London stations, but at Dover Marine.

Since the opening of the Marine station to the public, there have been no major changes, but considerable minor adjustments, especially in the arrangements for Customs examination and for the control of immigrants.

Other changes in the Dover area have already been mentioned. The Harbour station was closed in 1927, and subsequently the platforms, part of the curtain wall on the east side and the roof were demolished. A new Hawkesbury Street Junction signal box, replacing both the old Hawkesbury Street Junction and the Harbour signal boxes, was built on the east side of the line. Most of the buildings on the west side have survived, together with the clock tower in truncated form, which is used as a navigational mark.

In 1936, the train ferry service was inaugurated. It had first been proposed seventy-one years earlier by Sir James Fowler, whose scheme is described in detail in a report of 1868 by Captain Tyler of the Board of Trade. Partly on account of Admiralty opposition, the plans were finally abandoned in 1872. A second scheme was rejected by Parliament as being incompatible with the plans of the Admiralty and the Harbour Board. During the First World War, train ferries operated for military traffic from Richborough. After the war the perennial question of a Channel Tunnel came up, but was sufficiently dormant by 1932 to justify the Southern Railway in reaching an agreement with the Harbour Board for the construction of a train ferry dock. The tidal range at Dover, together with the need for a high degree of shelter, necessitated the provision of a wet dock basin on a site which was not ideal for rail access. It was on a short branch, leaving the former LCDR just south of Hawkesbury Street junction. Thus trains from the Chatham line had a direct run, but those for the Ashford direction had to reverse. The site also presented geological difficulties, as the excavations struck some fissures in the chalk through which water leaked. This delayed completion so that it was not until the October of 1936 that the train ferry service finally materialised, and rolling stock from the Continent was provided with easy access to the South East. (The Harwich train ferry had been open since 1924.) Much of the freight was highly rated, such as perishable fruit, and went up to London to Grande Vitesse Depot at Southwark. (After the war this was replaced by a new continental traffic depot at Hither Green.)

Sleeping cars, conforming to the British loading gauge, were manufactured to provide the 'Night Ferry' service between London and Paris. After suspension during the war, the 'Night Ferry' service was restored at the end of 1947, and in 1957, cars for Brussels were added to those for Paris. The combined effects of air competition, and the development of the motor ferry services have been to abstract passenger traffic from the railways to Dover. Construction of a Channel Tunnel would benefit the railways but harm the port of Dover. A greater proportion of the traffic of the LCDR main line now arises intermediately, but continental traffic, especially freight, is still a major source of revenue.

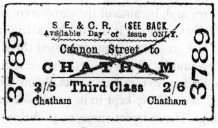

5 January 1911

3

Railways to Thanet

Once the SER was completed to Ashford, Folkestone and Dover, it was an obvious step to provide a branch to Canterbury, Deal, Ramsgate and Margate. All four places were well provided with steamer services to London although in the case of Canterbury, a journey on the Canterbury & Whitstable Railway was necessary to reach the water. Whereas a proportion of the Folkestone and Dover traffic was bound for the Continent and beyond, Margate and Ramsgate, being popular resorts for Londoners, were expected to produce their own traffic. Ramsgate did have a steamer service to the Netherlands, but the railway was never extended to the quayside and, in 1876, the service was transferred to Queenborough. Apart from this, Ramsgate harbour handled little more than local traffic until after the Second World War. In addition to being a resort, Deal developed some military traffic while Canterbury combined the functions of market town and tourist centre.

From Ashford down to Minster, the railway followed the valley of the Stour, but its character changed at Canterbury. Above the city, the valley through the chalk downland was comparatively narrow and, because of the sinuous course followed by the river, the railway crossed it in five places. In order to achieve a more direct line, at a few points it passed through projecting spurs of high ground by means of cuttings, but neither the earthworks nor the bridges were major works. Below Canterbury, the valley widened, the railway kept to its north side and there were no river crossings. The sharpest curve, of 41 chains radius, proved necessary at Grove Ferry where Section 26 of the SER (Canterbury & Thanet Branch) Act of 1844 had authorised the diversion of the river. However, for financial reasons the river was left where it was, and the railway curved round it. East of Minster, the line ascended from the estuarine marshes to the high chalk-land at the back of Ramsgate at a ruling gradient of 1 in 100. In order not to exceed this gradient, a chalk cutting over a mile in length was necessary. Ramsgate was a terminus and, until 1863, all trains had to reverse before running across the Isle of Thanet, mostly in a chalk cutting, to a well-placed terminus adjoining the seashore at Margate.

There have been important changes on the Isle of Thanet section but, apart from its electrification, the rest of the line has not changed a great deal since it was opened in 1846. It diverges from the main line at Ashford by a curve of 17 chains radius which, presumably, was acceptable on the assumption that all trains would have stopped at Ashford. A gentle rise at 1 in 400 brings the line to a summit in a cutting beyond which it descends to its first crossing of the Stour. A feature of interest at this point was a pump operated by a steam engine to provide a private water supply for the railway company's establishments in Ash-ford. For many years its siding was usually occupied by coal wagons. Four miles from Ashford the station at Wye, opened at the same time as the line, is reached. Somewhat inexplicably, while the racecourse is on the down side of the line, the special platform which served it was on the up side, leaving racegoers to find their own way over the level-crossing which adjoins the station. The goods facilities at Wye were withdrawn in 1963, but there is still some traffic to an oil depot opened at the time of the Second World War. Originally the station at Chilham was the only one between Wye and Canterbury but, under the spur of imminent competition from the new LCDR line, an additional intermediate station was opened at Chartham in 1859. (Incident-ally, Chartham had shown no great enthusiasm for the railway, and a clause was inserted in the Act forbidding the railway to come within 140 yards of the church.)

A second development on the section between Wye and Canterbury occurred in 1889, when the Elham Valley line was opened from Harbledown junction. As explained in Chapter 1, this was a 'defence line', constructed to protect Folkestone against invasion by the LCDR, and opened through rural districts between Folkestone and Canterbury. The location of Harbledown junction depended first on the need to skirt the western extremity of the built-up areas of Canterbury and second, on the desirability of placing the junction south-west of the bridge under the LCDR line, so as to avoid both the cost of constructing a second bridge and also the probability of LCDR opposition. The northern section of the Elham Valley line was closed to passengers in 1940 and to freight in 1947, but the typical SER signal box, with its weather-boarded sides, slate roof and sash windows, was not finally demolished until 1955. The bridge under the LCDR line was immediately beyond the junction, with a metal span resting on brick abutments. About three quarters of a mile separated the site of Harbledown junction from Canterbury West station and roughly halfway between the two was the site of another junction controlled by Canterbury Junction 'B' signal box. This was at one end of the wartime Canterbury loop described in Chapter 2.

The station at Canterbury was approached over a level-crossing with the road, which not only formed the main entrance to the city from the west, but was also part of the Dover Road. Its importance was recognised by special clauses in the railway's Act of Parliament. Normally, on the grounds that road vehicles could stop more expeditiously than trains, level-crossing gates were kept shut against the roads, but at Canterbury the reverse applied, with a proviso that, if the gates were ever closed against the road for more than five minutes, the company would be liable to a fine of 40s (£2). The inability of trains to stop in short distances without warning was recognised by a rule that all trains should stop short of the crossing and, when it was set in their favour, they could run on into the station at a speed not exceeding 4 m.p.h. (Incidentally, the same rule applied at the level-crossing at Wye.) It only affected down trains, as up trains would have stopped in the adjacent station. Needless to say, this statutory halt is no longer observed. Canterbury was one of the principal stations on the SER and, like Tonbridge and Ashford, had separate

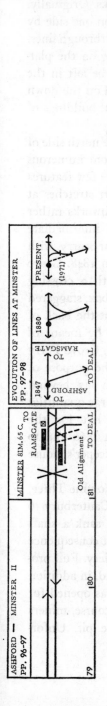
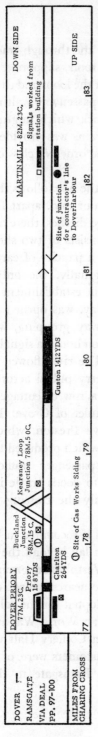
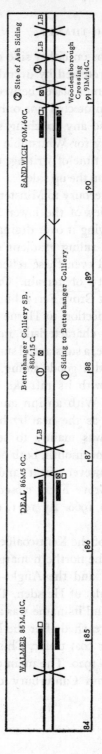
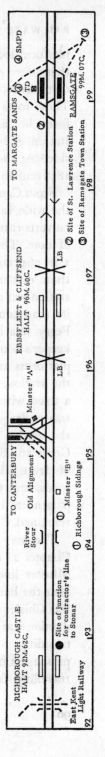

platform loops on either side of the through tracks. Originally, these were protected by overall roofs, supported on one side by cast iron columns placed between the loops and the through lines. These roofs protected not only passengers waiting on the platform, but also any coaching stock which might be left in the station. A bay for Whitstable trains was provided on the down side.[1] At the time of writing, the ordered, classical buildings of 1846 remain on the up side.

From Canterbury to Minster, the line follows the north side of the wide valley of the lower Stour and, apart from numerous culverts carrying it over drainage ditches, there are few features of note. The ruling gradient consists of two short stretches at 1 in 264, and even these reflect a paucity of earthworks rather than difficulty of terrain. Originally, the only intermediate station was at Grove Ferry, but the establishment at Sturry, with its road connection to Herne Bay, was opened in 1848. Grove Ferry was a characteristic railway grouping, with a crossing keeper's house, a substantial station house, a signal box, staggered platforms and a goods siding. The river flowed at the back of the station, with its raft-like ferry pulled across by means of a fixed wire. With an inn and a row of cottages, Grove Ferry was as large as the near-by hamlet of Grove. The purpose of the station was mainly to serve Preston, which lay beyond Grove and Stourmouth, both of which produced large quantities of fruit. However, fruit and passenger traffic left for the roads, and Grove Ferry closed to goods traffic in 1960 and to passengers in 1966. By 1971, only the crossing keeper's house remained.

The story of the Kent coalfield is recounted in Volume Three, Chapter 4. The northern margin lay beyond the Canterbury to Minster line, and the Anglo–Westphalian group sank a shaft near the hamlet of Hersden. The nearest village of consequence was Chislet and its name was adopted for the colliery. Full production was reached after the First World War and, in addition to sidings for coal traffic, Chislet Colliery Halt was opened for passengers in 1920. The main customers were, of course, miners travelling from Canterbury or Ramsgate to the pit. Unfortunately, by 1970, mining had ended, and although the halt remained open until 1971 coal traffic ceased. The now stagnant tip heaps, together with extensive gravel pits, give this part of the valley a distinctly industrial atmosphere. Strictly speaking, the Isle of Thanet is reached when the train crosses the Wantsum, now little more than a drainage ditch, about one and three quarter miles beyond Grove Ferry. (In the floods of 1953, water broke through from the sea and, for a limited period, Thanet became a real rather than a titular island.) Since 1847, Minster has been the junction for Deal.

Deal was an obvious candidate for a branch line in the 1840s, when, in addition to its traffic as a naval centre and resort, passengers occasionally joined or left sailing vessels laying in the Downs. Near-by was Walmer Castle, a residence of the Duke of Wellington, still one of the most influential men in the country and, subsequently, a somewhat mistrustful patron of the South Eastern Railway. A crossing of the Stour was unavoidable, but the alignment of the railway and the course of the river were adjusted to produce a crossing with a minimum span. Although navigation above Sandwich was already declining, the River Stour Commissioners insisted on a movable bridge, which for many years was swung annually to assert navigation rights. The bridge is now fixed but the approach embankments on either side remain the only significant gradients between Minster and Deal. Apart from this, the line was built over level, estuarine lands, moderate curvature being introduced to avoid re-crossing the Stour and demolition on the outskirts of Sandwich. The branch was built with double track but when it was found to be unnecessary, without the formality of informing the Board of Trade, the line was singled. This resulted in the insertion of a clause in the SER (Capital) Act of 1855 stating that the Board might require restoration of the double track on pain of a fine of £500 per day. In fact, it seems probable that the re-doubling was delayed until the extension from Deal to Dover was completed and the branch became part of a through route.

One intermediate station was constructed on the outskirts of Sandwich. Its substantial brick buildings survive on the east side

of the line. The terminal at Deal had similar, substantial buildings with the added refinement of an overall roof covering the
platform and the two tracks which adjoined it, thus forming a
convenient carriage shed. As explained in Chapter 2, the desire
of the LCDR to construct a branch to Deal was met by the extension of the SER Deal branch to Buckland junction, Dover,
undertaken jointly by the SER and LCDR companies. Two intermediate stations were opened, one at Walmer and one at Martin
Mill for St Margaret's Bay. The provision of spurs to enable the
line to be reached from the south was described in Chapter 2. At
the Minster end, a spur was put in to allow through running to
Ramsgate without reversal in Minster station. However, little or
no use seems to have been made of it until the rearrangment of
the Thanet lines in 1926. The junction at Minster was moved
farther to the east of the station, while the point of conjunction of
the two spurs was moved slightly north (see Diagram 9). The
effect of this was to reduce the eastern arm of the triangle, used
by trains running through from Deal to Ramsgate, to 23 chains
at 13 chains radius, while the new western spur curved at $8\frac{1}{2}$
chains radius, perhaps the most acute curve on a running line on
the former Southern Railway. The old western spur was retained
as a siding with no outlet at its southern end. From 1927, through
expresses from London via Dover and Deal ran over the eastern
spur at Minster towards Ramsgate. In addition to becoming part
of an important through route, the former Deal branch acquired
four branches.[2] The first pair to be built were the lines branching
off near Richborough Castle to Stonar, and that from Martin
Mill to Dover constructed in connection with the great harbour
of refuge at Dover. Thirdly, during the First World War, about
a mile from Minster, the important branch to the new military
port of Richborough diverged on the east side of the line. Its
position is now occupied by the line to Richborough power
station. Finally, a branch about two miles long from Bettes-
hanger colliery joined the main line a mile and a half north of
Deal.

Beyond Minster, the original line of 1846 ran on to Ramsgate
and to Margate. Whereas between Canterbury and Minster, and

on the Deal branch, earthworks are hardly to be found, this section was almost entirely on embankments or in cuttings, but even the provision of earthworks did not reduce the ruling gradient on to Ramsgate to less than 1 in 100. The single-storey buildings of the terminus at Ramsgate were virtually identical with those at Canterbury West, with the same recessed, classical entrance flanked by sash windows. However, while the layout at Canterbury was relatively spacious, the original Ramsgate station was decidedly cramped. Basically it consisted of arrival and departure platforms, with a two-span overall roof covering the inner ends opposite the main building. There were four tracks and room was found to insert a third platform, short and narrow, between the two centre tracks, so that all four were alongside platforms. It is only fair to say that this decidedly slender centre platform was normally reserved for local traffic. Until 1863, all Margate trains had to reverse at Ramsgate, but in that year a spur of 31 chains was constructed to permit through running. (This was doubtlessly attributable to the advent of the rival LCDR in Thanet.)

Mainly to cater for the very occasional train avoiding Ramsgate, in 1864 a station was opened by the road bridge just west of the spur, and named St Lawrence. During the 'railcar and halt' period, Ebbsfleet and Cliffsend Halt was opened in 1908 about one and three quarter miles east of Minster. The adverse economic conditions of the early thirties led to its closure in 1933. The SER Ramsgate station was over half a mile from the harbour but, from 1901, this disadvantage was reduced by the construction of an electric tramway which terminated in the station yard. Beyond Ramsgate it ran across Thanet, partly on reserved track, to serve Broadstairs and Margate. It was replaced by the buses of the East Kent Road Car Company in 1937. However, passengers by the SER route would usually have remained in their train to complete the 3¾ mile run across Thanet to a well-placed terminal near both harbour and beach at Margate. (See Diagram 11: Evolution of Thanet Lines.) The alignment was direct except for a slight inclination to avoid Nash Court. There were embankments at each end, with a total of three underbridges, while about two and a half miles were in a chalk cutting with six brick overbridges. A level-crossing, with a typical SER crossing keeper's house, was provided at Northwood.

Economic difficulties prevented the construction of station buildings similar to those at Canterbury and Ramsgate and, until 1858, Margate had to make do with a temporary wooden structure. By this time, funds permitted the erection of a modest but well-designed single-storey building. Old photographs show a frontage with slightly projecting end bays with Venetian windows and pediments, and a central section with an entrance flanked by two large sash windows on either side. The classical effect was completed by a balustrade running across the top. After its closure as a railway station, this quite elegant building was used, at various times, as a booking office for pleasure aeroplane flights, as an amusement arcade and as a snack bar. When I photographed it in 1954, it had been modified quite tastefully, one end bay being devoted to Cream Ices, the central section to refreshments, and the other end to the 'Casino Bar'. The SER station at Margate was finally demolished at the end of 1961. There were no normal intermediate stations, but platforms were provided to serve the Tivoli Gardens, now Tivoli Park.

Until 1863, the only serious competition the SER faced for Thanet traffic was from the steamboats but, from that date, it was up against the LCDR. The 'invader' had mileage advantages, distances from Victoria as compared to Charing Cross being 7 miles less to Ramsgate and 16 miles less to Margate. The LCDR had a far better placed station at Ramsgate, while its Margate site was not appreciably inferior. Competition, however, was limited to some extent by the continental agreement of 1865 by which revenue from journeys between London and all points on the coast between Margate and Hastings was pooled. There was no economic justification for the duplication of facilities in Thanet, and after the union it was only a question of time before some form of rationalisation was imposed. The LCDR line to Thanet had at least one thing in common with the LCDR main line to Dover in that it started as a local project and was blown up into a main line by speculative interests. George Burge who, together with Crampton and Morris, had taken the contract for the main line, had purchased a considerable amount of land at Herne Bay. Perhaps inspired by the successful speculative venture of Mr Burton at St Leonards, Burge envisaged a comparable development at Herne Bay. He was the contractor for the original Herne Bay Pier and was associated with the Herne Bay and Faversham Railway Act of 1857. (Herne Bay was served by road from the SER station at Sturry, but the route via Redhill and Tonbridge was very devious.) The line was planned as a single-line branch to Herne Bay but, in two stages, was extended and developed to become a main line to Thanet. The Margate Railway Act of 1859 authorised the first extension and the Kent Coast Railway Act of 1861 took the line through to Ramsgate. Apart from the section between Margate and Ramsgate, which included a considerable tunnel, construction costs were modest. For instance, the authorised capital for the 10¾ miles of line from Faversham to Herne Bay, was £80,000 compared with £700,000 for 30 miles of LCDR main line. Much of the line ran over marshes but, where higher ground came down to the water, near Whitstable and near Herne Bay, only moderate cuttings were provided, resulting in steep gradients. Despite their lack of depth, these cuttings were sources of difficulty as they penetrated weak clays.

Originally, the only intermediate station between Faversham and Herne Bay was Whitstable. Subsequently, a public goods siding was opened on the edge of the marshes at Graveney and, between the wars, Chestfield & Swalecliffe Halt was provided, following residential development between Whitstable and Herne Bay. Whitstable had had rail connection to Canterbury since 1830, admittedly of a rather limited character. But the new line gave a far quicker and more direct route to London. The original station was situated on the road from Whitstable to Canterbury, somewhat unusually placed on an embankment. Beyond Whitstable, it was decided to pass under the SER Canterbury & Whitstable line and this fixed the altitude of the foot of the bank ascending towards Tankerton. The depth of the cutting was sufficient to give a gradient of 1 in 82. Whitstable

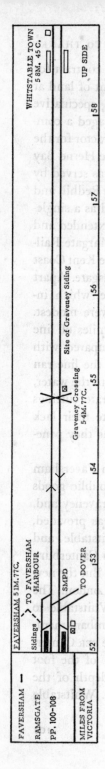
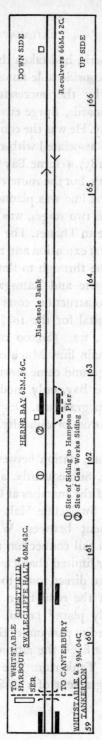
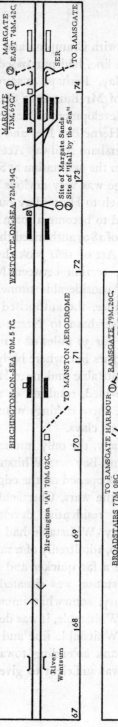
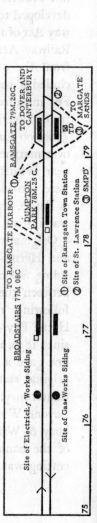

7 Ramsgate Harbour Station from above the end of the tunnel in the summer of 1913. This view shows the station buildings on the landward side of the train shed and also the proximity of the station to the harbour

8 Ramsgate Harbour Station from above the end of the tunnel in the summer of 1958. This view shows the train shed adapted to become 'Merrie England'; the harbour remains but the bathing machines have gone.

19 The original Margate Station of the LCDR in 1864, shortly after its opening. Both the station buildings and the station master's house on the right use bricks of different colours to form ornate patterns. Other highly decorative features are the windows, the chimneys and the iron finials at each end of the roof. A canopy protects the entrance and even the pump house, surmounted by its water tank, receives lavish architectural attention. A metal signal post with a semaphore arm appears to the right of the water tank. This station was demolished to make way for the present building, with the exception of the pump house and water tank. (From *The Illustrated London News*, Vol. 45, p. 88)

20 Etchingham Station on the SE line to Hastings shortly after its opening. The stations on this line form the best series in the South of England. They are nearly all contemporary, with three classical in flavour and three, including Etchingham with a mixture of Gothic and Tudor characteristics. (From *The Illustrated London News*, Vol. 20, p. 149)

offered traffic as a fishing port, specialising in oysters, as a general port, and as a seaside resort and residential area. The main residential districts were on the east side of the town and, when the inadequacies of the original station became notorious, a new station was opened just west of the bridge carrying the SER Canterbury & Whitstable line.[3] This was opened on the first day of 1915, with a footpath connection to a newly opened halt on the Canterbury & Whitstable. The new station handled passengers only and the original goods yard remained in use until its closure in 1964. The enlarged catchment area of the second station was recognised by naming it Whitstable Town and Tankerton. (The 'Town' was deleted in 1936, after the closure of Whitstable Harbour station.) While it was doubtless an improvement from the traffic point of view, the reverse was true for operating, down trains calling at Whitstable being faced with the problem of starting on a formidable gradient. The Herne Bay oyster industry, probably inspired by that of Whitstable, was served by a long siding to Hampton Pier.[4] A private siding used to carry coal for the Herne Bay gas works, but gas is no longer manufactured, although the site is indicated by the presence of gas holders. The station buildings on the down side at Herne Bay are original, characteristically located at a point of transition between cutting and embankment. In 1926 the up platform became an island, when an up loop line was constructed round the back of it. Colour light signals replaced semaphore on the Kent Coast line at the time of electrification, but the signal box at Herne Bay survived until 1971, able to take over the operation of the automatic signals if the need should arise. The up loop is now used for special traffic only and access is controlled by hand-worked points.

As explained above, the extension to a terminus at Margate, immediately to the west of that of the SER, was authorised in 1859. East of Herne Bay, comparatively high ground had to be crossed and the ruling gradient on Blacksole Bank was 1 in 93. Beyond the summit, the line ran down to the Wantsum which forms the boundary of the Isle of Thanet. Here there was four miles of almost straight and level track; over two and a half miles were absolutely straight and level. This section was inundated by the floods of 1953 and the earthworks which now protect it were completed after that date. The eight-mile gap between Herne Bay and Birchington was too lengthy for 'traditional' block signalling so, roughly at the midway point, in an isolated marshland setting was placed Reculvers signal box. (The Roman site for which it was named was called 'Reculver', but the railway authorities preferred, for their signal box, 'Reculvers'.) The branch to Manston Aerodrome diverged on the up side, near the site of Birchington 'A' signal box which was demolished in 1929.[5]

Birchington station was contemporary with the line, the fact that it was better placed for the new seaside resort than for the old inland village being reflected in its re-naming as Birchington-on-Sea in 1878. Nevertheless the station buildings, including a distinctive station house with prominent gables, were placed on the up side, facing the inland village. Westgate-on-Sea station was added in 1871. The signal box here remains to operate the level-crossing gates. The original plans for a terminal station at Margate did not materialise as, before it was built, the extension to Ramsgate had been authorised. It was not possible to extend from the intended terminus, so the curve towards Ramsgate was sited short of it. If the original site had been used, trains would have had to run into the terminal and then back out again before continuing to Ramsgate. (A similar arrangement was carried out for many years with Weymouth trains calling at Dorchester, LSWR.) So the first LCDR station at Margate was constructed on a curve, slightly farther from the beach than the originally planned terminus. Somewhat oddly, it was decided to build a second station on the east side of the SER with a junction facing Ramsgate. The most obvious explanation was the desire to compete for the local Margate and Ramsgate traffic, bearing in mind the advantage of better siting enjoyed by the LCDR at the Ramsgate end. In the event, the earthworks were completed by 1864 and retrospective parliamentary powers were obtained in 1865, but there seems to be no record of any trains using this short spur. The station building was let to the catering concern, Messrs Spiers and Ponds, who named it 'Hall by the Sea'. A photograph

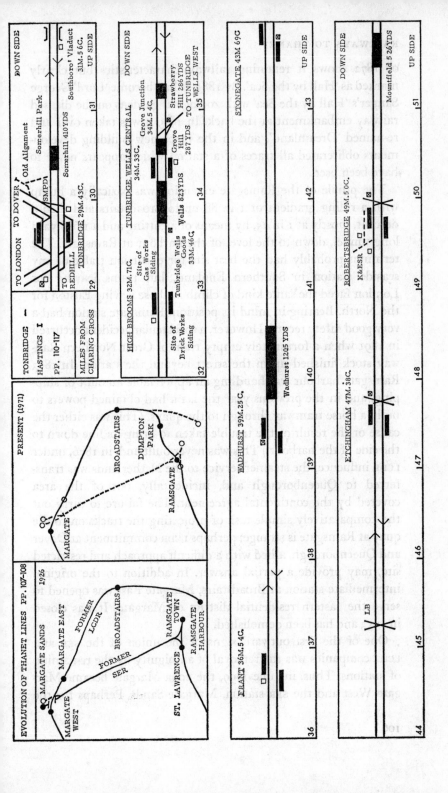

of 1872 shows it retaining railway characteristics but clearly marked as 'Hall by the Sea'. By 1885, it had become 'Lord' George Sanger's 'Hall by the Sea' with zoological gardens on the disused railway embankment at the back. In 1919 it was taken over and re-named 'Dreamland', and in the 1930s new building developments obliterated all traces of a station which appears never to have been used.

The profile of the Ramsgate extension was basically a hump with a ruling gradient of 1 in 88 up to Broadstairs and then a descent, mostly at 1 in 75, by means of a cutting and a 1,638 yard long tunnel, down to the level of the harbour at Ramsgate. The terminus probably had the best site for excursion traffic of any seaside station in Southern England, but trains leaving for London faced the same kind of climb as those leaving Euston for the North. Bearing in mind its position, Ramsgate station had a very good safety record. However, a spectacular accident occurred in 1891 when a fortunately empty train of Great Northern Railway stock finished up in the street beyond the station. In 1863 Ramsgate harbour was handling an appreciable amount of shipping, and in the previous year the LCDR had obtained powers to build a horse tramway through to the quays. (This was either the cause or the result of the trouble taken to bring its line down to the side of the harbour.) This was never built and, in 1876, under LCDR influence, the steamer service to the Netherlands was transferred to Queenborough and, incidentally, out of the area covered by the continental agreement. The failure to carry out the comparatively simple task of projecting the tracks on to the quay at Ramsgate is strange; perhaps LCDR commitment at Dover and Queenborough, allied with a difficult approach and restricted site, may provide a partial answer. In addition to the original intermediate station at Broadstairs, Margate East was opened to serve the eastern residential district of Margate. It was closed in 1953 and has been demolished.

One of the first outward signs of the union of the SER and LCDR companies was the removal of ambiguity by the re-naming of stations. Thus, in June 1899, the LCDR Margate became Margate West and the SER station, Margate Sands. Perhaps for the

sake of conformity, East Margate became Margate East. At
Ramsgate, the SER station became Ramsgate Town and the LCDR
establishment, which had rather inappropriately been called
Ramsgate and St Lawrence-on-Sea, became Ramsgate Harbour.
The Joint Committee completed plans for the rationalisation of
the lines on the Isle of Thanet but little progress had been made
by the outbreak of war in 1914 and it was left to the newly
formed Southern Railway to carry out a comprehensive scheme.
Basically this consisted of the construction of a new 1½-mile link
line which made possible the abandonment of the 4½-mile SER
line between Ramsgate and Margate and the concentration of
station facilities. The new line diverged from the LCDR on a 20
chain radius curve about one mile south of Broadstairs station
and just north of the entrance to the tunnel. Its other end joined
the SER about half a mile west of the Ramsgate terminus. Unfortunately, the junction at the LCDR end was considerably lower
than the SER line, so the new line, which was partly in cutting
and partly on embankment, climbed with a ruling gradient of 1
in 175. Like any scheme of its kind, the Thanet rationalisation
was not an unmixed blessing. For instance, the fine new station
at Ramsgate was not only more remote than the LCDR Harbour
station, but was constructed at the end of the new link line,
about a quarter of a mile farther away from the town than the
SER station. On the other hand, the new Margate station was
completed in 1926 on the same site as Margate West. Because of
the restricted LCDR site, the goods facilities of the abandoned
SER line at the Margate end were retained; a spur linked it to the
former LCDR line. New buildings were provided on the down side
at Broadstairs, but the existing buildings of 1863 were retained
on the up side.

At the east end of the link line, at Dumpton Park, a new
station was due to open at the beginning of July 1926 with the
rest of the new works. However, there were delays, and Dumpton
Park was not finally opened until Monday 19 July 1926. It consisted of an island platform in a cutting reached by a footbridge
from ample buildings in the early Southern style, at road level.
In a spirit of optimism, the excavations allowed space for the

addition of a second island platform. An interesting feature was the provision of concrete signal posts but these have now, of course, been replaced by colour lights. In the tradition of 'Hall by the Sea', the abandoned Ramsgate Harbour station provided a site for amusement facilities described as 'Merrie England'. The electric railway which ran through the approach tunnel has now been closed. If plans to extend this to Broadstairs had material-ised, albeit in an indirect way, the Harbour station would still have had rail access. The most recent stage of development of the Kent Coast line was reached with its electrification in 1959. Its character has changed from a line competing with steamers for seaside traffic to a commuter line. This is not to suggest that Londoners have ceased to go down to Ramsgate or Margate at summer weekends, but special day excursion trains are virtually unknown. The closely packed compartment stock, pressed into use at the height of summer, has disappeared as completely as the paddle steamers with which they once competed.

1880s

20 August 1909
(St Pauls is now Blackfriars)

3 January 1910

4

The South Eastern Main Line to Hastings

When the SER opened its main line to Dover, Hastings was served by stage coach from the intermediate station at Staplehurst. However, the end of this palpably temporary arrangement was foreshadowed when the Brighton, Lewes & Hastings Railway was authorised as a major part of the emerging Brighton company's network. Not content with this, in 1845 the Brighton, Lewes & Hastings obtained powers to extend to a junction with the SER at Ashford, thus completing the coastal route from Brighton to Dover. The revenue-earning potentialities of a line from Hastings to Ashford, with no town larger than Rye on the route, were slight and there seems to have been no great reluctance on the part of the Brighton company to transfer these powers to the SER. The interest that wanted the line most was the Government and, more especially, the Duke of Wellington, who was anxious to have a line of railway available to convey troops to any part of this most vulnerable stretch of coastline. The SER exploited the situation by offering construction of the Hastings to Ashford line as one of the 'sweeteners' accompanying its application for powers to build the North Kent line. The Government, in turn, made it a condition of authorising an SER line from Tunbridge Wells to Hastings, that the company should not open it until railway communication was established between Ashford and Hastings. (They also ordained the cessation of dividends pending completion of the line, if it were not opened within the statutory period.) On this account the Ashford to Hastings line is the best example in Southern England of a railway whose construction was encouraged for military reasons.

Faced with a commitment to build a line which was unlikely to pay its way, the SER sought to economise. Its plans for the Tunbridge Wells to Hastings line included a branch from Whatlington, about eight miles from Hastings, following the valley of the Brede to join the Ashford to Hastings line at Lidham Hill near Snailham. The SER proposed to substitute this branch for the authorised line which crossed the hills between Snailham and Hastings, traffic from Ashford joining its line from Tunbridge Wells at Whatlington, and then using it to reach Hastings. In this form, the line would have been cheap to build. In fact, the engineer's estimate was as low as £10,000 a mile for double or £8,000 a mile for single line between Ashford and Whatlington. Carried away by the prospects of this economy, the SER awarded a contract for the Whatlington to Lidham Hill line but, unfortunately, the Government proved adamant, and the contract had to be cancelled in favour of one for the original alignment between Lidham Hill and Hastings. It is of interest to associate such features as the 1 in 60 bank between Hastings and Ore with the intransigence of Russell's Whig Government.

The line from Hastings to St Leonards was constructed and owned by the SER, but in view of the fact that the powers to build it had been transferred from the Brighton, Lewes & Hastings company, its LBSCR successors had running powers which they were anxious to exercise. (A section of the 1848 SER and Brighton agreement applies to the completion of this link.) The reason for the Brighton company's anxiety was that, once completed, the link gave it a route from London Bridge to Hastings of 76½ miles via Lewes, compared to the SER route of 93 miles via Redhill and Ashford. By Thursday 13 February 1851, the line had been approved by the Board of Trade inspector and the SER service via Ashford was already running. In accordance with legal agreements, the link between St Leonards and Hastings was ready for use, but the SER signalmen appeared to have considerable difficulty in admitting LBSCR trains. Official protests were met by a statement that the SER could not be expected to handle the LBSCR trains without a timetable, so this was promptly provided. During Saturday and Sunday a number of the Brighton company's trains succeeded in reaching Hastings so, on Sunday evening, two locomotives and seventeen carriages and vans were sent through to form the first up train on Monday. This was effectively blocked by an SER locomotive and a number of wagons filled with earth. In accordance with a custom still prevalent, the LBSCR laid on an emergency bus service from St Leonards to Hastings, but the SER prevented the buses from entering the Hastings station yard. The deadlock lasted for some days until the inevitable negotiations began, leading to the creation of a traffic pool. After the opening of the direct SER route via Tunbridge Wells, the net receipts from Hastings traffic were divided between the two companies equally. Co-operation improved after the agreement of 11 June 1866 by which the intermediate station at St Leonards, Warrior Square, became a joint station, and new accommodation was provided at both St Leonards and Hastings to permit joint operation. (LBSCR trains called at Warrior Square from 1870.) Such extravagances as separate booking offices and staffs lasted until the two companies were merged in 1923.

To avoid demolition in an exclusive residential district of St Leonards, with the avoidance of gradients as a subsidiary influence, the one and a half miles of link line was almost entirely in tunnel—Hastings tunnel was 788 yards long and Bo-peep tunnel 1,318 yards. Because of the position of the intermediate station at St Leonards, instead of the tunnel descending gradually to the point of junction with the LBSCR, Hastings tunnel linked the two stations at 1 in 100, while Bo-peep tunnel ran on to the junction with the LBSCR line at 1 in 203. The excavation in the clays and sands of the Hastings Beds and Wadhurst Clay did not prove easy and the tunnels were built to substandard dimensions, without inverts. In 1848 work had to be suspended, as it was alleged that the tunnelling was abstracting water from the wells of the houses above it. Double track was provided, but the space between the tracks was less than usual and, for many years, trains were not allowed to pass in the tunnels. By November 1949, Bo-peep tunnel had deteriorated so far as to necessitate its closure for partial reconstruction. It was closed from 27 November 1949 until 5 June 1950 with emergency bus services linking Crowhurst, St Leonards and Hastings and also Bexhill West, St Leonards and Hastings. (Trains on the SER line were diverted to Bexhill West, while those on the LBSCR route terminated at St Leonards West Marine.)

The original Hastings station resembled a V facing St Leonards, one arm of which was a through platform intended mainly for the SER, and the other arm a terminal used by the LBSCR, who always treated Hastings as a terminus. It was located on the northern edge of the new resort district of Hastings, which was separated from the old town by Castle Hill. Spoil from the adjacent tunnels provided a foundation for the fan-shaped site which, in addition to the passenger station, was used for a goods depot and the SER engine sheds. Subsequently, an extra two-sided terminal platform was added to cope with the heavy summer traffic. The Southern decided to rebuild, and a new station was officially opened on 6 July 1931. Other improvements to the line from Tonbridge had been made to permit the use of the new Schools class locomotives, with heavier trains and higher speeds, and a special train was run from Charing Cross for the opening ceremony. It was hauled by Schools class no. E904 Lancing, which had been completed at Eastleigh Works in 1930. The new station consisted of two island platforms so that, when the electric service was introduced in 1935, there was no difficulty in running trains on to Ore. Locomotives were concentrated at the former LBSCR motive power depot at West Marina, where additional carriage sidings were provided, but the goods depot was not moved.

The electrification of 1935 gave a boost to the former LBSCR line but the SER line remained the shorter and more popular route. The railway from Tunbridge Wells to St Leonards was complete by 1852, but this was connected to the main line at Tonbridge by the Tunbridge Wells branch which had been opened seven years earlier. In view of the part played by Tunbridge Wells people in promoting the SER, it is not surprising to find a four-mile branch being opened to a temporary terminus in

1845. (An SER board minute of 29 July 1836 had referred to 'the proposed branch to Tunbridge Wells'.) The line was difficult to build and, despite considerable curvature, earthworks and an impressive 254-yard viaduct with thirty arches at Southborough, it had a ruling gradient of 1 in 93 and a maximum curvature of 20 chains radius. The position of Somerhill Park necessitated the branch diverging from the main line almost at right angles and climbing through Somerhill tunnel at 1 in 100. Instead of a direct junction, a similar arrangement was adopted to that at Folkestone. Trains for Tunbridge Wells ran into a dead-end siding and then reversed, but whereas at Folkestone they descended steeply, at Tonbridge they climbed. This time-consuming procedure was not too important while Tunbridge Wells remained a terminus, but after 1852, when through express trains to Hastings were involved, it became intolerable. In 1857 a new spur was constructed with a gradient of 1 in 53 on a curve easing from 14 chains to 27 chains radius. Heavy goods trains continued to use the original line, at least until the First World War, but subsequently it was put out of use and the track lifted.

There were no intermediate stations until 1893, when considerable residential development at Southborough led to the opening of a station at near-by High Brooms. This was called Southborough until 1925 by which time numerous passengers had discovered that the best way to reach Southborough was by bus from Tonbridge. On the London side of High Brooms, a large brick works with a private siding for many years provided traffic in coal and bricks. Between High Brooms and Tunbridge Wells goods depot, a gas works used to receive coal by rail. The goods depot was on the site of a temporary wooden passenger station, used between 1845 and 1846, until Wells tunnel was open. By the time the permanent station was completed at the far end of Wells tunnel, the plans for extension to St Leonards had already been authorised, and the buildings were confined in a cutting between the ends of Wells tunnel and Grove Hill tunnel. The goods depot was left at the old site, but a small engine shed was erected in the position now occupied by the down platform. The original station building of 1846, with the inevitable alterations and additions, survives on the up side. Before the First World War, when the SECR was enjoying an 'expansionist' period, plans were made for new buildings on the down side. Whereas corresponding plans for Margate were not completed until after the war, the new station at Tunbridge Wells, complete with eye-catching clock tower, was opened in 1911.

As soon as the SER had met its legal obligations by completing the Ashford to Hastings and St Leonards line, despite financial difficulties, it pressed on to close the gap between Tunbridge Wells and St Leonards. The fact that the line was built through difficult country when capital was scarce is reflected in its sinuosity and steep gradients. Where tunnels could not be avoided, they were built as economically as possible, leaving a legacy of operating difficulties. In Wadhurst tunnel (1,205 yards) 5 feet 3 inches was left between the tracks; in Grove Hill (287 yards) and Strawberry Hill (286 yards) tunnels, there was 4 feet 8 inches, and in Mountfield tunnel (5266 yards) only 4 feet 6 inches.[1] To add to the difficulties, the Hastings end of Mountfield tunnel is on a 35 chain radius curve, the track being super-elevated 3 inches. Over the years minor improvements have been made, beginning with the easing of curves carried out under the SER Act of 1876. The Southern Railway undertook a number of adjustments before the introduction of the Schools class locomotive in 1931. Nevertheless, special rolling stock has always been necessary, this being one of the reasons for the line being dieselised and not electrified.[2] Much earthwork and three of the tunnels were on the northern section of the line between Tunbridge Wells and Robertsbridge, so the contract for this was awarded first. In the event, it was ready five months earlier than the southern section.

The original stations were Frant, Wadhurst, Stonegate (originally Ticehurst Road), Etchingham, Robertsbridge and Battle. A feature shared with the stations on the Ashford line was staggered platforms, most of which survive to some degree. (Successive platforms extensions at Robertsbridge have almost eliminated the stagger.) Somewhat oddly, the station buildings are not identical in style. Wadhurst, Stonegate and Robertsbridge

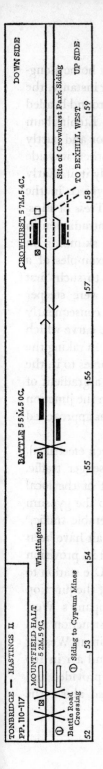
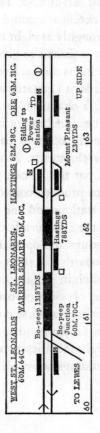
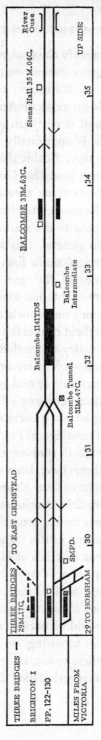
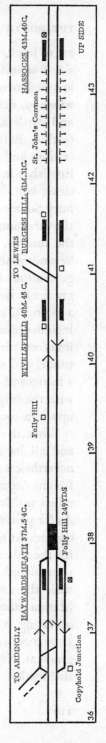

are of brick, vaguely classical, and would be quite at home along-side Rye and other stations on the Ashford line. For instance, the low pediment of Wadhurst, together with some round-headed windows, finds an echo in Appledore. But Frant, Etchingham and Battle are of stone, with a flavour partly Tudor and partly Gothic. Battle is marginally bigger than the other wayside stations and is more Gothic than Tudor, particularly in its Early English windows and the Early English chimneypiece in the ticket hall. The stations were all designed by W. Tress of Finsbury Square, London, and there is a degree of contradiction in the attention paid to the station buildings and the skimping on the tunnels. In general, this is one of the best examples of a 'second generation' main line, where, in contrast to such 'first generation' lines as the one to Brighton, there were steeper gradients, more adaptation to natural features, and consequently a saving of money on tunnels and earthworks. The curve which includes Mountfield tunnel is an excellent example. In taking the line from one valley to another roughly at right angles to it, the tunnel and earthworks were only sufficient to give a gradient of 1 in 100 and curves of 47 and 35 chains radius. Even the junction with the Brighton company's line at St Leonards was approached up a 1 in 100 grade on a curve of 11 chains radius.

While the Tonbridge to Hastings line has not been electrified, and all its original stations remain open to passenger traffic, nevertheless there have been developments. Most of the local freight depots have been closed, but the branch to the gypsum mines at Mountfield continues to produce considerable traffic.[3] As for passenger traffic, two new stations and one halt have been opened. At the end of the 1880s, the SER considered its provision for the suburban districts of Hastings and opened Ore station to the east and, in 1887, West St Leonards just short of the junction with the LBSCR and almost adjoining that company's West Marina station. From the point of view of construction and operating, it would be hard to envisage a worse position. West St Leonards lies in a cutting, on an 11 chain curve and a 1 in 100 gradient. Needless to say, no freight facilities were provided and the modest weatherboarded buildings were placed above the cutting and reached by a new approach road. The station opened at Crowhurst in 1902 was built as a junction for the new Bexhill branch.[4]

Mountfield Halt was opened in 1923, adjoining a level-crossing which had been provided with an original SER crossing keeper's house and a signal box named 'Battle Road Crossing'. It was a typical halt of wooden construction and illuminated by oil lamps until its closure in 1969. The survival of so many of the wayside stations has depended on the development of the beautiful country through which the line passes as a dormitory for London. Most of the station names were taken from the nearest large village, except in the case of Witherenden which took the name of the hamlet in which it was situated. This only lasted for a few months, when it was re-named Ticehurst Road, after a village a good three miles away. In 1947 a compromise was reached when it was re-named again, this time after the small village of Stonegate which is within a mile of the station. As mentioned above, standard electric stock could not be used on the Hastings line and multiple-unit diesel electric trains took over the services in 1958. There is a basic hourly service but, during the morning and evening peak periods, trains are divided, usually at Tunbridge Wells, one portion running as an express and the other serving the wayside stations. The existence of a diesel-operated main line in the Southern network is anomalous and it is highly likely that electrification will reach the Hastings line. Although it must be a matter of opinion, it is regarded by many as offering the most beautiful scenery of any of the main lines of Southern England.

9 June 1954

5

LBSCR lines to Brighton and East Sussex

Brighton achieved fame as a resort in the late eighteenth and early nineteenth century. Although it was ostensibly a health resort, offering both mineral and sea water combined with an attractive climate, many visitors were more concerned with pleasure than with health. Brighton had no sheltered water as a basis for a port and, although its piers were served by passenger steamers for some years, unlike Dover and Southampton, for the most part the town of Brighton generated its own railway traffic. Because of its position, just over fifty miles south of London, water transport was unable to compete with the overland route, in contrast with such resorts as Margate. Until the opening of the railway, Brighton was well served with stage coach services, with the journey time coming down to about four hours from London.

The Brighton railway was planned by Sir John Rennie, the second son of the famous civil engineer. His interest in railways was displayed in 1825 when he was involved with plans for a line from London to Bristol following a somewhat devious route via Brighton, Southampton, Salisbury, Westbury and Bath. (All of this route was subsequently followed by railways and it would be still possible to go from London to Bristol in this way if a passenger so wished.) This was the first of many proposals for railways planned to secure a lucrative passenger traffic. The peak years were 1836 and 1837. The stress was very much on Brighton traffic and the various lines were determined by attention to

1 A view on the up platform at Frant about 1905. All the original stations on the Hastings line had staggered platforms and, as stipulated by the notice partly obscured by the porter, passengers had to cross the line behind the train they had left accompanied by a 'servant of the company'. The view also shows a refuge siding, an oil lamp, ground signals and carriers for milk churns

2 View from the 12.20 train from Charing Cross to Hastings shortly before dieselization. It consists of special stock conforming to the loading gauge of the Hastings line, and includes a Pullman car. The train is passing through Mountfield Halt which, with its wooden platforms and oil lamps, is virtually unchanged since its opening in 1923. Battle Road Crossing is visible near the rear of the train in this view taken on 30 May 1958

23 St Leonards Warrior Square has the classical flavour found on some of the Hastings line stations which depends mainly on the pediments of the station buildings and the station master's house. The lengthy canopy is a later addition. Although LBSC trains called at Warrior Square from 1870, intending passengers are left in no doubt concerning the ownership of the station

24 One of the steam rail motor cars introduced by the LBSCR to run between Eastbourne and the West Marina Station at St Leonards in 1905

natural obstacles rather than the desire to serve other towns on the way. It was necessary to run across the 'grain' of the country, crossing in turn the North Downs, the High Weald and the South Downs. There were four 'passes' through the North Downs, one near Oxted, another, more popular, near Merstham, one near Betchworth and, farther west, the gap followed by the River Mole near Dorking. For penetrating the South Downs, most of the engineers used the Adur valley, with lines running between Horsham and Shoreham. Detailed reports have survived of the schemes for both years, those of 1836 being described by Gibbs who, being responsible for one of the lines himself, may have found impartiality a strain. (See Diagram 3: Proposed Railways to Dover and to Brighton, 1835–1836.) The routes of Stephenson and Cundy both used the Mole and Adur gaps and were about 13 miles longer than the direct route. Vignoles' line used the Merstham and Adur gaps and, with gradients of 1 in 94 and cuttings 110 feet deep, was an unlikely starter. The South Eastern engineer, Palmer, proposed a branch from their Dover line at Oxted, passing near Lindfield and penetrating the South Downs near Clayton. Gibbs evidently considered this to be the most dangerous rival to his own line, for it required less mileage and also served some important quarries. However, he noted cuttings at the ends of tunnels 124 feet deep with sides sloping at 1 in 1½ and queried their stability. His own line was associated with the Croydon company and, with almost excessive caution, Gibbs proposed three ways through the North Downs: one by Merstham, one near Betchworth and one by the Mole Gap. Beyond Horsham he used the Adur gap, his line following the same general course as those of Cundy, Stephenson and Vignoles. In the 1836 session, the plans for Rennie's direct line used the Merstham gap through the North Downs but, perhaps because Palmer had put in a claim for a line near Clayton, Rennie's crossing of the South Downs was near to that of the old road via the Newtimber gap. In the event, Vignoles' scheme failed to obtain financial support, Gibbs failed on parliamentary standing orders, the Cundy group fell out among themselves and only Stephenson and Rennie were left in the field. Neither line was sanctioned, so the various groups prepared themselves for the 1837 session.

There were some modifications, the most important being a move to the east by the South Eastern which enabled Rennie to take over the Clayton gap through the South Downs. The parliamentary committee selected Rennie's 'direct line' but their chairman, perturbed by the indifferent attendance of many of those voting, successfully moved an amendment for an independent report. Before this was issued, the contending parties had agreed on proportions for the allocation of capital in whichever scheme was successful. Section 136 of the Act specifies the division as follows: Rennie's £550,000, Stephenson's £550,000, South Eastern £330,000, Gibbs's £270,000 and Cundy's £100,000. This 'spreading of the load' gave the Brighton a very sound financial basis, this being one of the reasons for the rapid completion of their line. The independent report by Captain Alderson, recognising that through passenger traffic would predominate, paid special attention to terminals. At the London end, all the lines would have used existing stations, Stephenson to Nine Elms and the rest over the Croydon and Greenwich railways to London Bridge. Captain Alderson favoured London Bridge as the northern terminal, and Rennie's terminus for Brighton. As the allocation of shares indicated, the favourites were Stephenson and Rennie, the final decision going in favour of Rennie because, with a predominantly high-class passenger traffic, the saving in time achieved by a direct route was judged to be crucial.

The Brighton Act received the Royal Assent on 15 July 1837. Even more than the Dover or Southampton lines it reflected the view presented in *Our Iron Roads*, published in 1852 and written by the Rev. F. S. Williams: 'Select your termini and run your line between them as straight as you can. It is not even necessary that there should be a single house upon the route. Open the line and, as people flocked to the banks of that first great highway, a river, so they will flock to your railway.' The Brighton was the only line that followed this instruction. The Southampton deviated to throw off a line to Bristol, which failed to materialise, and the South Eastern deviated to throw off a line to Brighton which was built by the Brighton company. In fact, they were required to swing even farther to the south-west than they originally intended, nearly to Reigate instead of Oxted. This was necessary, as Section 135 of the Brighton Act stated that 'much expenditure of money and much intersection of country might be very advantageously avoided' if the SER and the Brighton used the same line to a 'point upon or to the northward of Earlswood Common'. The sharing of track was expected to be made easier by the shareholdings of the SER group in the Brighton company. The line was constructed almost exactly on the route specified in the original Act of Parliament. Although only just over forty miles of construction from Norwood to Brighton was necessary, there were very considerable works, including three long tunnels, at Merstham, at Balcombe and at Clayton. The work was not supervised by Sir John Rennie but by the resident engineer, John Urpeth Rastrick. The first sod was cut at Merstham in July 1838, and the line was opened throughout in September 1841, a considerably faster operation than with any of the other main lines in the south.

The Act included powers for branches to the two outports of Brighton—to Shoreham and to Newhaven via Lewes. The line to Shoreham was opened in advance of the main line, but no progress was made towards Newhaven. The powers lapsed and, in 1844, were taken over by a nominally independent company, the Brighton, Lewes & Hastings Railway. Despite its title, the line ran between Brighton and St Leonards with a branch into a terminus in Lewes. It ended at Bo-peep junction, about two miles short of Hastings, which was reached by running powers over the SER. At this time, St Leonards was growing rapidly so that, in 1837, a contemporary wrote: 'Under the superintendence of Mr Burton, a desert has become a thickly peopled town.' The only other place of size on the Hastings line was Bexhill, but this was a 'late developer', whose population only reached a significant level in the 1880s. The line was opened to St Leonards in 1846 but it was not until 1851 that the SER completed the link from Bo-peep junction to Hastings. The first LBSCR trains to run through were not given an easy passage.[1]

The cut-off line for the West Coast route to Portsmouth, avoiding the diversion to Brighton, was not opened until 1863, as a response to the LSWR Portsmouth Direct line. By contrast, the cut-off line to the East Coast route at Lewes anticipated SER competition at Hastings, being authorised in 1845 and opened in 1847. It left the Brighton main line half a mile to the north of Burgess Hill station and followed a route influenced mainly by physical features, to Lewes. So little importance was attached to intermediate traffic that, initially, no stations were opened on the new line. Its value was to bring Lewes and St Leonards 8½ miles nearer to London.

The Newhaven branch combined with the 'cut-off' line to make Lewes a 'crossroads'. It was authorised in 1846 by a composite Act which included an extension to Seaford and two other branches from the main line at Polegate, one to Hailsham and one to Eastbourne. The railway to Newhaven was intended to serve the port rather than the town, terminating at a wharf on the opposite side of the Ouse to the town centre. Like the cut-off line, the Newhaven branch had no intermediate stations, although separate establishments were provided for the town traffic and the boat traffic. After a few years, the LBSCR decided to link itself to a cross-channel service from Newhaven rather than Shoreham. The service from Littlehampton served points farther west on the French coast and Newhaven remained the LBSCR packet station for Dieppe and Paris. The line to Newhaven was opened in 1847, but the extension to Seaford was delayed until 1864. Of the other lines authorised, the Eastbourne and Hailsham branches were both opened in 1849. At the time, the market town of Hailsham was expected to provide almost as much traffic as the very small town of Eastbourne, with its new suburb by the sea. In 1881, the Hailsham branch became part of a new secondary route.[2] The Eastbourne line, however, progressed from branch line status until it came to be worked as part of the main line system.

Each of the lines will be described in their present condition, starting with the main Brighton line and then following the offshoots in the order of their construction. Three Bridges, 29¼ miles from London Bridge, is on the edge of London Transport territory. It became an important junction in LBSCR days, the branch to Horsham being opened in 1848. This was later extended to form part of the Mid-Sussex route. On the opposite side of the line the East Grinstead branch was completed in 1855 and later extended to Tunbridge Wells. In 1967, it was closed to all traffic.[3] Three Bridges station was opened to serve the small market town of Crawley, about one and a half miles to the west. After 1848, Crawley had its own station on the Horsham branch, but Three Bridges remained important as the main line junction. Like most of the Brighton line stations, as envisaged by the Rev. Williams, it attracted housing development and the inevitable inn, springing up on the Crawley side of the line. The station was constructed on an embankment, but the original engine shed was reached down a slope on the up side of the line. The usual developments, such as platform heightening and widening, took place and, by 1900, the up platform had become an island, with its outside face frequently used by trains from the Horsham direction. East Grinstead trains used a bay platform on the down side. At this time, the LBSCR seemed to relate visibility directly to height and placed their signals at the top of extremely tall posts. At the country end of Three Bridges there were three, one for the main line and one each for the branches. Another feature characteristic of the period was the provision of overall roofs, both for the up loop and the down bay.

Much of this was swept away when the line was quadrupled as far as Three Bridges in 1907 and on to the northern end of Balcombe Tunnel in 1910. The up island platform was enlarged to form a centre island platform and the site of the engine shed was filled in to embankment level to make room for a new island platform. The new engine shed was in the fork between the main and Horsham lines. The next spate of change came in 1932 when the main line was electrified. From 17 July 1932 until the extension of electrification to Brighton and Worthing on 1 January 1933, Three Bridges was the terminus for electric trains. It was also the location of the control room from which the eighteen substations between Purley, Brighton and Worthing were controlled. While Direct Current at 660 volts was fed to the third rail in the same way as on the suburban system, the substations were provided with mercury arc rectifiers instead of the rotary converters used in the London area. They were fed at 33,000 volts from a ring main at Croydon, at Three Bridges and at Brighton. The substations, with their impressive display of transformers and insulators, protected by high railings, now a familiar feature of any railway electrification scheme, attracted great attention when the Brighton line was first electrified. On a more modest scale were the huts, usually located between each pair of sub-stations, which did not contain equipment for transforming electricity, but merely switches and connections linking the up and down rails and enabling sections to be isolated. The increased service of electric trains necessitated re-signalling and the Brighton line set a pattern to be repeated on the Dover and Southampton main lines after the war. It was decided to install coloured light signalling between Coulsdon, 14¾ miles from London Bridge, Brighton and Hove, semaphores being retained for the time being between Hove and Worthing and on the London side of Coulsdon. Altogether, twenty-four signal boxes were abolished and, of the fifteen remaining, only six were open continuously. Simplification enabled the 393 semaphore signals on the running lines to be replaced by 186 colour lights. In most cases the new equipment was housed in existing signal boxes. Many, but not all, points were operated by electric point motors. The effect on Three Bridges was the closure and subsequent demolition of the North and South boxes and the retention of the former 'Central', located at the country end of the centre island platform. All signals were marked with code letters and a number, the letters indicating the box from which they were operated, or 'CA' if they were automatic, and the number corresponding to the lever which controlled them. The code letters for Three Bridges were 'CL' so, for example, the Three Bridges inner home signal on the up through line was CL81.

Between 1932 and 1970 changes were detailed rather than fundamental. After the closure of the East Grinstead branch, the down bay platform was rarely used, but despite this, the down side showed remarkably little change. The station building remained largely as built in 1841, alterations including such changes as a shortening of the chimneys. The canopy over the platform is certainly not original, but appears unchanged since photographs of the station were taken in the late Victorian period. Similarly, the up side platform is quite purely Edwardian, with a typical LBSCR-style valance on its canopy. Somewhat surprisingly, this feature is not repeated on the centre island platform of the same date. (This is not the result of war damage; the canopies on all three platforms were just the same in 1932.) By 1971, a new signal box had been opened and the goods yard and the engine shed were both closed, although the disused building was still standing.

The Brighton direct line surmounted each of its main obstacles —the North Downs, the High Weald and the South Downs— with a ruling gradient of 1 in 264. To achieve this, each of the three 'humps' leads up to a tunnel—Merstham for the North Downs, Balcombe for the Weald and Clayton for the South Downs. The profile of the line is remarkable for its regularity, the long stretches of unbroken 1 in 264 resembling the lengths of 1 in 330 which Stephenson planned for the London and Birmingham. The tunnels reduced the three summits to a level which made 1 in 264 possible, but the smoothness of the approaches to them necessitated a great deal of earthwork. Virtually the whole line is either on embankment or in cutting, and there are no level-crossings. Three Bridges is situated almost halfway up the north side of the middle 'hump' on the way to Balcombe tunnel. At this point, the line is embanked, but within two miles it is running in cutting through the wooded slopes of the High Weald. Beneath the surface lie the sand, sandstones and clays of the Hastings Beds which, compared with chalk, are structurally weak. This is reflected in the very gentle slopes of the sides of the cuttings as we approach the tunnel. In the 'high summer' period of the railways, the LBSCR had plans to quadruple the whole of their Brighton main line but, faced with the enormous expense of duplicating Balcombe tunnel, the Ouse viaduct and Clayton tunnel, they stopped short in 1910 at the north end of Balcombe tunnel. The convergence of the through and local lines involves conflicting movements, as typified by a photograph, taken in 1955 from a train stopped on the down local line, with a New-haven boat train passing on the down through, having been given precedence by the signalman in Balcombe Tunnel box. The summit adjoins the signal box and the tunnel itself is on the southern slope of the Wealden 'hump' which ends near Wivels-field. It is 1,141 yards long, at a maximum depth of 60 feet from the surface and, despite its brick lining and inclination, is very wet. Partly because of the adverse effect of continuous damp on an electrified line, a new drainage system was installed in 1932.

Scenically, the Wealden 'hump', especially the southern slope from Balcombe Tunnel down to Wivelsfield, is the most attractive part of the line to Brighton. While the sands and clays are re-sponsible for the wide embankments and cuttings, there are some stronger beds of sandstone, one of which is exposed in a cutting south of Balcombe. Between the tunnel mouth and the station, the only noteworthy things from a railway point of view are an overbridge built of stone instead of brick and, on the down side, a track paralleling hut. Balcombe station is an original of 1841, sited characteristically at a point of transition between embank-ment and cutting. The building on the down side looks original, with the inevitable additions such as the canopy cantilevered out over the platform. The re-signalling of 1932 left a signal box at Balcombe intact but only in regular use for the working of the goods yard. This closed in 1959 and, subsequently, the signal box was abolished. We pass the Ouse valley substation, and the site of Stone Hall signal box, both on the down side, and then run out on to the Ouse valley viaduct.

It was the strict adherence to the 1 in 264 gradient which necessitated this magnificent structure, rising nearly 100 feet above the valley. It is difficult to appreciate from a train what is described in the Sussex volume of the Buildings of England series as 'one of England's most impressive railway viaducts'. It has thirty-seven brick arches, each of 30-foot span, varying in height from 40 feet at the ends to 96 feet in the centre, and is 1,476 feet long. The piers are not solid, the brickwork being pierced by arches and inverts. Although the viaduct would be a monument to Rastrick purely as a structure, he did not leave it without embellishment. Instead of a plain brick parapet, a balustrade of Caen stone was erected and, at each end, four pavilions in a classical style. For anybody wishing to appreciate railway engineering at its best, a special journey to see the Ouse valley viaduct from the ground is strongly recommended. Half a mile down the line is Copyhold junction, named after a near-by farm, and the junction for the line to Horsted Keynes from 1883 onwards.[4] Originally, in order not to interrupt main line traffic, a separate double track was continued from the junction to Haywards Heath station. However, a signal box was opened and crossovers provided so that all four tracks were available for both branch and main line trains. In 1932, the junction was rearranged so that the branch down and up lines became a down local and a down through and the former main lines became up through and local. This reduced the possibility of conflicting movements for main line trains. In 1935 the line from Copyhold junction through Ardingly to Horsted Keynes was electrified, partly to provide a more convenient terminal than Haywards Heath for the local electric service from Seaford, but also as a step towards the electrification of the East Grinstead route between London and Brighton. The electric passenger service to Horsted Keynes was withdrawn in 1963, but the line remains open as far as Ardingly for special traffic.

Haywards Heath is another original station but, unlike Three Bridges and Balcombe, it retains nothing from the early period, having been completely rebuilt at the time of electrification. In its earlier form, it consisted of two side platforms, with bays on both sides at both ends. In connection with the rearrangement of the lines from Copyhold junction, the station was rebuilt with two island platforms, one for up traffic and one for down. A new signal box of traditional appearance was constructed on the up side of the line. Although adjoining a point of transition in the earthworks, most of the Haywards Heath platforms are on an embankment, and the entrance in brick and concrete, belonging very much to 1932, is at ground level. The local service from

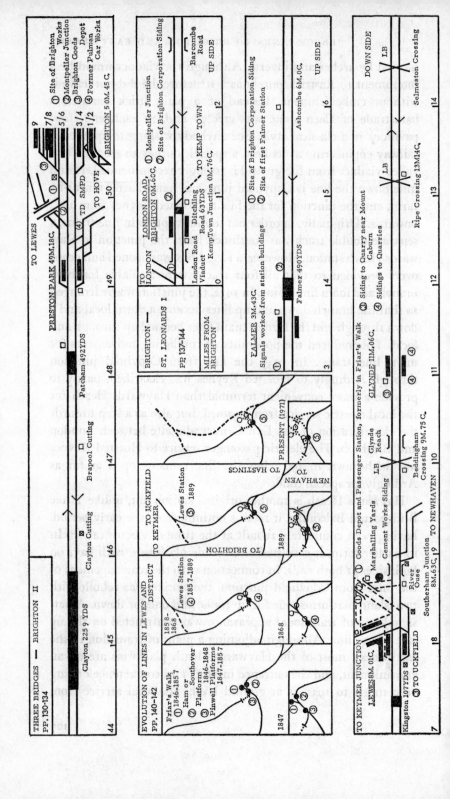

Seaford has been cut back, but Haywards Heath still enjoys an excellent train service, the only trains passing through without stopping being the hourly Brighton expresses. The cutting to the south of the station is a deep one, leading to the short Folly Hill tunnel. The Appendix to the Working Timetable gives the length as 249 yards and, incidentally, calls it Haywards Heath tunnel. The area is covered with expansive residential property, with considerable dependence on the railway for its commuting inhabitants.

Between Haywards Heath and Wivelsfield there is a transition from the heavily wooded, hilly country of the High Weald to the grassy lowland of the Weald Clay. The station at Wivelsfield was opened in 1886 as Keymer Junction, receiving its present name in 1896. The original name must rank as one of the most misleading ever perpetrated on passengers, as the village of Keymer was three miles away from Keymer Junction and only half a mile from Hassocks station. Wivelsfield was less than a mile north of the 1841 station at Burgess Hill and was presumably intended to provide a stopping place in the Burgess Hill residential district for East Sussex trains. (From 1862 until its closture in 1883, they had called at a station on the Lewes side of the junction.) A possibility would have been a new station at the junction but, instead, there were separate platforms south of it at Burgess Hill and north of it at Wivelsfield; the latter, however, were without goods facilities. Keymer is a conventional flat junction, with a substation in the fork between the two lines. Since 1932 it has been operated by Keymer Crossing signal box which is 215 yards down the Lewes line. Like Haywards Heath, Burgess Hill is an expansive residential district, a once rural area peppered with houses. The station has changed less than the place. The original building of 1841 is in use as a coal office. It was replaced by a pleasantly characteristic building of 1877 on the bridge over the railway. Basically, it belongs to the most conventional railway type, with end-sections with low gables at right angles to the road, and a central cross-section, parallel to it, which includes the entrance and booking hall. The goods yard was closed in 1964.

At this point, the line is climbing to the Clayton summit and, about one mile beyond Burgess Hill, it had to cross an extensive area of low lying land, inadequately drained by a tributary of the Abdur. It included the infertile expanse of St Johns Common. To maintain the required 1 in 264, an embankment over a mile long was required, absorbing nearly a million tons of spoil. Hassocks is another confirmation of the Rev. Williams's theory about railways and population—the Sussex volume of the Buildings of England series says, a little unkindly, 'no church and no identity'. It is true that the station was built in a somewhat remote spot, until 1881 taking its name of Hassocks Gate from that of a tollgate on a near-by turnpike road. It was, however, conveniently placed to serve the villages of Hurstpierpoint, Keymer, Ditchling and Clayton. The present buildings were constructed in 1880 but part of the original 1841 building has survived. The 1880 buildings are surprisingly lavish, approaching Midhurst in both scale and style. The station house is on the up side, but extensive station buildings were provided on both sides of the line. The most striking architectural feature is the fixing of strips of wood over plaster to give the effect of timber framing. On the house these form a chequerboard pattern but, in the gables of the entrance porches, they are curved and almost radial in effect. Presumably this is another case of promise of a startling residential development which was only partly fulfilled. (Christ's Hospital station is even more striking for the same reason.) Hassocks was the last of the original stations before Brighton as there were no stations on the seven miles of line through the South Downs. This reflects the fact that, largely due to the lack of water supply, there were no places for which to build them.

From Hassocks, the line of the Downs is clearly visible and a cutting heralds the approach to the scarp face. At the end is the northern entrance to Clayton tunnel which, like the Ouse viaduct, is one of the really impressive features of the railway to Brighton. The entrance suggests a pointed arch from a rather heavily built Gothic cathedral. But any hint of the sacred is balanced by the castellated turrets on either side, which are more evocative of a mediaeval castle. Wing-walls on either side join the main turrets to lower and simpler versions which terminate each end of the entrance. Mediaeval details, such as loops and modil-lions, contribute to what is often regarded as a folly. Whereas, on the Ouse viaduct, the embellishments are shaded by the func-tional elements, at the north end of Clayton tunnel the opposite is true. To add to the irrational, a cottage was built directly over the entrance, and is still inhabited. Surely nobody but a railway enthusiast could appreciate its position. A road runs parallel with the tunnel which at one point is 270 feet below the surface. A series of tip heaps and ventilation shafts mark its position over the 2,259 yards of its length. In contrast, the southern entrance is conventionally plain. It has a brick parapet capped with stone above the entrance and such details as a keystone, but little ex-pense has been incurred that was unnecessary. There must be, without doubt, some special reason for the extravagance, largely unseen by the public, at the northern end of Clayton tunnel.

The summit of the South Downs 'hump' is reached at the southern end of the tunnel, and the line begins the descent, still at 1 in 264, to the terminal in Brighton. At the time of the re-signalling, Clayton Cutting signal box, situated on the up side not far from the tunnel mouth, was retained and was still there in 1971. The line follows a natural valley and, at Patcham, emerges on to a low embankment, a location much favoured by railway photographers. The tunnel at Patcham was extended at its northern end, as specified in the authorising Act, to protect the estate of Major Paine of Patcham Place from the sight and sound of the railway (the converse situation to that experienced by the resident of the cottage at Clayton). Even with this ex-tension, Patcham tunnel is only 492 yards long. We emerge from the cutting at the south end, following the west side of the valley and penetrating the outskirts of Brighton. The only suburban station on the main line is Preston Park, opened in 1869. It has been enlarged and now consists of two island platforms, with the main line in the middle and loops on either side. The two signal boxes were on the up side. In 1932 the North signal box was closed and operations concentrated in the South signal box which became Preston Park. It controls the junction to the Cliftonville spur. The line was sited part way up the western side of a valley, and successive widenings have been achieved by cutting away into the chalk on the up side and embanking on the down. In succession, on the up side, are works of the former Pullman Car Company, now the home of steam locomotives in store, and the erstwhile paint shop of Brighton locomotive works. Since 1932 this has been used as a twelve-road shed for electric trains. The site of the steam motive power depot was also on the up side. In addition to the usual facilities, such as a coaling stage and inspection pits, this included a conspicuous water-softening plant adjoining a large water tank. These features have all been demolished, and most of the site is in use as a motor repair depot.

On the down side, beyond the Dyke Road overbridge, goods lines diverge to run obliquely down the valley side to the goods station. The East Coast line crosses over them before joining the main line at Montpelier junction. On a congested site, wedged between the main passenger line and the goods lines, was the Brighton company's principal works. Other companies usually selected an established place where labour was available, such as Nine Elms in London, or a convenient point on their system where plenty of land was available. A location fitting the latter description on the Brighton line was Horley, and land was purchased there. However, probably due to the persuasive powers of John Chester Craven, the influential locomotive engineer of the Brighton company from 1847 until 1869, their works were established at Brighton. The first locomotives were turned out in 1852. J. C. Craven was succeeded by William Stroudley in 1870 and a certain amount of rationalisation was achieved. In general, constructional and repair work was carried out on the down side of the line, while the activities of the operating department were concentrated on the up side. But there was no room for expansion and, in 1880, much of the marine work was transferred to workshops at Newhaven. A new carriage and wagon works was opened at Lancing in 1912 and subsequently Brighton works concentrated on the construction and repair of locomotives. This activity came to an end in 1922, the new Southern Railway deciding to concentrate work on locomotives at Ashford and at

Eastleigh. Brighton works did not close completely but, until the Second World War, did little more than running repairs to a locomotive stock declining in number with each successive electrification. After the outbreak of war, Brighton was re-tooled and the first locomotive from the revitalised works appeared in 1942. The last new locomotive to leave the works was a BR class 4 2–6–4 tank locomotive no. 80154, turned out on 20 March 1957. There followed a long period of declining activity, the last locomotive repairs being completed in 1958. Employment was maintained for a while by assembling BMW Isetta cars, but this also came to an end. Most of the remaining buildings were demolished in 1969 to make way for a car park.

The terminal station at Brighton is the nearest approach that Southern England can offer to the great terminals of the north, although even Brighton falls somewhat short of Liverpool Lime Street or Manchester Victoria. However, it does retain its original building of 1840, to the design of David Moccatta, who was responsible for virtually all the original architecture on the Brighton line. It is much obscured by the elaborate metal and glass canopy, added when the station was rebuilt in 1883. There have been modifications of architectural detail but, basically, the original building is intact. A striking survival is the elaborate clock case mounted in the centre of the façade. Inside is the train shed of 1883, consisting of two spans of most impressive overall roof. In its curvature it resembles York and Newcastle Central and its iron columns, although not quite approaching the elaboration of York, are magnificently executed. Somewhat oddly, the roof is surmounted by a pointed ridge so that, at the ends, there is an impression of a low gable. Brighton is one of the few stations that is impressive from a distance; from the east side the way in which it is terraced into the opposite side of the valley may be appreciated.

The arrangement of platforms was modified at the time of electrification. The island platform numbered 1 and 2 on the west side, used for the West Coast line, was lengthened to such an extent in the Hove direction that, apart from a short length at the terminal end of platform 2, it could not be reached from the main or East Coast lines. From an operating point of view, this effectively divided the station, with platforms 1 and 2 serving the West Coast line and the rest for the main and East Coast lines. (Short trains from the West Coast can use platform 3.) Platforms 3 and 4, 5 and 6, and 7 were all lengthened sufficiently to take twelve-coach trains. Platform 7 and 8 differs from the three more westerly platforms, having a cab road down its centre, a bay set into its end, and having the face numbered 8 much shorter than that numbered 7. Platform 9 was at the far end of the station and as short as 8, whilst 10 was shortest of all. It was rarely used and was finally closed in November 1971, its position being required for access to a new car park. All train movements are controlled from one signal box built into the wall of the old works in 1932. (The demolition of the works has left it in a position of unaccustomed exposure.) Brighton station has many features of detail which contribute to its unique character. There is, for instance, a four-faced clock suspended over the concourse, decorated with intricate ironwork, part of which forms the letters LBSCR.

While much of the 'atmosphere' emanates from the character of the station, it also owes a great deal to the trains, for trains on the Brighton main line always tended to be out of the ordinary. Perhaps more than any other, it was essentially a passenger line, with possibly the highest proportion of passengers with a variety of pleasures in mind. In Victorian and Edwardian times, its trains reflected the class structure, with a tremendous gulf between the luxury of the best and the harshness of the cheapest. Arnold Bennett noticed this, and put his feelings into *Clayhanger*. Edwin Clayhanger went from the Potteries to Brighton in search of Hilda and travelled down from Victoria on the Southern Belle.

Everybody who came towards this train came with an assured air of wealth and dominion. . . . All the luggage was luxurious; handbags could be seen that were worth fifteen to twenty pounds apiece. There was no question of first, second or third class; there was no class at all on this train. . . . When he sat down in the vast interior of one of these gilded vehicles, he

Brighton. Ordnance Survey Map 1874 Edition. This shows the main line running in
ast the Paint Shop, the West Coast line diverging from one side of the station, and the
ast Coast line branching off from Montepelier Junction, just north of the 'Locomotive
nd Carriage Factory'. The engine and carriage sheds were sited in the fork between the
ain and West Coast lines. The branch to the goods depot left the main line off the map
nd after passing under the East Coast line and over New England Road, skirted the
orks. Nearly a hundred years later, the basic layout remains the same, but the engine
ed and works are no more. (Scale 25 ins. to 1 mile; scale of inches shown at bottom)

26 Interior of Brighton Station about 1900. This shows the train shed of 1883 which is virtually unchanged at the present time. The platform numbered 3 corresponds roughly to the present Numbers 5 and 6. On the right of the platform a carriage awaits loading onto a carriage truck. In the right hand corner a line of horse cabs awaits the more affluent passengers

27 The 17.35 up 'Southern Belle' leaving Brighton hauled by King Arthur class No. 767 'Sir Valence' built by the North British Locomotive Co. in 1925. The train is passing the works, with its large water tank, and the new signal box is under construction. Standing in front of the sheds on the right is LBSC Gladstone class No. B172, built at Brighton in 1891 and the last survivor of its class. The third rail was in position by the time this photograph was taken on 30 April 1932

could not dismiss from his face the consciousness that he was an intruder, that he did not belong to that world.

It was not quite correct to say that there was no question of class on the Southern Belle; all the passengers were first class, and also paid a supplementary fare to the Pullman Car Company. The Brighton introduced the first train composed entirely of Pullman cars in 1881 but, at that time, there was insufficient support. However, single Pullman cars had been included in trains from 1875 and these continued to operate. From 1898, an all-Pullman train ran on Sundays only. In 1908, a train of seven Pullman cars was introduced and, apart from two wartime breaks, this has run ever since. Normally, a name is given to a service rather than a set of coaches, as with the Royal Scot, Flying Scotsman or Cornish Riviera Express, with departure times varying little over the years. The Southern Belle was unusual in that the name was applied to the train and not the service. (At the present time, on weekdays, there are four services in each direction.) Class barriers weakened and, after the First World War, the Belle included both first- and third-class cars. New stock was provided in 1925. When the line was electrified on the third rail system, it was decided to continue with steam locomotives for through trains from other lines and for goods, which only made up a small proportion of the total traffic. Electric locomotives were ruled out at this time, owing to the long gaps in the live rail at junctions, which would have left them cut off from an electricity supply. (The multiple-unit trains had pick-up shoes distributed throughout their total length and, even at the most complicated junctions, there would always be one shoe contacting the live rail.) A decision had to be made either to abandon the Southern Belle, to continue to work it by steam, or to build a new train of Pullman cars including coaches with powered bogies—that is, a multiple-unit Pullman train. The latter proposal was favoured and three five-car trains were ordered. The usual arrangement was to run two sets coupled together, the third being spare. In June 1934 there was a change of name to the more explicit Brighton Belle. After September 1939, the Pullman sets were downgraded to unnamed trains and, in 1942, were withdrawn and placed in store. Unfortunately, one of the sets had been damaged in an air raid in June 1940, and this delayed the full restoration of the Belle until October 1946. The three sets were usually confined to running between Victoria and Brighton, but at one period one of them ran down to Eastbourne on Sundays only. In 1969, by which time British Rail had purchased the Pullman Car Company, the Belle was repainted in BR livery. The first-class cars, which had borne names, became almost indistinguishable from the numbered third-class cars, the words 'Brighton Belle' being painted on the sides of all of them. (It may have been felt that the names—Vera, Doris, Hazel, Gwen, Audrey and Mona— savoured too much of the 1930s.) After this, the Belle was never quite the same and its withdrawal is due to take place in 1972.

It would be wrong to suggest that the Belle was the only train that lent distinction to the Brighton line. For instance, although by the time of electrification, third-class passengers were allowed on all the trains, there was still a high proportion of first-class seats. All the express trains included a Pullman car, seating sixteen third- and twelve first-class passengers. Commuting on the Brighton line had begun when the line was opened and, for many years, the most distinguished trains had been the 8.45 a.m. from Brighton to London Bridge and the corresponding down train at 5 p.m., known as the 'City Limited'. Third-class passengers had gained admission since the First World War, but they continued to be in a minority. This meant that the standard express trains were unsuited to this service and three special six-car sets were constructed. Normally two ran together to form a twelve-coach train with seats for 240 third-class and 276 first-class passengers. By the 1960s, the stock built for the electrification in 1932 was becoming due for retirement, and was replaced by more standardised trains, without Pullmans. At the same time, the standard hour which had been allowed for non-stop expresses for so long (including the war years) was reduced to 55 minutes for the fifty-one miles. The Brighton main line still has a remarkably good service of trains, but some of the sparkle has gone.

It must be confessed that the services to East Sussex, although distinguished in their way, never achieved the standards of the main line. In fact if, as seemed probable on more than one occasion, SER and the Brighton companies had amalgamated, the somewhat circuitous Brighton service to Hastings would, at best, have been of a very secondary nature. In view of the fact that, of their routes from Brighton and from Dover to London Bridge, two fifths of the Brighton and a quarter of the South Eastern was shared, it is remarkable that they did not combine. For instance, in November 1843 the South Eastern was seeking to lease both the Brighton and the Croydon companies, but both refused. Probably through lack of capital, the SER was unable to make a sufficiently attractive bid. Locomotive stock was pooled at this time, but in 1846 the pool was broken up, the locomotives being divided between the companies. In 1848, the two companies reached a territorial agreement which was not transgressed until 1888. After an outbreak of competition in the 1860s, amalgamation of the SER, LBSCR and LCDR almost materialised in 1868. Subsequent moves towards union finally succeeded for the SER and LCDR but the LBSCR remained independent until it became part of the Southern Railway. This, however, is not to suggest that intensive competition was rife in East Sussex. Many points were covered by traffic agreements for the pooling of revenue, including Redhill, Dorking, St Leonards, and Hastings. A special agreement applied to Eastbourne traffic.

There was a degree of symmetry about the western and eastern parts of the Brighton system, with Shoreham balancing Newhaven, Chichester corresponding to Lewes, Bognor to Eastbourne and Portsmouth and Southsea to Hastings and St Leonards. In detail, however, there were differences. The original powers included branches to both Shoreham and Newhaven, but only that to Shoreham was built and, as described above, in 1844 the Brighton, Lewes & Hastings Railway company was authorised to construct the East Coast route. Whereas the line to Shoreham required no major engineering works, that to Lewes was faced with the immediate problem of crossing the valley at Brighton. While the West Coast line diverged immediately north of the station, the East Coast line curved away a short distance to the north at Montpelier junction. The eastern end of the magnificent London Road viaduct is very near the junction and it stretches for about 400 yards across the valley. Nine semi-circular arches with a span of 30 feet are followed by an elliptical arch of 50 feet which is 67 feet above the London Road. Another seventeen semi-circular 30-foot spans brings the viaduct to the far side of the valley. About ten million bricks were used in constructing the viaduct and Rastrick, who was the engineer, was faced with one problem not encountered with the crossing of the Ouse Valley. The London Road viaduct was curved, so, to keep the sides of the arches parallel, all the piers are tapered, the northern ends being wider than the southern. The nine arches west of the main road curve at 10 chains radius and the seventeen to the east at about 60 chains radius. There are a number of points of similarity with the Ouse viaduct, including the piercing of the piers with arches and inverts. The viaduct was embellished with a handsome stone balustrade. During the Second World War, it received a direct hit from a bomb and, for some years, the newer brick marked the repaired section. It was considered worthy of ceremony when the 'first stone' was laid by the chairman of the company in May 1845; somewhat remarkably, the last arch was completed by March 1846.

The line reaches the far side of the valley and, at the point of transition from bank to cutting, only 60 chains from the terminus, London Road station was opened in 1877. It was purely a suburban station, with no goods facilities, served mainly by the trains for the Kemp Town branch. It was provided with a very good Victorian building resembling those at Kemp Town and at West Worthing, and has survived almost without change. The platforms are rather above surface level and the main building is elevated accordingly, so that, instead of going up steps to the platform, there is a fine, wide flight of steps at the front of the building. The line passes under Ditchling Road, through a 63-yard tunnel, and at the end of a cutting is Kemp Town junction. The branch to Kemp Town was opened in 1869, closed to passengers when the main line was electrified at the end of 1932, and closed to all traffic in June 1971.[5] The signal box was closed the following October. On the opposite side of the line was a private siding of Brighton Corporation which served their yard and their abbatoir. Until the 1930s, this handled appreciable quantities of livestock. The line follows the western slope of a dry valley, with the main road to Lewes in the valley below. The former cavalry barracks are passed on the up side and, for many years, this was virtually the end of Brighton. New housing has crept up the valley as far as the town boundary at Moulsecoomb. The railway crosses over to the east side, being carried over the main road by a bridge which, although minor by the standards of London Road viaduct, is still a very striking example of skewed construction. The three main arches are of brick, with the same kind of hollow piers as the viaduct, each with a span of 60 feet. The gradient steepens to 1 in 101, and this continues past the present Falmer station to the tunnel.[6] The original Falmer station at the east end of the tunnel was closed in 1865 and has gone without trace. Near-by was the site of a Brighton Corporation water pumping station, and at one time its coal was delivered to a private siding on the down side reached from the station siding.

The chalk downland has few villages and, for many years, Falmer had little traffic other than that emanating from the small village of Falmer and from the mansion in Stanmer Park. By 1930, it was decided to close the signal box and place the lever frame and instruments on the down side of the station, thus providing the station staff with an additional occupation. However, in 1958 a decision was made to establish the University of Sussex in Stanmer Park, the first building being ready in 1960. Especially in the early days, when many of the students were in lodgings in Brighton, Falmer handled a greatly increased traffic, later facilitated by the construction of a subway under the adjacent main road. Even with the construction of halls of residence, Falmer is still a much busier station than it was. Falmer tunnel, 490 yards, marks the summit of the line which then descends at 1 in 88 to Lewes. The alignment is entirely dependent on relief, every curve of the line reflecting the configuration of the valley. For purposes of traffic control, the section between Falmer and

Lewes was divided by a signal box at Ashcombe, but this was replaced by automatic intermediate signals in 1933. On the outskirts of Lewes, a spur of chalk is penetrated by Kingston tunnel, of 107 yards.

The evolution of the railways in Lewes is complicated, involving not only the line now being described, but also the 'cut-off' line from Keymer Junction and the railway to Uckfield. It would be very difficult to interpret what remains without an adequate historical background. (See Diagram 13: Evolution of Lines in Lewes.) The original line ran to a terminal station in Friars Walk, opened in 1846. The building was a fine one, five bays wide with four large Corinthian pilasters. It was used as a station for only eleven years, but continued in use as railway offices until recently. It was knocked down in 1967. A platform, known as Ham or Southover platform, existed from 1846 to 1848 on the through line. There were plans to construct a spur towards St Leonards, which would have given a triangular arrangement, reminiscent of Inverness. Instead, in 1847, some time after the opening of the extension to St Leonards, Pinwell platforms were opened beyond the junction with the terminal spur. However, most trains continued to run into the terminal station and back out to continue their journey, in a way once practised at Dorchester. Traffic at Lewes increased with the opening of two new lines—the Keymer 'cut-off' and the Newhaven branch, both in 1847. This, combined with the wish to develop the Newhaven boat train traffic, spurred the Brighton to open a new, through station at the junction of the lines from Keymer and Brighton in 1857. In the following year, the line to Uckfield was opened, joining the Keymer line north of Lewes.[7] When this was extended to Tunbridge Wells in 1868, partly to provide a through route from Brighton without reversal, a new approach to Lewes was constructed, joining the main line east of Lewes station. Although the abandonment of the terminal greatly facilitated operating, the sharp curvature, both at the end of the Keymer line and adjoining the former junction with the terminal spur, continued to impede traffic. In 1884 powers were obtained to build a new line which formed a chord, cutting off the old curve which was retained for goods traffic only. This necessitated the complete rebuilding of the passenger station and the new premises were opened in 1889. A new alignment was constructed for the Uckfield line.

Since then, changes have been less fundamental. At the time of the East Sussex electrification, in 1935, it was necessary to lengthen the platforms on the Keymer side of the station to take twelve-car trains. (Nos. 1 and 2, the down local and down through, from 500 feet to 760 feet and No. 3, the up through, from 580 feet to 793 feet.) As explained, the old line had been retained for goods traffic and these platform extensions 'pushed' the junction which served it to the mouth of a tunnel which adjoined the station. The tunnel was widened and a new signal box was opened. This stage represented the maximum development of Lewes as a junction with both an extensive passenger station and marshalling yards. (Somewhat surprisingly, there were no engine sheds; presumably Brighton and Newhaven were considered sufficiently close.) Subsequently, there has been some reduction. In 1969 the line to Uckfield was closed. In the same year goods facilities were withdrawn and, in June 1970, the tracks were removed from the East Yard. This severed the original line through Lewes which, after the diversion of passenger services to the new line in 1889, had continued in use for goods traffic. In the station, the down loop line on the Brighton side was closed in 1971 and, in early 1972 the London down loop was taken out of use.

But even with these reductions, Lewes has much of interest, with most of its features belonging to the LBSCR major rebuilding of 1889 or the Southern's electrification and 'facelift' of 1935. The station is one of the best examples of the type of building being constructed by the Brighton in the latter part of the Victorian period. In its use of different coloured bricks it recalled many of the buildings of the 1860s, but the dwarf balustrade, punctuated with decorative features, was closer to the 1840s. However, a feature which was repeated at Bexhill and Eastbourne belongs to neither decade. Almost from the Crystal Palace period, there had been a tendency to lighten interiors, and all these three stations had lanterns surmounting their roofs which illuminated the circulating area below in daylight hours. The building at Lewes is up at street level and, with the exception of the main platform which may be reached by a ramp, passengers descend from it by steps. There are rather more platforms on the Brighton side than on the Keymer line, down and up through with a reversible loop on the Brighton side and, since the closure of the down loop line, two platforms only on the Keymer side. (The reversible platform can be used for trains from Seaford terminating at Lewes.) Two of the signal boxes—that at the west end of the Brighton side and the large box at the junction—provide vintage examples of LBSCR styles. Most of the signal posts belong to the Southern period but the up starters on the Brighton side combine LBSCR posts with Southern upper quadrant arms. The Southern influence was represented at a more ephemeral level by station signs and more permanently by the electric sub-station by the junction signal box. A number of Sussex towns would compete for the maximum number of trains per hour per head of population—with a population of just over 14,000, Lewes has eight departures per hour, one to London, one to Eastbourne, one to Seaford, two to Ore and three to Brighton.

Three quarters of a mile from Lewes, on the far side of the Ouse, is Southerham Junction signal box. The box is responsible for the operation of the junction of the Hastings and Newhaven lines, the siding into a cement works and the lifting bridge over the river. At one time there was an appreciable amount of river traffic going up to Lewes, including barges and other small vessels to the cement works. The raising of the movable span was quite a performance, requiring at least thirty men for the removal of fishplates, signal wires and the like, and owners or masters of vessels were required to give 24 hours' notice to the station master at Lewes. In 1935, the bridge was damaged by a barge. This was in tow and slewed round in passing through the bridge, causing sufficient damage to necessitate the closing of the up line for two days. Electrification added to the difficulties of lifting the bridge. Commercial traffic on the river is now virtually extinct but, as a precautionary measure, the electric power cables were taken under the water. Although the actual junction

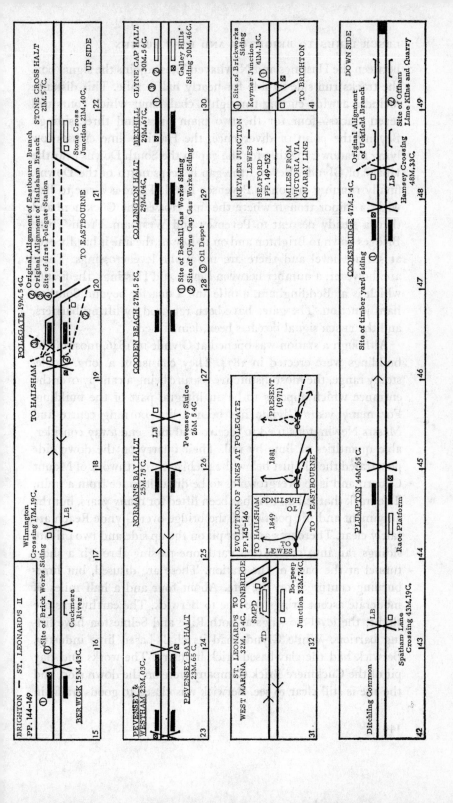

between the Hastings and Newhaven lines adjoins the signal box, the tracks run side-by-side for nearly half a mile. This distance includes a wide cutting through a chalk spur which contained seven tracks—four for the two main lines, and three sidings. Beyond the point of divergence, the Hastings line crosses low lying meadows, making for the gap in the South Downs near the village of Glynde. Beyond the gap it keeps north of the Downs, finally running out on to Pevensey Level. There is a rise to Berwick, a minor trough where the line crosses the Cuckmere and then a steady descent to Pevensey and Westham. From Three Bridges down to Brighton and on to Lewes, the line is hardly ever at surface level and there are no public level-crossings. There are, however, a number between Lewes and Hastings, the first of which is at Beddingham, a mile and a quarter beyond Southerham junction. The gates have been replaced by lifting barriers, and the LBSCR signal box has been demolished.

Although a station was opened at Glynde in 1846, most of the buildings were erected in 1874. They consist of a long, single-storey range, the most distinctive feature being a canopy over the entrance which appears to be an integral part of the building. For many years Glynde has been a lime-burning centre and Messrs Newingtons used to receive coal and send away considerable quantities of lime by rail. Their quarry on the down side penetrated the hill just below the prehistoric earthwork of Mount Caburn and is so overgrown as to be difficult to see from a train. The track that led up to it has been lifted for many years, but the alignment and the position of the bridge over Glynde Reach are fairly clear. There was another pit on the up side and two private sidings ran into the station yard, one passing through a short tunnel at the back of the station. These are disused, but lime-burning continues on the site. About four and a half miles of moderate ascent brings the line to Berwick. The earthworks are slight; the level-crossings at both Ripe and Selmeston have lifting barriers. While Glynde had its chalk-based lime industry, Berwick had the clay-based brick industry. The works and clay pit of the Cuckmere Brick Company were on the down side, and the site is still clear to see. Berwick was closed to goods traffic in

1963, but its signal box, which operates a level-crossing, is still in use. The river Cuckmere was not used as a navigation, and the fixed span over it has no unusual features. All the way from Glynde to Polegate there are magnificent views of the South Downs—Belloc's 'great hills of the South'. When the train crosses Wilmington crossing, now with its automatic lifting barriers, is the time to look for the striking figure, 226 feet high, of the Long Man of Wilmington, formed by exposing the chalk on the scarp of the Downs.

Polegate has an interesting railway history. A station was opened on the east side of the level-crossing in 1846 and served both Hailsham and Eastbourne by horse-bus connections. In 1849 branches were opened to both towns, facing in the Lewes direction. In 1881 the Hailsham branch was extended towards Tunbridge Wells.[8] It was required to provide the SER with a route from London to Eastbourne, but this would have involved a reversal at Polegate. The solution adopted was to build a new station about 300 yards to the east, and to re-align the end of the Hailsham branch so that it entered the west end of the new station with a junction facing Hastings. The re-siting of the station also necessitated the removal of the junction for Eastbourne to the east, and the re-alignment of the end of the Eastbourne branch. In 1969, the branch was closed and it became possible to restore the station to its original position, but this has not yet been done. There used to be three signal boxes at Polegate; one adjoined the level-crossing, one at the west end of the station operated the junction with the Hailsham line, and that at the east end of the station worked the junction for Eastbourne. After the closure of the Hailsham branch in January 1969, the box at the west end was disused. At the same time, the section of the original main line between Polegate and Stone Cross junction was closed, so that all traffic had to run in and out of Eastbourne. This meant that Polegate was no longer a junction and, after undergoing 'reduction', the east signal box was closed in 1971. Subsequently Polegate has been operated from the crossing box. As for 'railway fossils', the original alignment of the Hailsham branch has been largely obliterated by housing development but that of the Eastbourne branch is clearly marked by an existing siding. The 1881 station building is on the down side and, being at a lower level than the tracks, is not easy to see from passing trains. In general style, it suggests the 1860s rather than 1881, with its brickwork covered by painted plaster. Its appearance from the road has, if anything, been enhanced by the removal of a glazed canopy. The two island platforms are reached by a subway; each of them has waiting rooms and a generous amount of canopy.

Beyond Polegate the original line ran along the northern edge of Willingdon Level to Pevensey. For many years the Hailsham and Eastbourne lines had no through trains, a branch line service running between the two terminals with a reversal at Polegate, where connections were made with Hastings trains. The first move towards changing the Eastbourne line from branch to main line status came in 1871 when a spur was constructed from Willingdon junction on the branch to Stone Cross junction on the main line. Many years later, in 1905, a halt was opened a quarter of a mile east of the junction. Two parts of the former LBSCR system retain an unusually high proportion of stations which began life as halts—Portsmouth to Chichester and Eastbourne to St Leonards. For the latter service, four rail motor cars were constructed. These were basically powered coaches, carrying forty-eight passengers, two driven by steam and two by petrol engines. Whereas some trains on the LBSCR were first class only, the rail cars were third class only and, lacking class distinction, merely separated smokers from non-smokers. Needless to say, the accommodation reflected the class of passenger, the seats being made of perforated three-ply birchwood with oak frames. There was, however, some concession to the urge to decorate, in the form of carved oak pilasters and cream-coloured panels bordered with olive green and vermilion. The idea being to provide something approaching door-to-door transport, in addition to the stations on the main line at Pevensey and Bexhill, six halts were opened, at Stone Cross, Pevensey Bay, Normans Bay, Cooden, Collington Wood and Glyne Gap. In their original form, these consisted of short wooden platforms on each side of the tracks, equipped with name boards and oil lamps. There was no staff; fares were collected by the guard on the rail motor car, whose role was similar to that of a bus conductor. The service began on 16 September 1905 which was such a wet day that hardly anybody travelled. One can easily imagine the windswept platform of Normans Bay Halt, shining in the rain, with the occasional passenger bewailing the fact that, initially, the halts provided no more shelter than a bus stop. However, over the years, they have all either been closed or improved. The LBSCR were early converts from the single rail motor car to the far more flexible motor train. This consisted of suitably adapted locomotives and coaches—usually two coaches—operating as a unit which could be driven from either end. Halts were extended to accommodate trains and, in most cases, shelters were added. Stone Cross Halt survived long enough to have its up wooden platform replaced with concrete, but went out with steam trains in July 1935.

About one and a half miles east of Stone Cross is Pevensey & Westham, first opened in 1846. It is situated at Westham, but the neighbouring village, being noted for its castle, came first in the station name. The presence of a level-crossing at the west end of the station has ensured the survival of its signal box up to now. Pevensey Bay Halt was opened about three quarters of a mile to the east, on the road to Pevensey Bay, adjoining a level-crossing. From here the line ran across the almost uninhabited wastes of Pevensey Level to Bexhill. Somewhat surprisingly, a third halt was opened in a windswept position at Normans Bay. Its only neighbours in 1905 were a mission church, a Wesleyan hall, the Star Inn and a coastguard station. However, it did give access to a secluded stretch of beach and, somewhat surprisingly, is still in use. Half a mile beyond the halt, by a level-crossing, was Pevensey Sluice signal box which broke up the long gap between the Pevensey and Bexhill boxes. At this point the line begins to rise gently on an embankment towards the higher ground of Bexhill. The golf links provided some passengers for Cooden Golf Halt, which also served the small village of Cooden. From the point of view of traffic, this was probably the most successful of the six

halts, and was rebuilt by the Southern as a station in 1937. It did
not become a traditional station, lacking goods facilities and a
signal box, but it did have a typical Southern building of the
1930s complete with booking office down at road level. Of the
four halts that have survived, Cooden Beach alone receives hourly
calls from the London and Hastings express trains. Collington
Wood was only three quarters of a mile away from Bexhill, which
perhaps accounts for its opening in September 1905 being followed by closure in August 1906. It was, however, re-opened in
June 1911, trading under the new name of West Bexhill Halt.
When Bexhill (Eastern) became Bexhill West in 1929, West
Bexhill reverted to Collington. (The renaming of the former
South Eastern station was calculated to avoid confusion arising
from the location of a station called Eastern in West Bexhill.)
Like many former Southern halts, Collington has acquired a
small booking office on one of its platforms.

Bexhill became Bexhill Central to distinguish it from the
former rival SER terminal but, with the closure of the latter, is
again Bexhill. The construction of new buildings in 1901 was
probably not unrelated to the opening of the SER station in 1902.
Bexhill, like Lewes, belongs to its period, but slightly more so.
For instance, Lewes has lost sections of canopy whereas Bexhill's
not only survives most extensively but has typical LBSCR valanc-
ing. (The 1880s and 1890s were the 'high' period of canopies, both
over station entrances and on platforms.) Reflecting the changed
attitude to light of this period, is the rectangular lantern surmounting the roof of the main building, which is situated above
the platform at street level. From a railway viewpoint, Bexhill
has never been more than a major intermediate station, with the
usual goods facilities and a signal box at the London end. It was
closed to goods traffic in 1962. The works of the Bexhill Gas Company, with their own private siding, were on the down side, about
half a mile east of the station. A quarter of a mile farther on was
Galley Hill sidings, from which was served the Glyne Gap works
of the Hastings and St Leonards Gas Company. Adjoining the
works was Glyne Gap Halt, one of the six halts of 1905. This was

a typical wooden structure which remained in use until 1915, and which has gone, virtually without a trace.

The station arrangements at St Leonards began with a temporary terminus at Bulverhythe. The first permanent station was opened at West Marina in 1846, and was replaced by a second in 1882. From 1851, LBSCR trains were running through to Hastings.[9] West Marina was decidedly out of the way for local traffic but was retained and even developed, because it was the only station over which the LBSCR had exclusive control. Their motive power depot was on the down side of the line, and West Marina was their rail head for goods traffic. After the grouping, while the status of the station diminished, that of the motive power depot increased. Even after the electrification of the LBSCR route in 1935, it retained express steam locomotives for working the SER route to London. (In the period before the dieselisation of the SER line, these were examples of the well-known Schools class.) After dieselisation, a new depot was opened west of the old steam motive power depot, which has been demolished. Express trains did not call, and it is perhaps remarkable that West Marina station survived until 1967; the buildings have now been demolished. A quarter of a mile to the east, at Bo-peep junction, LBSCR trains joined the tracks of the SER. That company's line to Hastings is described in Chapter 4. Somewhat oddly, while the diesel trains for the SER route are stored at West Marina, on the former Brighton line, the electric trains on the LBSCR route are projected beyond Hastings to the suburban station at Ore, where a depot was provided on the former SER.

As already mentioned, the distance to Hastings by the LBSCR was reduced in 1847 by the opening of the Keymer 'cut-off' line. The location of the junction with the main line was based on physical features but, although convenient from a constructional point of view, it is perhaps a little surprising, first, that a sharp curve necessitating a severe speed restriction was incorporated in a main line and second, if there was to be a sharp curve, why the junction was not made at Burgess Hill Station. The Keymer line is by no means free of level-crossings, the first of which is only 10 chains from the main line. It is operated from a signal box

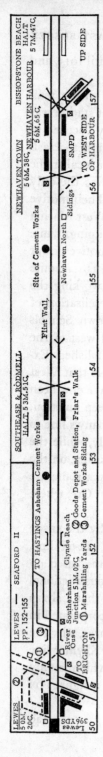
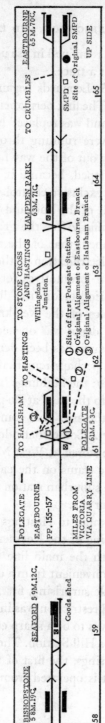
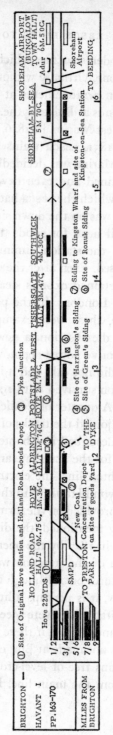
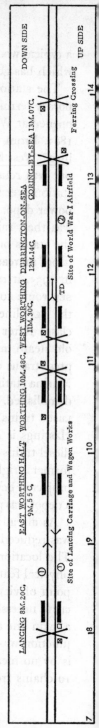

8 Lewes. Ordnance Survey May 1899 Edition. The original line from Brighton came in
on the left side and ran into the terminus in Friars Walk near the Goods Depot. The
extension to Hastings diverged short of the terminal and curved round to cross the River
Ouse at Southerham. The Keymer line ran under the town in a tunnel joining the line
from Brighton at the point where a new station was opened in 1857. The station shown
on the map is the present one, opened in 1889, together with the new line which short
circuited the original line, subsequently used for freight only. These changes also
necessitated a new connection to the Uckfield and Tunbridge Wells line. At the present
time the original line and that to Uckfield and Tunbridge Wells have both been
removed. (Scale 25 ins. to 1 mile; scale of inches shown bottom left)

29 The London Road viaduct carrying the East Coast line to Hastings away from Brighton. This view of 1846 shows the terminal station on the western side of the valley above the town. Details include a coach passing under the elliptical arch and a train crossing the viaduct. (From *The Illustrated London News*, Vol. 8, p. 53)

30 Luxury on the Brighton line. The interior of a saloon carriage in 1873

which also controls the junction. The site of Keymer Junction station, which was open from 1862 until 1883, adjoined the level-crossing. Its replacement by Wivelsfield on the main line has already been described. The large works of the Keymer Brick and Tile Company are still to be seen on the down side, but their private siding has been removed.

There is an ascent at 1 in 298 to the cutting on Ditchling Common, followed by an almost unbroken descent to Lewes at a ruling gradient of 1 in 143. The section from Keymer crossing to the first station at Plumpton was broken by the signal box at Spatham Lane crossing, now demolished. Plumpton was opened in 1863 and has modest, weatherboarded buildings which are difficult to date—they could belong to any year between 1863 and, say, 1890. The special thing about Plumpton was its race platform, a long, open platform on the up side at the Keymer end of the station. This is now overgrown but it still evocative of crowds returning home after the end of a day's racing. There is a level-crossing at the Lewes end of the station, with a conventional signal box, but also a crossing keeper's house, numbered 16, and probably contemporary with the opening of the line. Between Plumpton and Cooksbridge, the line crosses from one tributary valley of the Ouse to another, and there is a slight break in the descent to Lewes. Cooksbridge was opened in 1848 and at least part of the station house may be original. Wikeley and Middleton distinguish extensions of 1894. The goods yard was closed in 1961. A private siding to Messrs Chatfield's timber yard had been reached from it, and this also has been closed and lifted. The signal box and level-crossing remain at the Lewes end of the station. Hamsey Crossing signal box has been demolished and automatic lifting barriers installed. Just beyond its site, on the down side, was the junction with the original line to Uckfield.[10] We are carried over a side channel of the Ouse by a fixed bridge. The navigable channel is on the east side of the line, and we cross a short branch leading to a disused wharf. This was the terminal of the tramway serving the Offham lime kilns.[11] A chalk spur separates the 'cut-off' line from Lewes station and this is penetrated by a tunnel of 396 yards. The ground had been built over

L

for many years, and a clause was inserted in the authorising Act making the company responsible for any damage attributable to subsidence above the railway. As already described, the south end of the tunnel was widened in 1935 to enable the platform of Lewes station to be lengthened.

The 'cut-off' line was opened in the October of 1847 and the Newhaven branch followed in December. Leaving the main line beyond Southerham bridge, it follows a course between the navigable Ouse and the road which follows the side of the valley. It crosses two meanders of the river which were short-circuited by new cuts. Apart from a slight hump over Glynde Reach, it is virtually level. About half a mile after crossing Glynde Reach, Asheham cement works is passed on the down side. It has an overhead cableway which passes over the railway to a wharf on the Ouse, and also has a private siding, both of which were disused by 1971. The only intermediate station between Lewes and Newhaven is Southease & Rodmell Halt, opened in 1905. The two villages are both on the west bank, but there is a minor road crossing the valley at this point. Southease signal box was originally named Itford crossing, after a near-by farm, and the signalman still sells railway tickets through his window. The authorising Act contained a clause requiring the construction of high walls at certain points where the railway ran alongside turnpike roads to screen railway locomotives from the doubtlessly apprehensive horses. The horses have long since gone, but a flint wall, about 15 feet high, still separates the railway from the road near Durham Farm. Just north of South Heighton, on the far side of the road, is the site of a cement works which, when it was open, had a private siding. Newhaven was of special importance during the First World War, being out of range of the enemy guns, and therefore much used for the shipment of munitions. We pass the extensive sidings at the back of the North Quay on the up side. Entry and exit from the sidings was controlled by Newhaven North signal box, which was taken out of use in January 1934. The signal box by the level-crossing, once named the South signal box, controlled the crossing gates on the very busy A259 coast road, and also the junction for the Harbour

Tramway. This passed over the swing bridge, shared with road traffic, to serve the western side of the harbour. Weight restrictions on the bridge precluded the use of any steam locomotives other than Brighton Terriers and these continued to work the traffic on the Newhaven Tramway until its closure in 1963.

Newhaven Town station is on the opposite side of the river to Newhaven. The town is quite uncharacteristic of Sussex, having the atmosphere of a Victorian port. It is neither seaside- nor commuter-based, most of its inhabitants being associated with the port and the ships that use it. So it is not surprising that only minor changes have been made to the station since 1847. The original flint building is on the up side, with additions of various periods, mostly of wood. Beyond the station, on the up side, was the steam motive power depot and, beyond that, workshops of the marine engineering department, first of the LBSCR and then of the Southern railway. Until a few years ago, their site was dominated by the tall sheerlegs which were used mainly for lifting engines and boilers out of ships under repair. The Harbour station is just over a quarter of a mile beyond the Town station and is in two parts. A normal side platform arrangement is used by the scheduled, public service from Seaford, but there are two special terminal platforms on a short branch for the use of boat trains. Most of the buildings associated with the boat train station were brought into use in 1886 and the long transit and customs sheds are typical of their period. Alongside the through station was the large block of the London and Paris Hotel which was finally demolished in 1958. In the early 1960s traffic on the Newhaven to Dieppe route was declining, but in 1964, the construction of a link span made it possible to introduce car ferry services. These have done much to increase the trade of Newhaven but do not, of course, contribute to railway traffic. Beyond the boat train terminal, tracks extend to the harbour works and to the area of gravel waste resembling the Crumbles at Eastbourne, which was once used as a source of ballast.

Although the line was authorised to go to Seaford, unfavourable conditions prevented its getting there in 1847 and it was not until 1864 that the extension was made. A sharp curve of 10 chains radius diverges from between the through and the terminal platforms of the Harbour station, and the line crosses the marshes to the site of Bishopstone station. This was a remote establishment, nearly a mile away from the village whose name it bore. Lacking goods facilities, although it was opened with the line, it almost anticipated the halts of the Edwardian period. In fact, in 1922, it became an unstaffed halt. By 1938, the district to the west of Seaford was developing rapidly and a new station was opened to serve it. The old station, now officially a halt, was closed at the same time, with the new establishment taking its name. Somewhat surprisingly, the following Easter the halt re-opened with the name 'Bishopstone Beach'. Under war conditions, its survival until the beginning of 1942, is more surprising. Although no buildings remain, the platforms for the first Bishopstone are plain to see. Two other survivals are a concrete name board which looks as though it was erected for the re-opening at Easter time in 1939, and the Newhaven Harbour up distant signal, which has an LBCR post.

The town of Seaford is elevated on the edge of chalk downland and the line climbs up from the marshes at 1 in 100 to reach it. The second station to be called Bishopstone was at the end of a cutting, near the main A259 road. It was typical of its period in every way, being designed to handle passengers only. Its entrance and booking office have a slightly dumpy tower, perhaps owing something to London Transport architecture, e.g. Hounslow West. There have been no great changes since 1938. Just under a mile from Bishopstone is the terminal at Seaford. The station building on the down side has altered little since 1864. The canopy over the entrance is an addition and there have been alterations to the doors but, basically, it remains a solid, three-bay building of its period, almost without embellishment. On the railway side, Seaford consists of a single platform with a bay on the north side. The buildings are alongside and not across the end of the track and, on a number of occasions, there were moves towards extension to Eastbourne. The goods yard was closed in 1964, and the impressive and characteristic LBSCR goods shed and warehouse have been leased to Seaford Urban District Council.

The inclusion of the Seaford extension as a main line could be challenged as, for most of the day, it has only a local service of electric trains. However, each morning and evening there are through trains to London.

One main line of East Sussex remains to be described. As mentioned above, the Eastbourne line was opened at the same time as the Hailsham branch and, until the introduction of through coaches about 1875, was operated as a branch line. The change in status reflects the growth of Eastbourne which, in the 1840s, was a very small town, about a mile and a half inland. (This centre is now called Eastbourne Old Town.) The hamlet of Southbourne was near the site of the present civic centre, and there was a small group of houses on the front known as Sea Houses. The first plan was for a line following the scarp foot of the Downs through Willingdon to an inland terminus at the old town centre. Instead, partly as a speculation and partly because it was cheaper to build, the line was located farther east across Willingdon Level with a terminus at the hamlet of Southbourne. This change of plan was most important for Eastbourne, as it encouraged the growth of the new seaside town. The first terminal was situated to the west of the present station, on a site now occupied by Upperton Road. The original timber-framed building was removed to a new site, where it finally became a depository for a local firm. After this re-alignment, there have been no further changes in the basic geography of the line.

As explained above, the re-siting of Polegate station necessitated re-location of the northern end of the Eastbourne branch; some sidings remain to indicate the old alignment. The spur of 1871 to Stone Cross junction, giving a direct run from Eastbourne to St Leonards, comes in on the down side at Willingdon junction. The signal box here became redundant in June 1930 when Hampden Park took over the working. Hampden Park is a rather plain, weatherboarded station of 1888 serving a detached suburb of Eastbourne. Beyond Hampden Park the line crosses Willingdon Level in a straight and level line, with no earthworks. The steam motive power depot was on the up side, about three

quarters of a mile from the terminal. The site had been purchased for a carriage and wagon works, but local opposition to
industrial development was strong enough to bring about the
move to Lancing instead. The original engine shed, almost opposite the present signal box, was both cramped and in a position
wanted for other purposes, so the available site was used to construct a new shed in 1911. Electrification of the main line, followed by a diminishing demand for steam locomotives, led to its
decline, which was hastened by bomb damage received in the
Second World War. It was finally closed in April 1968 and
demolished in 1969. The small Locomotive signal box, which
controlled the movements of the engines, became disused in
April 1968, but was not abolished until September 1969. On the
down side is the site of the Crumbles branch, perhaps better
regarded as a long siding, although locomotives working on it
were required to carry a staff marked 'Gas Works and Ballast
Hole Line'. The order of premises served was as follows: Davey
& Mannington and Lunsford & Co.: Bainbridge and Shell Mex:
Eastbourne Corporation electricity works: Eastbourne gas works:
Lewis Gasson and the Ballast Hole. There was a progressive with-
drawal. The end of the line went out of use, with a decline in the
demand for ballast; the last user was the gas works and the
Crumbles branch has now been lifted.

The terminal station is approached by a sweeping curve, with
sidings concentrated on the up side. Basically, the station consists of two island platforms served by four tracks, which is
identical with, for instance, Littlehampton. But in fact, Eastbourne is grander than this basis would suggest. For instance, the
eastern platform, numbered 3 and 4, is wide enough to carry a
roadway and also a flowerbed. Movements are controlled from
one signal cabin at the end of platforms 3 and 4, with a manual
72-lever frame. There are signs of damage for those who seek
them. For instance, the canopy on platforms 1 and 2 was damaged
by aerial bombardment; the signal gantry at the end of the platforms has had a girder replaced after a Motorail train ran into a
platform occupied by another train. But the main part of the
station retains all its Edwardian seaside charm—Eastbourne and

Bognor have perhaps more than other stations this slightly nostalgic atmosphere. There are parts from many periods, but the strongest contribution is from 1886. To begin with, Eastbourne has a lantern over its circulating area, bigger and more elaborate than either Lewes or Bexhill, especially notable for the ornamental ironwork it bears. Then there is a clock tower which, while not aspiring to the standards of Nottingham Victoria, is still tall enough, with its spire, to catch the eye of the traveller. While much belongs to the period before the First World War, especially at the time of electrification, the Southern left its mark, including the decoration of the booking hall. But this does not detract from the claim for Eastbourne as the most characteristic of the seaside stations of the South.

LC&DR, 1880s

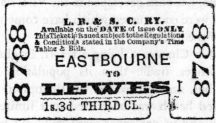

24 August 1912

LB&SCRY, 1 September 1921

6

LBSCR Routes to Portsmouth

The LBSCR system developed like an inverted letter T with its main line as the vertical between London and Brighton, and its East Coast line to Hastings and the West Coast to Portsmouth forming the crosspiece. Later, the system was complicated by an infilling of the angles between the stem and the arms. This chapter is concerned, first with the West Coast route from Brighton to Portsmouth and then with the Mid-Sussex line which provided a more direct route from London to Portsmouth, avoiding going round two sides of a triangle. The towns of Little-hampton and Bognor both developed in the Victorian period and short branches were constructed which have come to be worked as extensions of the main line.

As explained in Chapter 5, being a resort, Brighton attracted far more passenger traffic than its population would have accounted for but, unlike Dover or Southampton, it was not a port. Its exposed beach was only used to a limited extent for landing cargoes and its passenger piers could not be used when the weather was bad. Some use was made of Newhaven, but most of Brighton's traffic passed through the port of Shoreham. This was at the mouth of the Adur, about six miles west of Brighton. Coastal drift tended to block the entrance, but over the years between 1817 and 1820 the bar was pierced. What had been the lowest part of the river was blocked off at the seaward end to become an enclosed basin, while access to Shoreham and neighbouring Kingston was facilitated. There was a greater incentive to improve communications between Shoreham and Brighton and, in 1820, there were plans for both a horse railway and a turnpike road, of which only the latter materialised. In 1823 William James produced his famous plan for railways in Southern England, including a link between Shoreham and Brighton. Other proposals followed and, as summarised in Chapter 5, most of the plans for railways to Brighton passed through Shoreham. The direct route to Brighton, which was authorised in 1837, made good its omission to include Shoreham on its line by agreeing to include it on a branch. Further, a section of the Act was designed to ensure that the branch was not neglected for the sake of the main line and, in the event, it was opened in May 1840, one year and four months before the main line was completed.

Although Shoreham was an objective in itself, the Sussex coastal plain was a rich agricultural area with a number of growing resorts and established towns, of which Chichester was the principal. A subsidiary company of the London & Brighton, the Brighton & Chichester, obtained its Act in July 1844 to carry the line on from Shoreham, over the Adur and for 22¾ miles over the coastal plain to Chichester. In the August of the following year, it was authorised to extend its line to the great naval base of Portsmouth. Apart from crossing two rivers, the Adur and the Arun, construction was unusually simple. Worthing was reached in 1845, Chichester in 1846 and the final sixteen miles on to Portsmouth were opened in 1847. This gave Portsmouth its first, but somewhat indirect route to London and, as will be explained in Chapter 7, the inhabitants were not entirely happy. However, the alternative western approach, via Eastleigh and the Southampton railway, was little better, so the LSWR and LBSCR companies came to an agreement to pool the Portsmouth revenue and provide an unsatisfactory service to their mutual satisfaction. Needless to say, their attitude was not shared by the people of Portsmouth and, perhaps inevitably, in 1859, the Direct line to Portsmouth was opened and, to the fury of the LBSCR, operated by the LSWR. The immediate and abortive countermeasures of the LBSCR are described in Chapter 7; in the longer term, it improved its own route so as to reduce the mileage from London

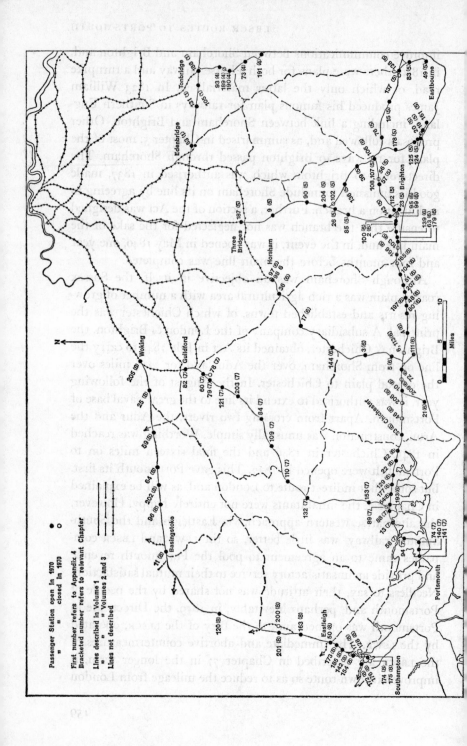

Passenger Station open in 1970 ●
" " closed in 1970 ○

First number refers to Appendix 4
Bracketed number refers to relevant Chapter

Lines described in Volume 1
" " " Volumes 2 and 3
" " not described

N

0   5   10
Miles

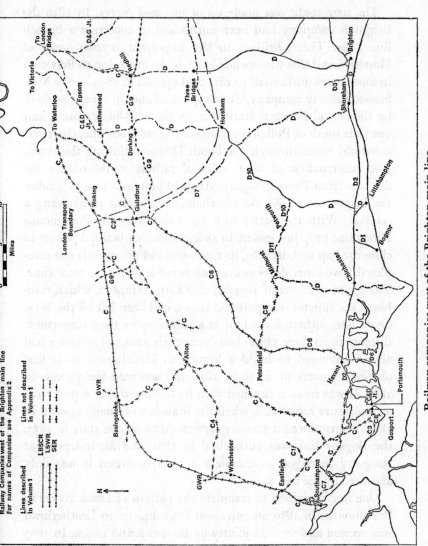

Railway companies west of the Brighton main line

Railway Companies west of the Brighton main line
For names of Companies see Appendix 2

Lines described | Lines not described
in Volume 1 | in Volume 1

LBSCR
LSWR
SER

N

Miles
0   5   10

To Victoria

To London
Bridge

To Waterloo

D&G Jt.

Epsom

C&D Jt.

Leatherhead

Dorking

Effingham Jt.

G9

G9

G/D

Three Bridges

Horsham

Brighton

Shoreham

D3

D2

Littlehampton

Bognor

Chichester

D1

D6

Havant

Portsmouth

Gosport

D

London Transport
Boundary

Woking

Guildford

C2

C

C

C

G9

D7

D10

D10

Midhurst

Petworth

Midhurst

C5

C6

Alton

Petersfield

C

C

GWR

Basingstoke

C4

Winchester

Eastleigh

Southampton

GWR

C7

C1

C3

C8

C&D Jt.

D6

Bridge from 95 to 87 miles. This was, in fact, rather better than it sounded, as the congestion of the line between Croydon and Redhill was avoided, and also the reversal at Brighton.

The new route was made up of bits and pieces. In 1846 the Brighton company had been authorised to construct a branch line from Three Bridges to the important market town of Horsham and this was opened in 1848. An extension to Petworth in Sussex was authorised in 1857 and opened in 1859 by the Mid-Sussex Railway company.[1] It was operated and, in 1862, absorbed, by the LBSCR. Between Hardham, on the Mid-Sussex line about one mile south of Pulborough, and the West Coast line, there was a natural route through the South Downs following the Arun. The construction of nine miles of railway could reduce the distance from Three Bridges to Arundel junction from 40¼ miles via Brighton to 30¾ via Horsham, in addition to avoiding a reversal. With the battle with the LSWR over the Portsmouth Direct line only just ended, in 1860 the LBSCR obtained powers to close the gap and, in 1863, its new route to Portsmouth was completed. Two other developments occurred at about the same time. The growing resort of Bognor, and Littlehampton, which combined the functions of port and resort, had been left off the West Coast line, although stations at a rather more than respectable distance from these places had borne their names. The LBSCR had always intended to build a branch to Littlehampton—it first obtained powers to do so in 1846 and repeated the process in 1860. It was more concerned with its possibilities as a port than as a pleasure resort and, when the branch was finally opened in 1863, it introduced a steamer service. After a false start in 1853, the Bognor line was authorised in 1861 and an independent company managed to complete it by 1864 when it was duly absorbed by the LBSCR.

One line remained to complete the pattern of LBSCR routes to Portsmouth. In 1859 an extension from Epsom to Leatherhead was opened and worked jointly by the LSWR and LBSCR. In 1863 the LBSCR obtained powers for an extension from Leatherhead to Dorking. An independent company, the Horsham, Dorking & Leatherhead, had been authorised in 1862, so the LBSCR acquired its powers and opened the line from Leatherhead to Horsham in 1867. For trains from London Bridge, the route via Dorking was about one and a half miles longer but, for Victoria trains, it was half a mile shorter. There was, however, an important saving in time by the avoidance of the congested line between Croydon and Redhill. This completed the network of main lines leading through West Sussex to Portsmouth. There were, however, three secondary lines, all of which have been closed. The first, opened in 1861, ran from Itchingfield junction to Shoreham through Steyning.[2] This provided an alternative but roundabout route between London and Brighton and was usually served by local trains. It was closed in 1966. Next in chronological order was the line from Chichester to Midhurst, opened in 1881 and closed to passengers in 1935.[3] Although there were junctions at both ends, this was always treated as a branch line. Finally, from 1887 until the end of 1938, there was a branch line from a point west of Hove to the Devil's Dyke.[4] There were no other lines operated by the LBSCR in Sussex, although an independent company eked out a precarious existence between Chichester and Selsey from 1897 to 1935.[5] All the main lines were electrified before the Second World War, from Brighton to Worthing in 1933 and the rest in 1938. Revenue has always depended largely on passenger traffic and an increase in both the total and the commuting population has helped to keep the lines open, despite the abrasive efforts of road transport and continental holidays. Services are notable for their frequency and reliability rather than speed; the 'standard' express trains from Victoria to Portsmouth Harbour by the Mid-Sussex route make twelve stops and average about 40 m.p.h. If the Portsmouth Direct line always appeared to be a runner-up to the Southampton line, this was equally true of the Mid-Sussex line and the main line to Brighton. But this is not to say that the West Sussex lines lack attractions or character.

Any review must start with the 'senior' line—that is the six miles between Brighton and Shoreham. Brighton station is described in Chapter 5, and it will be remembered that the platforms for the West Coast line form a separate terminal unit. The line is cut into the side of a chalk hill, curving sharply to the west with a large area excavated on the up side to make room for the motive power depot. After penetrating the 200 yards of Hove tunnel, we pass the site of the newly-closed Holland Road goods depot. This was the goods yard of the original Hove passenger station opened with the line in 1840 and closed in March 1880. In 1905, just beyond the overbridge at the west end of the yard, Holland Road Halt was opened. It survived until 1956 but has left virtually no evidence of its existence. Beyond its site a double-track line comes in on the up side. This is the important Clifton-ville spur, opened in 1879 to enable trains from Littlehampton and Worthing to avoid running in and out of Brighton. A station had been opened, and named Cliftonville, to serve a rapidly growing residential district about half a mile west of the original Hove in 1865. When the spur was opened, this became the nearest point to Brighton touched by the London to Worthing trains, so it was re-named West Brighton. Its upgrading was followed by the closure of the original Hove, and some enlargement of the premises. There were more alterations about 1893, followed by two more re-namings—to Hove and West Brighton in 1894 and finally to Hove in 1895.

Although the tracks for Brighton and those for the Cliftonville spur separate nearly half a mile east of Hove, the actual junction adjoins the station and is controlled by Hove 'A' signal box. The platform on the up side is an island. A large goods depot was situated on the up side of the line, west of the passenger station. This met the fate of so many goods stations, being closed in 1968, but in this case revival came in the form of re-opening as a coal concentration depot in 1971. Aldrington is a typical halt, opened in 1905 and now reconstructed in concrete. At its western end, the branch line to the Devil's Dyke diverged and, until 1932, Aldrington was named Dyke Junction Halt. The alignment of the branch is indicated by the premises of Messrs Harrington, who for many years had a private siding. Only a mile away is Portslade and West Hove station—the 'West Hove' was added to the name in 1927. The present substantial buildings were opened in 1881, but passenger facilities were first provided here when the line was opened in 1840. There appears to have been a closure in

1847 through lack of traffic, followed by a re-opening in 1857 when houses began to go up in Portslade-by-Sea. The original platforms were on the opposite side of the level-crossing to the present station, but nothing is left of them. The goods yard was closed in 1968. Factories on either side of the station—Messrs Green to the east and Ronuk to the west—had private sidings, which have been removed. Fishersgate was opened three quarters of a mile west of Portslade in 1905 and is one of only two stations on the Shoreham line which has not changed its name—unless one counts the recent dropping of the suffix 'Halt' as a name change. The second establishment with constant nomenclature is Southwick. The West Coast line is notable for its lack of earthworks but, at this point, the line is on an embankment and buildings were added in 1899 at ground level, with steps leading up to the platforms. Until 1951 there were some remains of earlier buildings but, by 1971, not only these, but most of the 1899 buildings had been demolished. Partly because of its elevation, and partly because of its proximity to Kingston, Southwick never handled goods traffic.

Kingston-on-Sea was closed to passengers in 1879, but in 1840 was probably surpassed in importance only by Shoreham. At this time there was a regular steamer service from Kingston Wharf to Dieppe. Normally the steamers called at the Chain Pier at Brighton but if, for any reason, this was not possible, then a special train was run to or from Kingston. In 1847 the Dieppe service was transferred to Newhaven, but Kingston Wharf continued to handle freight. Its connection with the main line was restricted, consisting of a short incline with turntables at each end, up or down which wagons were passed, connected to a chain which was operated from a stationary engine. The turntables made it impossible for wagons with a wheelbase of more than 11 feet 9 inches to reach the wharf and there was also a height restriction. The line passed under the main road and, because of this, the Appendix to the Working Timetable ruled: 'Goods must not be loaded in box wagons which exceed 11 feet in height from rail level.' Having descended the incline, wagons were moved on the wharf by horses. This went on until 1938, when the incline was replaced by a line descending obliquely at 1 in 82. The horses were displaced by small shunting locomotives, such as the SECR P class. Kingston Wharf finally closed after 128 years, in 1968. Somewhat remarkably, the station house survives, although there is no sign of the platform. The growing awareness of the attractions of the seaside was reflected in a change of name from Kingston to Kingston-on-Sea in 1870. This, however, did not attract sufficient passengers to save the station but, under its new name of Kingston Wharf, goods traffic continued on a satisfactory scale. It was the promise of traffic from Shoreham which encouraged the construction of the railway in 1840 and it is indicative of the rise of road transport that, in the 1960s, when Shoreham's traffic was expanding, the rail connection to the waterside was not carrying enough traffic to justify its retention. Like all the stations, Shoreham has undergone change since its opening in 1840. Its name was changed to Shoreham Harbour in July 1906 and, finally, to Shoreham-by-Sea in October 1906. One seeks a rule to determine whether places in Sussex should be *on* Sea or *by* Sea, but fails to find it. (The railway used 'Kingston-On-Sea' but the Ordnance Survey prefer 'Kingston-by-Sea'.) The station buildings at Shoreham underwent major reconstruction in 1892. Although modest in size compared with Hove, the building has some interesting details. Both the chimneys and the eaves are adorned with elaborate plasterwork and the pointed moulding over the windows is suggestive of the Saxon influence seen in Sussex churches. The goods yard was closed in 1965.

After 130 years, there is very little between Brighton and Shoreham which can be regarded with certainty as belonging to the early days of the line. As each of the stations has been mentioned, varying degrees of rebuilding have been recorded. The main function of the line has changed from what was considered as a connection between a town and its port, a Liverpool & Manchester on a very small scale; it has become more like a suburban railway, with the port of Shoreham making increasing use of road transport. But the basic character remains of a line starting some distance inland and running down obliquely to its nearest approach to the water's edge at Kingston Wharf. The gradient of

1 The port of Newhaven viewed from the footbridge of the Harbour Station. The boat train platforms are ahead; the line on to Seaford diverges to the left. Details include semaphore signals, a level crossing and a 'traditional' signal box operating by means of points and wires. On the marine side, a link span is visible on the right, a Southdown bus is behind the loading gauge and a vessel is beside the cranes on the quay. This was the view on 1 July 1969

2 A down Hastings train at Stone Cross Halt hauled by LBSC B4 class N. 2054 built at Brighton Works in 1900. One of the platforms has been rebuilt with concrete but retains its oil lamps. The junction signal of Stone Cross Junction and the South Downs were visible in the background when this photograph was taken on 9 October 1933

33 The circulating area of the station opened at Bognor in 1902. This carefully posed photograph was taken shortly after it was completed. It has changed little since then, and reflects something of the Edwardian high summer of the LBSCR

34 Platform for Midhurst trains at Petersfield viewed from the footbridge adjoining the level crossing. Q1 class locomotive No. 33002, built at Brighton in 1942, is at the end of the platform. Petersfield Signal Box is visible on the left of the picture which also shows traditional level crossing gates. It was taken on the 4 February 1955

1 in 264 is the same as that selected by Rennie as the ruling gradient for his main line. Being the first passenger railway in Sussex, in its early years the Shoreham branch attracted a great deal of pleasure traffic which could combine a first experience of rail travel with a visit to the Swiss Pleasure Gardens. Now, although hemmed in by housing, the Shoreham branch retains some of its individuality and Shoreham continues to mark the end of a distinctive section.

The next section consisted of the 22¾ miles to Chichester, with traffic from the market town of Arundel, the port of Little-hampton and the resorts of Bognor and Worthing. The first obstacle was the crossing of the River Adur above Shoreham. A fine suspension bridge had carried road traffic since 1833, and there was a second wooden bridge about three quarters of a mile farther inland at Old Shoreham. The Duke of Norfolk owned and collected tolls on both, and the railway met this problem by purchasing the old wooden bridge and paying the Duke com-pensation for any reduction in tolls on the newer, suspension bridge. (The suspension bridge was replaced by the present bow-string girder bridge in 1923.) The railway bridge was approached on an embankment more costly than usual, as there were no cuttings from which spoil could be extracted. This may partially explain the end section consisting of brick arches with a girder span over the main road. From 1861 to 1966, Shoreham Junction, just east of the bridge, was the point of divergence for the trains to Horsham. The signal box was closed in 1932 and, subsequently, the points were operated from Shoreham 'B'. At present the line is still open as far as the cement works at Beeding.[6] The bridge over the Adur consists of fourteen spans resting on circular iron columns. On the far side was a flat and featureless marsh, ter-minated by the slightly higher ground of Lancing. The Edwardian period was notable for land speculation—for instance activities on the Isle of Sheppey are described in Volume Three, Chapter 3. By means of suitable financial arrangements, the rail-way was persuaded to erect Bungalow Town Halt in 1910, named in anticipation of extensive bungaloid growth. This did not occur to the desired extent. But on the up side of the line, an airfield

M

was opened. After military use during the First World War, it was used by an aircraft manufacturer. Somewhat oddly, in 1933, when Shoreham became a civil airport and the railway was electrified, because of the lack of support from 'Bungalow Town' the halt was closed.[7] However, the Southern Railway was interested in the development of feeder rail services for air transport and, in 1935, the halt was re-opened as 'Shoreham Airport' with the modest terminal buildings of the airport near-by. The name reverted to Shoreham Airport (Bungalow Town) Halt, presumably to make it clear that both air passengers and bungalow residents were welcome. But not many came and, after the German occupation of the Channel Islands, air services terminated and, in July 1940, the halt was finally closed. About two concrete posts on the down side are almost all that remains. But, in a way, this was the forerunner of Gatwick Airport and of the Southern Region's newest station, Southampton Airport.

Lancing station is typical of the West Coast line in at least two respects. First, it is alongside a level-crossing and secondly, its buildings are of mixed period and style, although some additions of 1893 are prominent. At the beginning of 1971 Lancing was distinctive in a temporary way, retaining Southern Region green enamelled signs in contrast to the standard BR black and white which was established elsewhere in Sussex. Beyond the station on the down side was the carriage and wagon works, erected on the nearest available piece of ground near Brighton and on the LBSCR system. About a hundred acres of land was purchased in 1902 and, when the works was opened in 1912, it covered about sixty-six acres. It was envisaged that many of the employees would require housing in Lancing, but this proved to be incorrect as they preferred to retain houses in Brighton with the opportunity to let rooms to summer visitors. This situation lay behind the running of the famous Lancing Belle which, in contrast with the Brighton Belle, conveyed workmen to and from Lancing, not in Pullman cars, and was not advertised in the public timetable. The Lancing Belle made its last journey on 3 July 1964, after which workmen had to use the public services. In the 1930s the Southern concentrated repair work at Lancing, employing 1,400 men to repair about 2,200 carriages a year. The two main shops stood on either side of the yard, each measuring 400 feet long by 250 wide. Painting and frame-building was carried on in the western shop; other operations, including upholstery, in the eastern. There were a number of other premises, including the smith's shop and the timber-drying shed and, on the opposite side of the railway, stood a conspicuous water tower. The icy blasts of the Beeching era were unlikely to spare a relatively small establishment like Lancing, and the last coach to be repaired— CK S5750S—left the works on 11 March 1965. The site has now been acquired for other industrial purposes.

About a mile and a half farther on, in 1905, Ham Bridge Halt was opened to serve a growing suburb of Worthing. Subsequently it has been rebuilt in concrete and, in 1949, given the less suggestive name of East Worthing. At this point the line was sufficiently far inland to avoid the built-up area of Worthing and its station was built on the road connecting the Regency resort with the old village of Broadwater. The first station was a severe looking building, without embellishment and repellent rather than inviting. It lasted until 1870 when new buildings were provided immediately to the west. The most striking features of Worthing's second station were the canopies which ran the whole length of both platforms, supported by walls at the back and by iron columns. (Curtain walls were provided where buildings were lacking.) Almost invariably in Southern England, platform canopies are level, the edges being decorated with wooden valances. But at Worthing, the canopies consisted of a series of ridges and furrows of the type commonly found on the Midland or Great Eastern Railways. The third reconstruction period began in 1909 and most of the second station has gone; but, by happy chance, a short length of its ridge and furrow canopy has survived on the down platform. The third Worthing in some respects looks more like a station of the 1920s than a late Edwardian design. There is a gable over the main entrance which contains a large semi-circular window similar to that at Ramsgate. Perhaps because of its late date, Worthing has suffered less from unrelated additions than most of the West Coast stations and, until 1968, the impression of coherence was enhanced at night by the gas lights, which fitted so well its Edwardian atmosphere. Traffic is sufficiently heavy to require more than two platform faces and the up platform is an island. The platforms are connected by a subway lined with white glazed tiles, which was extended to the north of the station to provide an alternative exit and also to serve a possible third platform. In steam days there were water cranes at the ends of the platforms, for which a water-softening plant was provided. Re-naming did not occur until 1936 when, to give both distinction and status, Worthing became Worthing Central. By 1968, status had been superseded by economy and the 'Central' was dropped. Most of the goods facilities, including a large shed, were east of the station and were closed in 1970.

By 1889 West Worthing was considered ready for a station, and the original buildings remain, albeit with modifications. From 1933 until 1938, this was the limit of electrification and electric train sheds were provided on the up side. For services terminating at West Worthing, a shunting neck was provided between the up and down tracks, enabling trains to be stabled without crossing either of the running lines. The coast between Worthing and Littlehampton is much developed. This had begun before the First World War and continued unabated between the wars. The area afforded limited employment opportunities apart from horticulture and the tourist trade but, for the unusually high proportion of retired residents, this was immaterial. After the Second World War, the area continued to grow, being favoured by those without fixed work places, such as company directors with dispersed 'empires'. There are, however, no postwar stations. Durrington-on-Sea, which takes its name from a village two miles inland, is typical of its 1937 date. Goring became Goring-by-Sea in 1895. It retains its signal box and level-crossing gates, but its goods yard was closed in 1962. Lack of architectural detail makes it difficult to decide if any part of the buildings belongs to the opening date of 1846, but it would seem unlikely. The gap between Goring and the next station at Angmering, two and a half miles, is greater than any to be found east of Worthing.

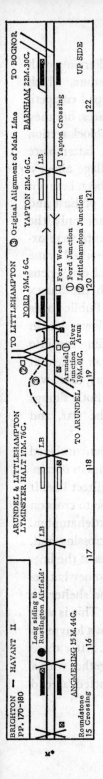

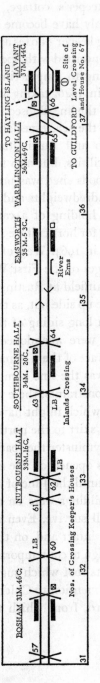
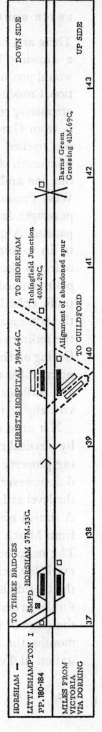

There are, however, two level-crossing sites, one at Ferring, with a crossing keeper's cottage, and one at Roundstone, which would probably have become station sites but for road competition. Crossing keeper's boxes are provided at both places, but they are merely concerned with operating the gates—the block section is from Goring to Angmering. The station at the latter place was opened in 1846, taking its name from the village about a mile north of the line. Subsequent development has been between the line and the sea, especially round the villages of East and West Preston and Rustington. At Angmering, not only the passenger facilities, but also the freight arrangements were expanded. A goods shed was provided with a hand-worked crane to lift 20 hundredweights and an unusual number of cattle pens reflected the holding of a cattle market (although the Sussex plain is noted for horticulture rather than livestock). Public goods traffic ceased in 1964. West of the station, on the down side, in the latter stages of the First World War, a long siding ran into the military airfield at Rustington. (There was also an airfield at Goring on the up side but, as this adjoined the railway, there was no need for a long siding of the Rustington type.) Both sidings and airfields were abandoned after the end of the war, and virtually no trace of them remains.

Not only was the line along the Sussex coast unencumbered by physical constraints; there were very few difficulties in obtaining property which might have deflected it from a direct line. It did, however, skirt to the north of Rustington House to cross on the level at Lyminster the road from Arundel to Littlehampton. A station was opened on the east side of the level-crossing and, from March until the June of 1846, was the terminus of the line. The main buildings were on the down side and, somewhat remarkably, still survive. Even more surprisingly, the shelter on the up side is intact and, on the down side, a shed. This is very similar in design to contemporary goods sheds but has a louvre on the ridge of its roof which suggests an engine shed. After three months, the extension to Chichester was opened, together with a station at Ford, from which the company constructed a road over the one and three quarter miles to Arundel. So the station at Ford was called 'Arundel' and what had been 'Littlehampton & Arundel' became 'Littlehampton'. This arrangement lasted until the May of 1850, when 'Arundel' became 'Ford' and 'Littlehampton' became 'Arundel & Littlehampton'. The reason for this is not readily apparent but the most probable explanation is that, although 'Ford' was nearer to Arundel, its road connection was not favoured. In August 1863, both Arundel and Littlehampton were provided with their own stations, and on 1 September Arundel and Littlehamton closed. This was not, however, the end of railway facilities at this point for, in 1907, Lyminster Halt was opened here. The wooden platforms of the halt were located adjacent to the level-crossing and, after its closure in 1914, were removed. But the buildings of the original station survived and, whereas all the stations that have remained in use underwent modifications, Arundel & Littlehampton remains to give a very clear impression of what a station of 1846 looked like.

Beyond the station, the line swung slightly north to the point selected for crossing the Arun at Ford. When the line was constructed, masted vessels, such as collier brigs, were still going up to Arundel, so a movable bridge was necessary. This was something of an engineering wonder, and numerous drawings and descriptions have survived. One was included in F. S. Williams's *Our Iron Roads* published in 1852. It states:

> ... the Company was bound to leave a clear waterway of sixty feet for the passage of shipping, and this had to be accomplished by a contrivance called a telescope bridge. The rails, for a length of 144 feet, are laid upon a massive timber platform, strengthened with iron, and trussed by means of rods extending from its extremities to the top of a strong framework of timber rising 34 feet above the level of the roadway in the middle of the platform, the framework being ornamented so as to appear like an arch. Beneath this central framework and one half of the platform are mounted 12 wheels, upon which the whole structure may be moved backwards and forwards so as to be either clear of the river or to project its

unsupported half across it, to form a bridge for the passage of trains.

This original drawbridge carried a single track which, initially, would not have been a significant complication, as the line from Arundel & Littlehampton to Chichester was not doubled until 1857. After this, points were provided at each end of the bridge until it was replaced in 1862. The new bridge was of iron and carried a double track. These improvements would have become necessary sooner or later, but the particular timing was related to the rearrangement of tracks in connection with the new branches, in one direction to Arundel and Pulborough and, in the other, to Littlehampton. The new bridge had two fixed spans, the western of 70 feet and the eastern of 30 feet. The centre, movable span was 90 feet long and this could be tilted and drawn back over the western span. The bridge was strengthened in 1898 but was operated in the same manner until the last opening on 5 April 1936. The winding back of the movable span only took a few minutes and, in its tilted position, it almost ran back on its own. However, it took considerably longer, in the words of the Appendix to the Working Timetable to 'detach the fishplates and disconnect the signal and track circuit wires and gas and water pipes at each end of the bridge'. Commercial traffic up to Arundel declined after the First World War, and most pleasure craft could pass under the span. For instance, in *A History of the Southern Railway*, Dendy Marshall states that the bridge was not opened between 22 September 1919 and 4 May 1928. To ensure that vessels were correctly positioned to pass through the opening of 40 feet, wooden piers were provided, converging on the gap from each side of the river, one of which carried a gangway from which vessels could be guided by ropes. The signalling arrangements for trains were probably simpler than those for boats. 'On a vessel approaching the bridge, the Bridgeman will hoist on the flagstaff at the east end of the bridge a white flag to denote that the vessel is seen. If the bridge can be safely opened, a black ball will be hoisted. When the bridge is actually open, a red flag will be hoisted and kept flying until the bridge is about

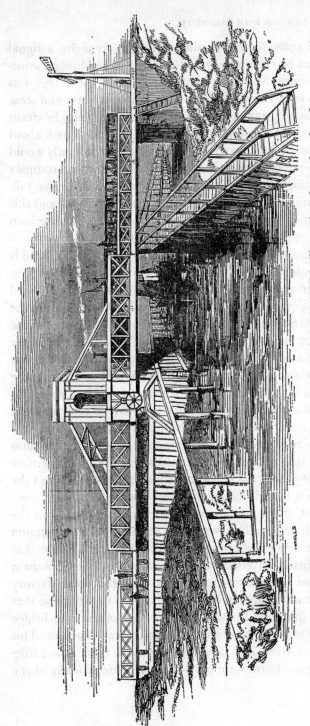

35 The drawbridge over the Arun called the 'telescopic bridge'. This illustration shows the piers for guiding vessels under the bridge, and the gangway. Details include an early semaphore signal on the approach to the bridge and a sailing vessel beyond. The rather short passenger train has a guard seated on the roof. (*Illustrated London News*, 14 November 1846)

to be closed again for the passing of trains.' At night, a signal lamp, worked by the opening and shutting of the bridge, somewhat surprisingly, showed a white light when the bridge was closed and a red light when it was open. (The colours would seem to be more appropriate to the trains than to shipping.) In steam days, the complete operation of opening and closure took about thirty minutes. When electrification was planned, not only would this disrupt services using the bridge, but even more complex was the cutting off of the electricity supply from the live rail. Instead, powers were obtained to substitute a fixed span and this was installed in 1938, in contrast to the bridge at Southerham which remained movable after electrification.

By the standards of the West Coast line, the history of Ford is simple. It became Ford instead of Arundel in 1850, Ford Junction in 1864 after the branch to Littlehampton was opened, Ford (Sussex) in 1923 to distinguish it from Ford (Devon) also on the newly-formed Southern Railway and now, after the closure of the Devon station in 1964, it is Ford again. The building is rather too plain for easy dating, but some of it is early. The down platform is an island with a loop line. There is still a level-crossing with a signal box at the east end of the station. Until 1930, this was Ford East signal box, but after that date it took over the functions of Ford West, Ford Junction and Littlehampton Junction and was re-named Ford. The arrangements of the junctions on the east side of the river have changed. When they were opened in 1863, both the new connection to Pulborough and the Littlehampton branch joined the West Coast line at Ford junction, just east of the bridge, with their junctions facing in the Chichester direction. This was quite suitable if Littlehampton was to be served by a shuttle service from Ford, but meant that through trains from either the Pulborough or the Shoreham directions had to reverse to reach it. In 1887 this unsatisfactory arrangement was ended by diverting the West Coast line so that it joined the line from Pulborough so far east of the river bridge that there was room to construct a triangular junction. This enabled trains from any direction to run straight into Littlehampton. Signal boxes were provided at all three corners of the triangular junction: Ford Junction near the bridge on the west side, Littlehampton Junction to the south and Arundel Junction, which controlled both the junction of the West Coast and Pulborough lines and the eastern apex of the triangle. As part of the original line of the West Coast route was in a cutting, its position is still visible.

Yapton station was opened with the line in 1846, closed in 1847, re-opened in 1849 and finally closed in 1864. Although it only served a rural community, its station buildings were very similar to those of Arundel & Littlehampton station and have also survived. However, they have undergone rather more extensive alterations. Just over two and a half miles separated Yapton from the original Bognor station which the company apparently hesitated to name. Having been opened as Bognor, perhaps concerned by that resort being three and a half miles away, the company switched to Woodgate, in which hamlet the station was situated. However, in a year it was back to Bognor again, which it remained from 1847 until 1853. For its last eleven years, until closure in 1864, it reverted to Woodgate. An original station building and a crossing keeper's cottage remain. Both Yapton and Woodgate were closed when the branch to Bognor was opened from a new junction station at Barnham, roughly midway between them. The basic layout at Barnham is the same as that at Ford, with a side platform on the up side and an island on the down, on the outside of which a connecting train for Bognor could be waiting. Whereas nearly all stations have some character, Barnham has a strong character, being very much a product of the 'high summer' of the railways. It has all the features which distinguished the LBSCR as a 'passenger-minded' company, including ample canopies and a refreshment room which is still open. The losses—goods traffic in 1964 and the water crane that used to stand in the down siding—have not detracted greatly from its atmosphere.

From Barnham to Chichester, six and a quarter miles, is the longest stretch without a station on the West Coast line. The closure of Woodgate, a mile and a quarter to the west, has already been mentioned. The present appearance of the country, which is intensely farmed, but not 'suburbanised', gives an indication of the character of the scenery between Ford and Shoreham—and the rivers Arun and Adur—before the First World War. It appears almost flat, but the variations between a few feet above sea level near the south-running streams and a maximum of about 40 feet on the ground between them, give rise to moderate gradients—1 in 204 is the steepest—and to shallow cuttings. Drayton station, about three miles beyond Woodgate, was closed to passengers in 1930, an early victim of an economy drive. Until Singleton station was opened in 1881, Drayton was the nearest station for Goodwood, whose races brought it lucrative but very intermittent traffic. At present, a level-crossing and signal box mark its position. There used to be two level-crossings between Drayton and Chichester, the first of which was replaced by a bridge when the Chichester by-pass road was constructed, just before the Second World War. Its signal cabin, Portfield Ballast Pit signal box survives, and a siding for an oil depot is in use. Whyke Road box still operates a level-crossing manually. The West Coast line has far above the national average number of level-crossings per mile and the mile to the west of Whyke contains another two. Of these three, Whyke and the crossing adjoining the east end of Chichester station are worked from signal boxes, but the third is operated manually. There is a striking contrast between, for instance, a modern Portsmouth express and the appearance of a gateman coming out from his cabin to open the gates for it.

The first Chichester station was a simple, wooden affair, opened in 1846 and replaced by the permanent station west of the level-crossing in 1847. Chichester is a small but historic cathedral city which attracts many visitors and, perhaps, this was one of the reasons for BR's rebuilding its station in 1960. Fortunately this was before the austerity of the Beeching era had robbed new construction of any hint of extravagance, and the new station suggests an opulent BR which had ceased to exist by the early sixties. In particular, the booking hall on the up side has a spaciousness which makes the comparable facility at Worthing look decidedly meagre. From 1897 until 1935 the modest terminal of the West Sussex Railway was sited in a yard on the down side.[8] Apart from goods traffic generated by Chichester itself, there used to be extensive marshalling yards on both sides of the line which, with the decline of local goods traffic, have largely been lifted. Fishbourne Crossing signal box is typical of the products of Messrs Saxby and Farmer, with shallow top lights to its windows. Many have survived on the LCDR and LBSCR systems but very few have retained their maker's plate, a pleasing feature of Fishbourne. This was the junction for the line to Midhurst, now open for freight only as far as Lavant.[9] The Portsmouth extension was provided with a series of character-istic crossing keepers' houses which, although different in detail from those farther east, were numbered in a continuous series from Brighton. Until very recently, the numbers have appeared on the painted stucco of the houses, with white figures in a red disc. The house adjoining Fishbourne crossing was no. 53, followed shortly by no. 54 and, adjoining Fishbourne Halt, no. 55.

Each end of the West Coast line, from Worthing to the east and Chichester to the west, had an intensive rail motor car ser-vice, associated with various halts. The Portsmouth to Chichester service began in 1906 and Fishbourne Halt was opened at the same time. It was originally a simple, wooden structure, with oil lamps, but has now progressed to concrete and electric light. Its future prospects may have been considerably enhanced by the discovery near-by of a Roman Palace, which is now on view. A mile and a half to the west is Bosham, a respectable distance from the waterside village associated with King Harold. This was one of the original stations of 1847 but the present buildings were erected about 1903. Again, this was a 'complete' country station with level-crossing, signal box and a goods shed contained a 30-hundredweight crane. Most of this remains, although freight traffic ceased in 1963 and the shed is no longer used by the rail-way. A good series of crossing keepers' houses adjoins the various crossings between Bosham and Emsworth. No. 60 and no. 61 are isolated, but no. 62 adjoins Nutbourne Halt. The next crossing, at Inlands Road, has passed through three phases. At first it was operated from house no. 63, then from a crossing keeper's box and now it has automatic barriers. House no. 64 adjoins South-bourne Halt which resembles Fishbourne and Nutbourne in both opening date and appearance. But, while the other former halts are served by the hourly stopping trains, Southbourne has the distinction of hourly calls from the Victoria and Portsmouth expresses. The signal box at the adjacent crossing is a block post and, since the closure of Emsworth signal box, the section to Warblington extends for about two and a half miles. The line continues to be without curves and virtually level, although this is achieved by a short and shallow cutting just west of South-bourne, and an embankment adjoining the crossing of the river Ems. This marks the boundary between West Sussex and Hamp-shire. Emsworth had flour mills, oyster fisheries and a small port; now it is a residential centre with a strong interest in yachting. The station was opened with the line in 1847, but the age of the buildings is difficult to assess. The station offices would seem to be of a different date from the house. (Wikely and Middleton suggest 1872 and 1891 extensions.) With the loss of its signal box and goods yard, Emsworth has moved closer to a 'halt' atmos-phere, although the extent of its buildings proclaims its early origin. One station remains before the junction at Havant. Warblington Halt was opened as Denville in November 1907, slightly later than the other three halts on this section. Although the halt was almost the same distance from either place, in the following month its name was changed to Warblington. Just under three quarters of a mile to the west is the present Havant station. The Portsmouth extension continued to Portsmouth, but is described in Chapter 7.

The construction of the link line between Mid-Sussex at Hard-ham junction and the West Coast line at Arundel junction has already been described in historical terms. If history be the criterion, then the line from Horsham to Hardham junction, being part of the original Mid-Sussex Railway, should be described with the rest of the line to Midhurst. However as, since 1863, it has formed part of a main line route to Bognor and to Portsmouth, there is a case for its inclusion in the present chapter.

As explained above, the railway reached Horsham from Three Bridges in 1848. In 1859 the extension to Petworth was opened and a new through station was constructed. With some alterations and additions, this lasted until 1938. In its later days it consisted of a side platform with the main buildings on the up, or western side, and an island platform on the down side. The buildings inclined to a Gothic rather than Classical style with pointed windows on the ground floor. The general arrangement was the common one of two end-sections with their axes at right angles to the line of the railway, linked by a centre section in which the entrance was placed. When the Mid-Sussex electrification was planned, the Southern decided that Horsham station should be rebuilt. The down island platform was widened and lengthened and provided with new minor buildings such as waiting rooms. The original buildings were demolished and a track inserted at the back of the up platform to convert it to an island. The new entrance on the up side was in the characteristic 'Odeon' style, with entrance doors that might well have been suggestive of a pleasurable visit to a super-cinema. While there was a degree of conscious modernity to blend with the 'electrified railway' image, the extensive use of brick as opposed to concrete is, perhaps, one reason why the 'new' Horsham has aged rather well. Another pleasing feature is the curvature of the entrance buildings to fit the curve of the forecourt. A new signal box replaced both Horsham Junction and Horsham West. The motive power depot, which included a roundhouse, survived until 1964, but has now been demolished. While the main lines, both from the Dorking and Three Bridges directions, and on to the coast, were electrified from 1938, steam lingered for the branch line services to Guildford and to Brighton via Shoreham. The Guildford line was worked by steam until its closure in 1965, but the Brighton line was dieselised before its services ended in 1966. While the steam trains were running, Horsham was very much a 'frontier' station, both as a terminus for what were in effect outer suburban services, and as a changing point from main line expresses for the delights of minor lines. Now, with the engine shed demolished and, since 1970, the goods yard closed, the atmosphere has become even more dominated by the 'Southern Electric' period.

South of Horsham, the line descended and curved to run on the side of the valley of the Arun. This was an undulating stretch of line which provided special problems with loose-coupled goods trains, the couplings being alternately in tension and compression as the summits and troughs were passed. To avoid this, the Appendix to the Working Timetable instructs the guards of goods trains to 'partially apply the brake in the rear van when leaving Horsham and apply it fully when passing East Street underline bridge', thus keeping the couplings in tension and avoiding 'snatching'. Christ's Hospital was the junction for the Guildford branch.[10] The original triangular junction of 1865 lost its southern arm in 1867. The station, south of the junction, with platforms both on the main line and the branch, was opened in 1902 in anticipation of major building developments. In the Sussex volume of the Buildings of England series, it is described as 'one of the best examples in Southern England of an unaltered Late Victorian railway building'. Unfortunately, since this was written, the tracks and buildings have been removed from the branch platforms and the goods yard has lost its track, although its shed survives. Nevertheless, if Horsham brings back memories of 'Southern Electric' days, Christ's Hospital is above all the station to evoke the 'high summer' of the LBSCR. From its incredibly expansive platform canopies to its frosted glass windows, from its gas lamps to its deserted white-tiled subways, it is a monument to its builders and its period.

Between Christ's Hospital and Billingshurst the Arun describes a wide loop, but the railway follows a fairly direct but undulating line, with a ruling gradient of 1 in 100. Itchingfield junction, for the line to Shoreham, was just over half a mile south of Christ's Hospital. The tracks have been lifted and the signal box, which stood in the fork between the two lines, has been demolished, but the site is still plain to see on the down side. Although, as far as Hardham Junction, the present main line was built by the somewhat impecunious Mid-Sussex company, the undulating Wealden country, demanding an alternation of embankment and

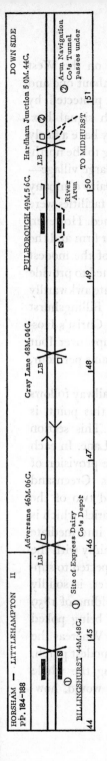
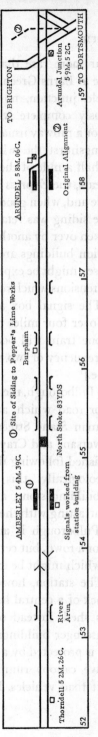
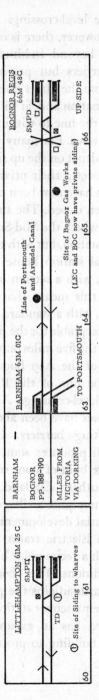
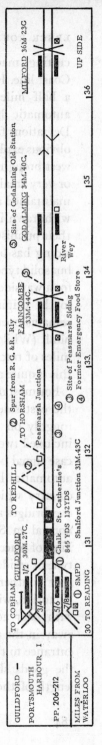

HORSHAM — LITTLEHAMPTON II
PP. 184-188

DOWN SIDE

Adversane 46M.06C.   Cray Lane 48M.04C.   Hardham Junction 5 0M.44C.

PULBOROUGH 49M,5 6C.

Billingshurst 44M.48C.

LB   LB   LB   LB

① Site of Express Dairy Co's Depot

River Arun

① Site of Siding to Pepper's Lime Works, Burpham

② Arun Navigation Co's Tunnel Passes under

TO MIDHURST

44   145   146   147   148   149   150   151

Amberley 5 4M.39C.   North Stoke 83YDS

ARUNDEL 5 8M.06C.   Arundel Junction 5 9M.5 2C.

Signals worked from station building

River Arun

Original Alignment

TO BRIGHTON

TO PORTSMOUTH

52   54   55   56   57   58   59 TO PORTSMOUTH

BARNHAM 63M 0IC   BOGNOR REGIS 66M 48C

BARNHAM —

BOGNOR PP. 188-190

MILES FROM VICTORIA VIA DORKING

Line of Portsmouth and Arundel Canal

Site of Bognor Gas Works (LEC and BOC now have private siding)

SMPD

UP SIDE

TO PORTSMOUTH

60   61   63   64   65   66 48C

LITTLEHAMPTON 6M 25C

Thorndell 5 2M.26C.

SMPH

TD

① Site of Siding to wharves

GUILDFORD —

PORTSMOUTH HARBOUR I

PP. 206-212

MILES FROM WATERLOO

TO COBHAM   GUILDFORD 30M.27C.   Chalk St. Catherine's 845 YDS 132YDS   Shalford Junction 31M.43C

TO REDHILL

Spur from R.G.&R. Rly

Peasmarsh Junction

② TO HORSHAM

③ Site of Peasmarsh Siding

④ Former Emergency Food Store

SMPD

TO READING

30 TO READING   31   32   33

FARNCOMBE 33M.44C.   GODALMING 34M.40C.

MILFORD 36M 23C

River Wey

⑤ Site of Godalming Old Station

UP SIDE

34   35   36

cutting, made level-crossings far more rare than on the West Coast line. However, there is one at Barns Green, about one and a half miles beyond Itchingfield junction, now protected by automatic barriers but previously complete with signal box. Deviations from the direct line for a railway usually have a fairly obvious explanation and, at Billingshurst, the swing to the north-west brought the line to within half a mile of the large village—or very small town. For many years, the Express Dairy company maintained a depot on the up side and, when goods facilities were withdrawn in 1964, their private siding was retained. However, their premises have now been taken over by another firm and the siding has been closed. The station buildings are of the modest but solid type which the Mid-Sussex might be expected to provide for a wayside station, but with extensions which relate awkwardly to the original station house. The signal box at Billingshurst remains open, with a section of over four miles to Christ's Hospital. (While this means that one train will occupy over four miles of track, with a standard frequency of two trains per hour, this is quite acceptable for the line.)

For most of the five miles on to Pulborough, the railway follows the east side of the A29 Bognor road which, at this point, is roughly on the line of the Roman Stane Street. This section included two level-crossings, Adversane and Cray Lane. In each case signal boxes have been abolished following the provision of automatic lifting barriers. Geologically, this is Greensand country which produces some building stone, and two of the overbridges are built of stone contrasting with the brick which is normal in Southern England. Pulborough is an intermediate kind of place, not quite a village or a town, but certainly with the type of residential development which might be expected to support Southern Electric trains. The station, however, is solidly Victorian, with a rectangular block of a central building of 1859 with later additions. The goods shed, instead of being poked away in the yard, adjoins the passenger buildings. Whereas the entrance to the passenger station is protected by a modest porch, the goods shed has an expansive canopy running the whole length of the building to protect road vehicles. It would, however, be wrong to imply that Pulborough has kept everything. The up platform was an island and this was the usual point for the arrival and departure of the Midhurst trains. Now there are no Midhurst trains and the loop has been severed.[11] The terminal function of Pulborough was reflected in its turntable and its three water cranes (at each end of the up platform and at the country end of the down). The goods yard was closed in 1966 and, although Pulborough retains its signal box and is a stopping place for the Bognor and Portsmouth expresses, it is no longer a place where passengers 'changed for the branch'.

Beyond the station, the line crosses the Arun, which at this point only carried a limited commercial traffic, being part of a loop short-circuited by the Arun Navigation, with its tunnel at Hardham. The site of Hardham Junction is marked by a level-crossing with automatic lifting barriers; an antique signal box stood on the down side just beyond the crossing. In addition to Hardham Junction, at one time Thorndell signal box broke up the five miles between Pulborough and Amberley. From Hardham Junction to Arundel Junction we follow the 1863 link line of the LBSCR. The line is at no point more than a mile from the Arun and the only significant gradients are to be found near Amberley, where the line intersects higher ground in cutting across meanders of the river. Just beyond Hardham Junction the Arun Navigation tunnel is crossed, the track being only 8 feet above the crown of the arch, but the waterway is not visible from the train. The line of the South Downs and the way through them made by the river and followed by the railway are visible as we cross the meadows bordering the Arun. Amberley, with its castle, controlled the northern entrance to the gap in the same way that Arundel Castle covered the southern entrance. Amberley station is on the road about half a mile to the south of the village. As at Pulborough, the goods shed formed part of the main group of buildings until it was demolished. It was of the type in which road vehicles went into one side of the shed, rather than sheltering under a canopy projecting from the side. Because of this, the two sides each consisted of an unbroken series of three large blind arches. The passenger buildings consist of a low, single-storeyed range, running parallel with the railway with a station house at one end at right angles to it. On the platform side a canopy stretches the full length while, on the road side, the entrance is protected by a modest porch, small enough to be domestic in character. The signal box was on the up side but, as part of the economy drive of the period, the signal frame was moved into the down side buildings early in 1934. The interest of Amberley was not confined to its public railway facilities, for a private siding left the goods yard to run for over a quarter of a mile into Messrs Peppers' lime works. Traffic, mainly coal in and lime out, was exchanged in the goods yard, Messrs Peppers retaining their own locomotive. For many years, this was the type of machine manufactured by Aveling and Porter as a road locomotive which, by changing the wheels, was adapted for use on rails. Messrs Peppers have now gone out of business and the siding has been removed.

From an engineering point of view, there was a concentration of work between Amberley and Arundel. Within the confined space of the gap in the downs, the railway was brought closer to the river, and crossing two loops necessitated the provision of four bridges. The Arun was still navigable so, rather than provide movable bridges, the railway crossed on fixed bridges and built new channels for the navigation which not only cut off the loops, but also avoided the low railway bridges which crossed them. In addition to the four bridges, there was a very short tunnel of 83 yards at North Stoke, just south of Amberley. The position of the town and the great estate of Arundel Castle, kept the line east of the river at this point. The station, which was for a short time called New Arundel, was only half a mile from the town. Perhaps, with its aristocratic patronage in mind, Arundel was on a bigger scale than Amberley. The main building was of brick with a slate roof, with the two end-sections projecting and the centre section recessed. Rather unusually, the end-sections did not have gables; their roof ridges ran at right angles to the centre section but they were hipped at the ends. A limited amount of alteration took place at the time of electrification. A new signal box was built, and a canopy of glass and steel was cantilevered out over the station entrance. The bay platform on the down side has frequently been used for connections from Bognor and Portsmouth trains to Littlehampton and it is used in this way at the time of writing.[12] Some high ground south of the station is traversed by a cutting. From there the railway crosses low lying meadows to Arundel Junction where it joins the West Coast line.

Two short branches completed the main lines of West Sussex—one and three quarter miles from Arundel Junction to Littlehampton and three and a half miles from Barnham to Bognor. The Littlehampton line was constructed by the LBSCR and was opened in August 1863, a little late for the summer season. It will be remembered that, until the West Coast line was deviated in 1887, the Littlehampton branch trailed in on the east side of the bridge over the Arun, so that traffic from the east had to reverse at Ford. Presumably this inconvenient arrangement was prompted by a desire for economy, as only one junction and signal box was required to serve both the Mid-Sussex and the Littlehampton lines. When the inconvenience became intolerable, in 1887, as already described, the one junction was replaced by three, and trains could run on to the branch from any direction without reversal. The line itself was cheaply built over low lying ground, terminating on the edge of the town. As mentioned above, although holiday traffic was anticipated, the LBSCR were perhaps more concerned with the development of Littlehampton as a port. Their service from Newhaven to Dieppe, to some degree, competed with the Folkestone and Dover route; from Littlehampton they planned to serve points farther west competing with the routes from Southampton and Weymouth. Destinations selected for the Littlehampton services were Honfleur (competitive with the LSWR Southampton and Le Havre service), St Malo (competitive with another LSWR service) and Jersey (already served from Southampton and Weymouth). None of the services was successful and they were either withdrawn or transferred to Newhaven. Apart from the railway steamers, Littlehampton developed a modest general traffic, including coal and gravel. When the somewhat primitive floating bridge was replaced by a conventional bridge in 1908, this was constructed below the wharf and had to be built with a movable span.

At present, railway Littlehampton is perhaps more interesting than tidy. The passenger terminal consists of two island platforms. These are normal, although the canopies are rather shorter than might be expected. At the end is a concourse fringed by some hut-like buildings which built in 1938 and intended as a temporary expedient seem to have become permanent. Improvement may have swept through places like Chichester, but it has missed Littlehampton. Lack of architectural distinction does not mean lack of interest, and there are some intriguing relics. For instance, at the entrance to the forecourt, a large enamelled notice headed 'Southern Electric' offers, among other facilities, 'Through Connections for Bath, Bristol and South Wales' which, while true in a sense, is not as true as it used to be. The engine shed was on the down side of the station not, as might have been expected, well beyond the ends of the platforms, but almost level with the concourse. It remains in use as an office and store. A magnificent goods shed, doubtless constructed with continental traffic in mind, is situated on the up side. Two storeys high, it seems to combine the functions of transit shed and warehouse. Its elaborate brickwork, with most ornate arches, is in contrast to the austerity of the passenger station. The semi-circular windows in the tops of the arches— the rest is brick filled—are strongly reminiscent of the goods shed at Steyning, described in the Sussex volume of the Buildings of England series as 'Georgian in proportions and delicacy'. A characteristic LBSCR signal box, with a valance round the eaves, is to be seen on the down side at the London end of the station. Such relics of steam days as a turntable and a water crane have been removed and, far more important, the sidings down to the wharf have been severed. But on a winter evening it does not need too fertile an imagination to picture an LBSCR paddle steamer departing for Honfleur.

The Bognor branch is different in many respects. To begin with, Bognor was purely a resort and residential centre; only in recent years has it attracted some manufacturing industry. Not only Bognor, but also its neighbours—Aldwick, Felpham and Middleton—have all grown considerably since the First World War. Despite, or because of, a comparatively slow rate of growth until about 1900, there were a number of proposals for a railway to the town. That of 1853 came to nothing but, under the Bognor Railway Act of 1861, the line was built, and opened in 1864. Perhaps the biggest single boost came when King George V selected the Sussex resort for convalescence and, after his departure, in 1929, Bognor became Bognor Regis. The name of the railway station was altered accordingly. In 1960 another boost came with the opening of a Butlin's Holiday Camp to the east of the town. As might be expected, the original branch was opened with a single line. The section from Bersted crossing to the terminus was doubled in 1902 and the rest of the branch in 1911.

It was almost as simple a line to build as the Littlehampton branch, but not quite, as it had to cross a moribund canal, two streams and two roads. The moribund canal was the Portsmouth and Arundel, and Section 40 of the 1861 Act required a swing bridge over its line. There is no movable bridge over the dried-out bed of the canal at the present time, and it seems unlikely that there ever was one. The line of the canal is crossed about half a mile from Barnham, the first stream at about one mile and the second, Aldingbourne Rife, near the gas works. The Bognor gas works were situated on the up side, about a mile from the terminus and, for many years, received coal and fed coke and by-products on to the railway by means of a private siding. LEC and BOC retain a siding in roughly the same place. The first of the level-crossings is a minor one, just beyond the gas works, but the second, Bersted crossing, is on the A259, a main road into Bognor. Separate boxes used to control the crossing and the station, but a new box was erected shortly before the Second World War, in typical Southern style, to operate both the crossing and the station. The engine shed, complete with turntable, and the goods shed, were on the east side of the station. The first terminus of 1864 was not only decidedly simple, but, in 1897, had its roof blown off. This was repaired but, at the end of September 1899, fortunately at the end of the season, the whole thing was burned down. A temporary structure appeared for 1900 but, by 1902, the present station was complete, an excellent example of an Edwardian seaside station. It is of red brick with a number of gables, the somewhat confusing roof line being dominated by a clock tower. Outside there is an ample canopy and inside, beyond the various offices, a circulating area covered with an overall roof incorporating sufficient glass to dispel any suggestion of gloom. Two island platforms accommodate the traffic.

Having surveyed the West Coast railways, it may be asked if there are any special characteristics. There are some obvious features, such as the high proportion of passenger revenue and the proliferation of level-crossings. A striking fact is the complete avoidance of station closures on the main lines during the Beeching era. In 1971 services were, in general, at least as good as those introduced at electrification in 1938. For Bognor and Portsmouth, there was an hourly express service from Victoria, with the trains dividing at Barnham. Littlehampton had an hourly express, also from Victoria, via Haywards Heath, Shoreham and Worthing. In addition, Bognor and Littlehampton had an hourly semi-fast service via Three Bridges and Horsham, also from Victoria. There was a feeder service linking Littlehampton and Ford to Arundel to connect with the Bognor and Portsmouth trains, but this did not appear in the timetables introduced in May 1972. In 1971, the standard service along the coast each hour consisted of a train from Brighton to West Worthing, Brighton to Portsmouth (slow), Brighton to Littlehampton and Brighton to Portsmouth (fast). In 1972 this was altered to Portsmouth slow via Littlehampton, a Bognor Regis direct, and a Portsmouth fast. Even this gives an intensity of service which would not be equalled in many parts of the country. Bognor with 34,000 people, and Littlehampton with 18,000, each have had, for many years, a half-hourly service to London, a standard which Birmingham only achieved in 1972.

6 Train for Southampton running on line of the Portsea Canal between Portsmouth
and Fratton. The road on the right is Canal Walk and the public house Canal Walk
Cellars. The train which consists of Multiple Unit Diesel Set No. 1129 was seen from
Somers Road Bridge on 18 September 1968

7 Portsmouth and Southsea Station. The ground level station of 1866 with its three
platforms is on the right; the high level island platform of 1876 is on the left. The site of
the former goods depot was occupied by sidings for empty trains when this photograph
was taken on 18 September 1968

38 Southampton Ordnance Survey, 1910 Edition. The original level crossings were with
Bevois Street (just off map), Chapel Road, Marsh Lane-Chantry Road and Itchen Bridge
Road. In 1882 the Central Bridge was opened to replace the last two crossings. As well as
the main line, the Chapel Tramway serving the Gas Works and various wharves, and the
lines in the docks are shown. The old horse tramway is shown but by 1910 the electric
tram route had been cut back to the railway station to avoid the level crossings in Canute
Road, and electric trams were running over the Central Bridge down to the Floating
Bridge. The terminal station is shown as it was before the extensive rebuilding which
followed the First World War. (Scale 25 ins. to 1 mile; scale on top left)

7

The Direct Line to Portsmouth

Whereas the main lines to Dover, Brighton and Southampton initiated the railway network, the Direct line to Portsmouth consisted mainly of a rather cheaply constructed link between existing railways. This chapter is concerned with the 49¾ miles between Woking and Portsmouth Harbour, of which 32½, between Farncombe and Havant, were constructed by the Portsmouth Railway company. From its opening, the trains on the Portsmouth company's line were provided by the LSWR but, in addition to using the track of the independent company, the trains used a section of the LSWR, a section owned jointly by the LSWR and LBSCR, and a length owned by the latter company alone. The way in which this situation arose is made clear by consideration of the history of the main lines to Portsmouth.

Portsmouth was late in getting its first railway—six years later than Brighton and seven later than Southampton. The delay was caused partly by physical obstruction, Portsdown Hill lying across the direct line to London, but more by the reluctance of the military authorities to permit a development which might weaken the landward defences of the great naval base. Lack of railways, however, did not reflect a lack of proposals, at least two of the earlier schemes belonging to the period of horse railways of the type usually associated with mineral traffic. Convicts provided the labour for a number of projects in Portsmouth during the nineteenth century and, in 1803, R. A. Edlington produced a plan 'for erecting a penitentiary house for the employment of convicts to which are added a plan for a rail-way from London to Portsmouth on a construction superior to anything seen in this country'. In the same year William Jessop carried out a survey for a line from Blackfriars bridge in London down to Portsmouth. By 1823 early steam locomotives were in operation with varying degrees of success on a number of horse railways. William James had the misfortune to appreciate their possibilities in association with a new kind of railway before the circumstances were propitious, and so most of his plans failed to materialise. He produced his 'Report or essay, to illustrate the advantages of direct inland communication through Kent, Surrey, Sussex and Hants to connect the Metropolis with the ports of Shoreham (for Brighton) Rochester (for Chatham) and Portsmouth by a line of engine railroad, and to render the Grand Surrey Canal, Wandsworth and Merstham Rail Road, Shoreham Harbour and Waterloo bridge shares productive property, with suggestions for diminishing poor rates and relieving agriculture'. James did not carry out detailed surveys, but his lines would have included an end-on junction with the Surrey Iron Railway and the Croydon, Merstham & Godstone, two horse railways which, by 1805, linked Wandsworth on the Thames, via Croydon to Merstham on the North Downs. The Grand Surrey and the Croydon Canals together linked the Thames at Rotherhithe to Croydon, and would presumably have received some of the traffic from 'Kent, Surrey, Sussex and Hants'. Waterloo bridge was involved by means of a plan for a line from its southern end to join the Surrey Iron Railway. Operation might well have been by steam locomotives on the more level sections, with stationary engines hauling the trains up cable-operated inclines, in which changes of level could be concentrated. Seventeen years later, James's scheme was described as 'the first railway ever projected in England, even before the Manchester & Liverpool Railway' and the proposer as 'the celebrated William James, the Father of Railways who, in a letter to George IV, advocated a line between Chatham and Portsmouth'.

None of the early schemes materialised and, probably to its disadvantage, Portsmouth was to obtain its first rail communica-

Railways to Portsmouth

Lines open by 1845
Lines opened after 1845

Brighton
Reigate
Three Bridges
Epsom
Leatherhead
Horsham
Shoreham
Worthing
Woking
Dorking
Guildford
Shalford
Littlehampton
Pulborough
Arundel
Godalming
Haslemere
Bognor
Chichester
Selsey
Alton
Midhurst
Petersfield
Hayling Island
Havant
Portsmouth & Southsea
Portsmouth Harbour
East Southsea
Cosham
Basingstoke
Fareham
Gosport
Stokes Bay
Lee-on-the-Solent
Winchester
Eastleigh
Southampton

SER Rly
RG&R Rly
L.B.S.C.R
LBSCR
LSWR
LSWR
A&A Line
Meon Valley Line

N

0   5   10
Miles

Railways to Portsmouth

tion by means of branches from both the Brighton and the Southampton lines. The access from Brighton has been described in Chapter 6, and that from the Southampton line is discussed in Volume Two, Chapters 3 and 7. Portsmouth's first, and decidedly limited, rail communication was provided from the Southampton direction when, in February 1842, the LSWR opened their line from Eastleigh to Gosport via Fareham. Portsmouth passengers were able to use the new floating bridge to cross the Harbour to Gosport Hard and then find their own way for about three quarters of a mile to the station. Its position was determined by the fortifications, which the railway was not permitted to penetrate. Needless to say, this situation was considered unsatisfactory. Firstly, although the floating bridge was reasonably reliable, it always gave way to Her Majesty's ships and, on occasion, had been put out of action by anchored vessels dragging over its cable. Anybody wishing to catch the night mail train at a time when the floating bridge was not operating had to cross the harbour in an open boat. But of even greater importance was the extent to which Portsmouth's commercial traffic, especially to France and the Channel Islands, was being lost to Southampton. There was no question of the port expiring, as cargoes such as Jersey potatoes could reach many places by road, and this traffic increased during the 1840s. But this was despite the lack of a railway to Portsmouth; until it came, progress was limited.

Ultimately, rail connection came from three directions: firstly the eastern route via Brighton and Chichester, completed in 1847; next, the western approach via Fareham on the Gosport line; and thirdly the direct line via Haslemere which finally materialised in 1859. The LSWR might well have been content to serve Portsmouth via Gosport, but schemes for both the direct and eastern approaches persuaded it to forward its own proposals. These included a branch from Fareham via Cosham to Portsmouth and a direct line from an end-on junction with its line to Guildford, passing Godalming and Midhurst to reach Chichester and then traversing the coastal plain to join the western approach line near Cosham. Powers to build the lines were to be sought by an LSWR subsidiary company—the Guildford, Chichester, Portsmouth & Fareham Railway. The necessary plans were deposited with Parliament in 1844, as were those for the two rival lines, the Direct Portsmouth & London, and the Brighton & Chichester Railway (Portsmouth Extension). Neither of these was independent, the Direct line being associated with the London & Croydon Company and the eastern with the London & Brighton. There was, however, one genuine independent, the London & Portsmouth Railway company. This had first appeared in 1838, with plans deposited under the title of London & Southampton, Portsmouth Branch Railway, with Robert Stephenson and Thomas Ellis Owen as acting engineers, although the first survey was carried out by G. Hennet and Francis Giles. (Thomas Ellis Owen was an engineer, architect and property developer of Southsea whose involvement with railways was virtually confined to those associated with Portsmouth and Southsea.) The 1838 scheme appeared in a revised form in 1844 and, before it went to Parliament, was considered by the Railway Commissioners with the other plans.

The newspapers of the time bear plentiful comment. For instance, the *Hampshire Telegraph* reported a meeting held in September 1844 to support the Direct London & Portsmouth. A speaker demanded to know '. . . who had heard of Southampton as a port till it got the railway which had enabled her to put Portsmouth in the background? Why should not Portsmouth have her docks as well as Southampton?' By April 1845, much to the displeasure of most Portsmouth interests, the Railway Commissioners reported in favour of the LSWR proposals. Portsmouth Corporation appointed a special committee to follow the Bills through Parliament and also decided to petition in favour of the Direct Portsmouth & London Company. This presumably reflected a consensus of opinion; (Councillor J. Hopkin was the company's solicitor). Thomas Ellis Owen had assisted with the plans for Stephenson's line but, after the adverse report of the Railway Commissioners, this was withdrawn. Of the other two companies, the land agent for the Brighton & Chichester (Portsmouth Extension) was a member of the Corporation and only the LSWR was unrepresented. The Commons passed all three Bills despite numerous petitions and counter-petitions. For instance, the Guildford, Chichester, Portsmouth & Fareham (LSWR) Bill was petitioned against by individuals such as the Duke of Richmond and other owners of property on the line and also corporate bodies, including the Portsmouth and Arundel Navigation company and the Mayor and Corporation of Portsmouth. The House of Lords failed to pass both the Direct Portsmouth & London and the Guildford, Chichester, Portsmouth & Fareham, but the Brighton & Chichester (Portsmouth Extension) received the Royal Assent in August 1845 for their lines to both Portsmouth and Fareham.

In 1845, ready for the next parliamentary session, both the GCPFR and the DPLR re-submitted their plans, but the latter concern had changed in two respects. First, its London & Croydon sponsors had amalgamated with the Brighton company who, despite its association with the authorised extension from Chichester, changed from opposition to limited support. Secondly, the Direct London & Portsmouth had intended to run its trains by the atmospheric system. This used stationary engines spaced at intervals along the line, which extracted the air from a tube laid between the running rails. Trains were propelled by the pressure of the atmosphere bearing on a piston in the tube which was fixed to the train. The system was tried out, notably on the London & Croydon and the South Devon Railways, but was not successful and when the Direct Portsmouth & London returned to the parliamentary battle in 1845, it was proposing to use conventional steam locomotives. It continued to receive the support of Portsmouth Corporation and, in June 1846, its Bill received the Royal Assent. While the GCPFR commenced from the end of the Guildford branch, and the DPLR started from the Croydon company's Epsom branch and ran via Dorking to Godalming, the two routes came together on the mainland north of Portsea Island. With the abandonment of the atmospheric system, the DPLR track could be used by other companies and it was decided to award the GCPFR running powers over the DPLR between Godalming and Cosham. The company was therefore

authorised to construct its lines from Guildford to a junction
with the DPLR at Godalming and from Fareham through Cosham
to Portsmouth, the Royal Assent being given in July 1846. Dis-
appointed at this result, the GCPFR sold out almost immediately
to the LSWR.

In this way, much of the possible duplication on the mainland
was avoided, but not so on Portsea Island itself where three
different companies, the LSWR, the DPLR and the Brighton &
Chichester (Portsmouth Extension) all ran across to the town of
Portsmouth. On amalgamation with the Croydon company, the
Brighton became the London, Brighton & South Coast, and this
company took over the Brighton & Chichester (Portsmouth
Extension). It had few construction problems and passenger
trains from Brighton reached Havant in March 1847 and the
terminus on Portsea Island in the following June. The LSWR
powers were for a line down the west side of the island, passing
between the dockyard which was largely on reclaimed land, and
the built up area of Landport, to a terminal near the Unicorn
Gate. In 1847 a better-sited terminal near the junction of Edinburgh and Commercial Roads was authorised but neither this
nor the rest of the LSWR on Portsea Island was ever constructed.
By this time, reaction to the 'Railway Mania' of 1845 had set in
and money was hard to get. The situation was exacerbated by an
intimation that the Board of Ordnance would demand £12,000
to 'restore the equilibrium of defence' which would arise from
the penetration of Hilsea fortifications. Under the circumstances,
the LBSCR and LSWR came to an arrangement. The LBSCR did not
construct the authorised line from Cosham to Fareham and the
LSWR abandoned its line from Cosham on to Portsea Island and
Portsmouth. It was decided that the LBSCR line would be able to
carry the traffic from both the western (LSWR) and eastern
(LBSCR) routes. The DPLR was, by now, in a state of suspense
although some moves were made towards joint ownership by the
LSWR and LBSCR. Meanwhile, four and a half miles of line, together with the stations at Cosham and Portsmouth, were transferred to a joint committee consisting of three representatives of
the LSWR and three of the LBSCR. Revenue arising from traffic

between London and Portsmouth was to be paid into a pool, after the deduction of 30 per cent to cover running expenses, and this was to be divided in the proportion of five-eighths to the LSWR and three-eighths to the LBSCR. The pooling arrangement, despite heavy strains of the type to be described, survived in various forms until the two participants were finally joined in the Southern Railway in 1923. And so, when the first LSWR train reached the Portsmouth terminal at the beginning of October 1848, it used the joint line from Cosham.

The people of Portsmouth now had a choice of two routes to London, of 95¼ miles via Brighton or 94¾ miles via Eastleigh. In fact, during the period when only the Brighton route was complete, with journey times of between three and four hours to London, Portsmouth inhabitants were little better off. One disgruntled passenger asserted in the *Hampshire Telegraph* in February 1847, 'We'd better cross to Gosport'. Even when the alternative western route via Fareham and Eastleigh was opened, journey times to London compared unfavourably with those from Southampton. While this was partly the inevitable result of the greater distance, matters were not helped by the absence of competition, as the two companies not only pooled the receipts from London traffic but also agreed on their timetables.

The powers for constructing the Direct Portsmouth & London were still in being, but whether the established companies, secure in their monopoly, would ever have taken it over is an open question. In the event, in 1852, plans were deposited for a new, independent Portsmouth Railway. This was shorter and also cheaper than the Direct London & Portsmouth which it superseded. In accordance with their powers of 1846, the LSWR had opened their line from Guildford to Godalming in 1849 and the new company proposed to fill the gap of 32½ miles between that point and Havant on the LBSCR. The main difference was that the Portsmouth Railway planned nothing east of Godalming and also was to be constructed with steeper gradients and more curvature. Money was to be saved in at least three ways. First, the route mileage was reduced and, secondly, only a single track was to be provided. Thirdly, although, especially in its crossing of the South Downs, the route was less favourable, earthworks were reduced by a sinuous alignment and a ruling gradient of 1 in 80. This was supported by a 'momentum' theory, that trains could gather sufficient speed on the down grades to carry them over the up gradients. (Presumably where there was no down grade to give momentum, as with a train approaching the South Downs from Havant, there was supposed to be enough time for it to gather speed, although it is less clear how the theory would apply to a train approaching from the north which had stopped at Petersfield.) In fact, the 'second generation' main lines were often built with steeper gradients and lighter engineering works, reflecting both the greater difficulty of attracting capital and the greater knowledge of the capabilities of the conventional steam locomotive.

The Portsmouth Railway enjoyed the support of the town and a public meeting in its favour was held in December 1852. Among its influential backers was John Bonham Carter. On the professional side, the eminent contractor, Thomas Brassey, was behind the new line which, despite the hostility of the two established companies, obtained its authorising Act in July 1853. The moribund Direct Portsmouth & London decided that there was no opening for two direct lines, and was wound up in 1854, the new company assisting in the realisation of its assets. (These consisted mainly of land.) While, with the aid of Brassey and the town of Portsmouth, independent construction was feasible, operation of the new line presented greater problems. Clearly, co-operation with the LSWR was needed on the London side of Godalming and with the LBSCR on the Portsmouth side of Havant. There was, however, one other possibility. In 1849 the Reading, Guildford & Reigate Railway had been opened and, at Shalford, this was a little under three miles from the northern end of the Portsmouth Railway.[1] The line was operated by the South Eastern Railway, with trains running from London via Dorking and Guildford to Reading. South Eastern trains could have reached the Portsmouth Railway by means of a spur line at Shalford and either a short independent line or running powers over the LSWR to Godalming. In fact, an embankment to carry the spur line was constructed at Shalford, but it never carried rails.

An arrangement with the South Eastern might have solved the problem at the London end, but this would only have enabled trains to get as far as Havant. For the Portsmouth end, powers were obtained in 1858 to build an independent line from Havant to Hilsea, at the north end of Portsea Island, and then to run over the joint LSWR and LBSCR line into Portsmouth. Neither of these plans materialised. First, the SER hesitated to provoke the LSWR and LBSCR by invading their 'territory', and backed out of the Shalford scheme. Secondly, the LSWR became so apprehensive that either the SER or the LBSCR might come to an arrangement with the Portsmouth, that it decided to lease it itself, reaching agreement in August 1858. The Bill to authorise the LSWR to either lease or absorb the Portsmouth was passed in 1859 and contained clauses cancelling most of the favourable fares and freight rates which had attracted so much support from the town of Portsmouth. It became clear that the LSWR intended to charge the same fare for the 74-mile direct route as it was charging for the 95-mile western route. Portsmouth people felt that they had been betrayed by the railway company that bore the name of their town, and petitioned vigorously against the bill. In particular, they accused the Portsmouth Railway of abandoning its promises of favourable conditions, including concessions to third-class passengers, in order to persuade the LSWR to take over its line. In fact, the Portsmouth company had little choice, for its line had no future other than adoption by one of the established companies. Parliament accepted this, but recognised Portsmouth's misgivings by including some protective clauses in the Act. One fear was that the LSWR would not use the new line as a direct route to London and this was met by requiring it to provide at least six through trains a day in the summer, and four in the winter. Further, their average speed was not to be less than that of similar trains on the Southampton line. When the receipts exceeded £45,000 per annum, the line was to be doubled. (Doubling was completed in 1878.)

It was assumed that the LSWR would enjoy all the powers of the

PORTSMOUTH & LONDON & SOUTH-WESTERN RAILWAY COMPANIES' BILL.

PETITION AGAINST THE BILL.

To the Honorable The Commons of the United Kingdom of Great Britain and Ireland in Parliament assembled.

The Humble Petition of the undersigned Inhabitants of the Borough of Portsmouth,

Sheweth:

THAT by the Portsmouth Railway Act, 1853, powers were given to the Company thereby incorporated to construct a Line of Railway from Havant, in the County of Southampton, to Godalming, in the County of Surry, for the purpose (as expressed in the Preamble of the said Act), of affording an additional and expeditious means of communication between London and Portsmouth, Chichester, the Isle of Wight, and other places.

That pending the progress of the said Act in your Honorable House, a large and influential Public Meeting was held at Portsmouth, for the purpose of taking the same into consideration. and that the support of your Petitioners thereto was obtained upon the distinct pledge of the Promoters of the undertaking to insert in the Bill a reduced Tariff of Charges, both for Goods and Passengers, and to afford other advantages in regard to Passenger traffic, and particularly in reference to Third Class Passengers, as set forth in the said Act, and to work such Railway as an independent Line.

That a Reduced Tariff of Charges for the purposes aforesaid, and provisions in reference to the conveyance of Second and Third Class Passengers were accordingly inserted in the said Act, and your Petitioners believed that the Line of Railway thereby authorized was intended to be managed and worked as a Line separate from and independent of that of the other Companies whose Lines communicate with the Borough of Portsmouth.

That by the Portsmouth Railway Amendment Act, 1858, all the provisions which were inserted in the Act of 1853, as regards the Rates and Tolls on Goods and Merchandize, and the Charges for Passengers, were thereby Repealed, and an Amended Schedule of such Rates, Tolls, and Charges substituted, by which the same were largely increased, and the provisions relating to the Conveyance of Third Class Passengers were also repealed.

That your Petitioners believe that such alterations were in reality effected by the Portsmouth Railway Company for the purpose of enabling them to make a more advantageous bargain than they could otherwise have made with the London and South Western Railway Company for the transfer of the said Porismouth Line to them, and for which (as your Petitioners believe) negotiations were then contemplated or actually in progress, and your Petitioners submit that such proceedings were contrary to good faith and most injurious to your Petitioners.

That a Bill is now pending in your Honorable House, entituled, "A Bill for authorizing an Amalgamation or Lease of the Portsmouth Railway with or to the London and South Western Company and for other purposes," whereby it is proposed to provide for the Amalgamation of the undertaking of the Portsmouth Railway Company with the undertaking of the London and South Western Railway Company, or in the event of the two Companies not agreeing to such Amalgamation, for leasing the undertaking to the London and South Western Company, with powers at any time thereafter for the said Companies to carry an agreement for Amalgamation into effect.

That under some arrangement already entered into between the two Companies, the London and South Western Company have entered upon the working of the Portsmouth Railway and the Fares and Rates already charged by them for the conveyance of Passengers and Goods by the Line of the Portsmouth Railway Company, being a distance of 74 miles only, are the same as are charged by them for the conveyance of Passengers and Goods on their own Line from London to Portsmouth, being a distance of 95 miles.

That your Petitioners altogether object to the proposed Amalgamation and Lease as injuriously affecting them, and depriving them of the advantages which they would enjoy if the said Portsmouth Railway were worked as an independent Line, and is calculated to augment the Rates of Fares, and to be above that which would be charged if the same were worked as an independent Line; and your Petitioners submit that such Amalgamation or Lease is in violation of good faith on the part of the Portsmouth Railway Company and inconsistent with the understanding on which the support of your Petitioners was obtained, and that the Interests of your Petitioners and the other Inhabitants of the Borough of Portsmouth and its Neighbourhood will be greatly prejudiced thereby.

That the preamble of the said Bill is incapable of proof.

That there are divers Clauses and Provisions in the said Bill which very seriously affect your Petitioners and the other Inhabitants of the said Borough of Portsmouth, and that other Clauses should be inserted therein for their protection, should the same be allowed to pass into a Law, especially with reference to the Rates and Tolls to be charged on the said Line now belonging to the Portsmouth Railway, and the Conduct, Management, and Regulation of the Traffic thereon, and the accommodation to be afforded to your Petitioners and such Inhabitants in respect thereof.

Your Petitioners, therefore pray your Honorable House that the said Bill may not be allowed to pass into a Law as it now stands, and that they may be heard by their Counsel, and Agents, and Witnesses before the Committee of your Honorable House to whom the said Bill stands referred, against the Preamble of the said Bill, and against such of the Clauses and Provisions thereof as affect the interests of your Petitioners and such Inhabitants as aforesaid, and in favor of the insertion of Clauses therein for the protection of the same, or that such other relief may be given to your Petitioners in the premises as to your Honorable House shall seem fit.

And your Petitioners will ever pray, &c.

39 In the 1850s, the acquisition of railway facilities was not only a question of prestige but also of economic prosperity for people such as the 'Inhabitants of the Borough of Portsmouth'. As their petition indicates, they regarded the transfer of the Portsmouth Railway to the London and South Western as an act of betrayal.

company whose line it leased, including running powers over the LBSC from Havant to the joint line. However, the LBSC did not take this view, and took measures to prevent the running of the first train by obstructing the junction at Havant. The violence and drama of the occasion have improved with the telling, with efforts to justify the title 'Battle of Havant', a name bestowed on the event some time after its occurrence. In fact, although there was an impressive confrontation of opposing staff, the violence seems to have been confined to the forcible ejection of a Brighton driver and guard from a locomotive. The 'battle' was transferred to the courts and, while the verdict was pending, passengers by the Direct line used a replacement bus service, operating from a temporary station just short of the junction. The buses were hauled by four horses and covered over seven miles to Portsmouth in the very creditable time of 25 minutes. The LSWR made no greater use of the line than was required by law and ran only four trains a day. It was not until 24 January 1859, after the courts had ruled in favour of the LSWR, that through trains reached Portsmouth over the long-awaited direct line.

The LBSCR lodged an appeal and, considering the traffic agreement no longer binding, resorted to a period of intense competition which lasted from March until August 1859. It introduced return fares to London of 10s (50p) first class, 8s (40p) second class and 5s (25p) third class. The LSWR reacted by putting on two excursion trains over the direct line at 8s (40p) first class, 5s (25p) second class and 3s 6d (17½p) third class. These were scheduled to cover the distance in 1¾ hours which, considering the present express timing of 1½ hours, seems somewhat incredible. The LBSCR was already allowing free travel by boat on to Ryde or Cowes in the Isle of Wight; next it provided a paddle steamer to take passengers on to Southampton. (It is of interest to speculate whether anybody actually made the journey from London Bridge to Southampton via Brighton.) The appeal decision in June gave a reserved judgment in favour of the LBSCR, so the replacement bus service between Havant and Portsmouth was resumed. The only beneficiaries from this cut-throat competition were the public, so it is not surprising that, in August 1859, the two railway companies reached a new agreement. Fares were to be equal by all three routes and net receipts were to be pooled and distributed according to a previous agreement. (This was based on the average of actual traffic from 1854 to 1856.) However, in view of the extra traffic arising from the direct line, the LBSCR was to contribute £15,000 per annum towards the rent payable by the LSWR to the Portsmouth Railway company. The LSWR abandoned the powers to build an independent line from Havant to Hilsea and, instead, agreed to pay the LBSCR £2,500 per annum to use its line. An Act authorising the amalgamation of the Portsmouth Railway with the LSWR was passed in 1859.

After this disturbance to the status quo, the LBSCR developed its own new London to Portsmouth route. This ran by Dorking and Pulborough and reduced the distance to London Bridge from 95 miles via Brighton, to 87, which was still 13 miles longer than the direct line (see Chapter 6). There have been no new through routes to Portsmouth since the completion of the LBSCR route in 1867. There were plans, however, including the Basingstoke, East Hants & Portsmouth Railway of 1887 and the Portsmouth, Basingstoke & Godalming of 1895. While these were nominally independent, the two established companies saw in them the possibility of the Great Western reaching the Portsmouth area in much the same way that, by its association with the Didcot, Newbury & Southampton, it approached the neighbouring port. The response of the LSWR was to occupy the routes with 'blocking' lines—the Basingstoke and Alton[2] and the Meon Valley.[3]

While there have been no more rival routes to Portsmouth, the Direct route benefited from the opening of three branches, all now closed, and some important extensions. The branches ran from Petersfield to Midhurst,[4] from Havant to Hayling Island and from Fratton to East Southsea.[5] The line on to Portsea Island was stopped short of the old fortifications and much effort went into securing extensions. The first was a single line, crossing over the main road outside the station, on the level. This is shown on a plan of 1858 and curved round to coincide with the present Dockyard branch where it crosses Edinburgh Road. It was primarily a goods line although, in a later form, it carried special passenger traffic. Plans were made for an extension to the Camber Dock which would have skirted the old fortifications. The Admiralty felt that it would have weakened the defences and proposed an alternative line to the Clarence Pier. This was never built but, in 1862, plans were deposited for a street tramway which went some way to serving the same purpose. Like similar undertakings in Fleetwood and Glasgow, the track was constructed to a gauge of 4 feet 7¾ inches so that railway wagons could use it. The Landport & Southsea Tramways Act was duly authorised and, after some delays, the line was opened in June 1865. It was provided with single track, laid in the road, with passing loops. The usual 'train' consisted of a single-deck passenger car with a trailer for passengers' luggage, drawn by two horses. Although local traffic was not refused, the preamble of the Act states that the main aim was 'the quick transfer of traffic, both passengers, goods and passengers' luggage to and from the Isle of Wight'. Although this tramway was connected to the railway, if railway wagons ever used it, it was very infrequently and the railway interest continued to press for access to the waterside. Plans of 1863 proved abortive but, by 1871, most of the old fortifications had been demolished and new plans were deposited. These were for a conventional double-track railway leading down to the harbour at a point occupied by the Albert Pier. There was little chance of the authorisation of what would be a busy passenger line crossing Commercial Road on the level, and an end-on extension could not have gained sufficient height to clear it. So the new junction was located outside the station, a little farther east than the original junction of the Dockyard branch, opposite the engine shed. The line climbed at 1 in 61 from Blackfriars junction to a new platform south of the original terminal and over the line of the original Dockyard branch. Having reached this elevation, it maintained it for the mile down to the harbour, crossing three roads, one of which existed and two of which were projected. The harbour extension was opened in 1876 and completed the line from Woking to Portsmouth Harbour.

For many years, the direct line to Portsmouth was a 'poor relation' as far as the LSWR was concerned, with services inferior to those on either its Southampton or its West of England main lines. This was partly because of the inferiority of its alignment and, perhaps, partly a subconscious attitude to a line that had been 'wished' on them. It is possible that the existence of the traffic agreement with the LBSCR did not encourage enterprise, but it will be remembered that, in places like Southampton and Bournemouth, the LSWR had the even greater security of a monopoly position. The great change came after electrification by the Southern Railway, in July 1937, when the service was dramatically increased to three trains an hour—one express and two stopping. In 1971 the standard service consisted of three trains an hour—an express calling at Guildford and Havant only, a fast train calling at Woking, Guildford, Godalming, Haslemere, Petersfield and Havant, and a stopping train calling at all stations. Although the line was built as a through route, especially since 1937, intermediate traffic has developed on a considerable scale.

Inevitably, the line bears the marks of its history. Whereas the main lines to Dover, Brighton and Southampton have the air of grandly conceived projects, the Direct line to Portsmouth is an attractive conglomeration of bits and pieces. The first section to be traversed after leaving the Southampton main line at Woking is also chronologically the first. As explained in Chapter 8, but for the attraction of Bristol, the Southampton line would almost certainly have gone through Guildford and, even after they had settled for the Basingstoke route, there was an intention to provide a branch to Guildford. In the event, the necessary powers were obtained by the Guildford Junction Railway company in 1844, which surely achieved a record with an Act of 347 sections for about five and a half miles of line. A special feature of the plans was the intention of reverting to wooden flangeless rails, on which trains were directed by means of guide wheels. (There is a strong likeness between the proposed arrangement and that in use on the Montreal Metro and certain lines in Paris, except that the Metro uses concrete rails and rubber-tyred wheels.) The wooden rails were never put to the test, as the LSWR intended the Guildford Junction as their first step towards Portsmouth, and therefore required normal track. Prosser, who developed the idea, later constructed a test track on Wimbledon Common. Meanwhile, the LSWR purchased the Guildford Junction, whose line was opened in May 1845. It was a relatively simple line to build, taking a direct route over country only requiring the construction of moderate earthworks.

Guildford station was opened on the west side of the River Wey, just short of the Farnham Turnpike Road, in a situation very comparable to the original Maidstone terminal of the SER. However, when the Maidstone line was extended to Strood, a junction was constructed outside the original terminal and a new through station was built. On the other hand, at Guildford, end-on extension was possible, and the station has been on the same site since 1845. In 1849 two important developments were the construction of the Guildford to Farnham line with a junction facing Guildford at the London end of the station, and the extension through tunnels in the opposite direction to Godalming. The SER-operated Reading, Guildford & Reigate used the Godalming branch between Shalford junction and Guildford and the Farnham line between Guildford and Ash junction.[6] So that, from 1849, Guildford saw the trains of both the LSWR and the SER companies. In 1865 the line from Horsham was opened, joining the Godalming branch at Peasmarsh junction and bringing LBSCR trains into Guildford.[7] At this time, the operating facilities were still limited, consisting of two through platforms and a loop on the outer face of the up platform. An additional platform was added on the up side for local trains. By the 1880s a major reconstruction was necessary, the work being completed about 1884. The buildings of 1845 on the down side were demolished and replaced by a fairly typical range of LSWR-style buildings. The gables were plain by LSWR standards, but a degree of elaboration was provided by a bay window at first-floor level. At the present time the building remains substantially unchanged. The engine sheds on the up side were swept away, the site being used for additional platforms, a coaling stage and loading docks.

206

There are now four platforms serving six through tracks and one terminal. The platform faces, and not the tracks, are numbered as follows—1: a bay on the down side, at the London end of platform 2; 3 and 4: an island platform; 5 and 6: another island; 7 and 8: a third island which, somewhat oddly, is separated from 5 and 6 by only one track. This leads to the slightly surprising situation of trains arriving or departing from platforms 6 *and* 7. Another complication arises from the signalling permitting trains to leave some of the platforms in either direction. Beyond 7 and 8 was a coaling stage for locomotives, sited there because of the very constricted site to which the engine shed had been moved. This was excavated from the chalk on the up side between the bridge carrying the Farnham Road and the tunnel mouth. In order to use the site to best advantage, the shed combined a roundhouse with a normal seven-road shed.

After the reconstruction, operation was carried out from three signal boxes—North, Yard and South. Their work was increased in 1885 when the new line from Hampton Court junction to Guildford via Cobham was opened. It was by this route that the live rail first reached Guildford, electric trains being extended from Claygate in 1925. Trains from this line have usually terminated in Guildford, using the no. 1 bay platform. The Southern built a new footbridge, spanning all the platforms and leading to a second station entrance in Guildford Park Road. In 1937 the North signal box ceased to act as a block post, and Guildford Yard signal box became an extremely complicated box. It was regarded by signalmen as something of a test piece— 'if you could work Guildford Yard box you could work anything'. All this ended in April 1966 when a new box replaced not only the Yard and South boxes, but Shalford and Peasmarsh junction as well. The sites of the signal boxes are merely gaps, but the site of the engine shed is now earning revenue as a car park. Although Guildford is still a very busy junction station, it cannot boast the range of services it once offered. At local level, the service to Horsham ended in 1965, being worked by steam locomotives until the end. This was the service that, at one time,

o

brought LBSCR trains into Guildford; the Reading, Guildford & Reigate line brought SER and, later, SECR trains. Although the RGRR was intended as a by-pass to London for trains from the Midlands and North to the South East, apart from a period in the 1860s, there were no regular through passenger workings until 1897. There was a break from 1916 until 1922 when they were restored, generally with Great Western coaches and Southern coaches running north and south on alternate days. Various destinations were served, but the northern terminus was usually Birkenhead. In the South, Brighton, Eastbourne, Hastings, Folkestone, Dover, Deal, Ramsgate and Margate all had through coaches, at least during the height of the holiday period. The normal through trains were withdrawn in September 1939, although a special service from Ashford to Newcastle ran from 1940 until 1945. Restoration came in 1957 and, once again, Guildford saw locomotives and trains from what had become the Western Region. However, this traffic was waning, and, after November 1959, it ran in the summer only until it was finally withdrawn in 1964. From January 1965, the Southern Region service from Reading to Redhill and Tonbridge was operated by multiple-unit trains. But, while it is no longer possible to travel through from Guildford to such destinations as Deal or Birkenhead, it still handles a variety of services. In addition to the basic three trains an hour on the Portsmouth line, there is an hourly service on the RGRR and two trains an hour to Waterloo by the new line via Effingham Junction and also via Aldershot and Ascot, giving twenty-four arrivals and departures per hour in the off-peak period.

The circumstances under which the LSWR extended the line from Guildford to Godalming have already been described. As it was not possible to fit in the railway alongside the River Wey, the ridge of the North Downs was penetrated by two tunnels. The first, Chalk tunnel, not surprisingly penetrates chalk, its original length of 938 yards having been reduced to 845 yards when excavations were carried out at the north end to make room for the new engine shed. After a short open section, the line enters St Catherine's tunnel, which takes its name from a ruined mediaeval chapel. Although only 132 yards long, this tunnel was built through sand and has caused the closure of the line on at least three occasions. (Perhaps the first would better be described as a delay in opening, from August to October 1849.) The RGRR line of the SER came in on the down side, the junction being controlled by a venerable LSWR wooden signal box. Its lower part was encased with brick, presumably to give the signalman some degree of protection during air raids. The junction is still in use but, since April 1966, has been operated from the new box at Guildford; the Shalford Junction box has been demolished. The significant embankment, which would have enabled SER trains to run towards Portsmouth, has already been mentioned. The site of Peasmarsh junction, a threshold of LBSCR territory, is just south of the end of the embankment, and just north of an overbridge. Beyond the bridge on the up side there was formerly a public siding which, after 1965, handled coal traffic only and, in 1969, closed completely. On the same side, a quarter of a mile farther on, is one of the emergency food stores, constructed with a private siding during the Second World War and now used as a depot by the GPO.

As originally built, the Godalming extension was designed to join the Direct Portsmouth & London Railway, after crossing the River Wey. As explained above, the DPLR was not constructed, so the railway terminated above the left bank of the river, near a roadbridge which gave access to the town. The station consisted of a single side platform and a solid brick station house with so few embellishments that it is difficult to associate it with any particular style. It was rectangular in both plan and elevation, with a hipped roof. The sash windows on the first floor had keystones in their lintels. When the Portsmouth Railway was opened, it began from a junction about a quarter of a mile towards Guildford, and the company opened its own Godalming station in 1859, much closer to the town centre. Until 1897 Goldalming kept both its terminal and its through stations but, in that year, the old terminus was replaced by a more elaborate establishment on the Guildford side of the junction, serving the Godalming suburb of Farncombe, whose population had grown to almost equal that of the original town. The new station had no goods facilities and the old terminal remained open for freight traffic until 1969; the track from the junction has now been removed. Farncombe was built between two level-crossings, and at present each of them is operated from a signal box. The station buildings, although they lack the elaborate gables of Worplesdon or Brookwood, have sufficient decoration to give a Tudor atmosphere. The site of the junction between the Godalming extension of 1849 and the Portsmouth Railway of 1859 is in a cutting, and therefore easily located, despite the removal of the tracks to the old terminal.

The line crosses the Wey to enter the Portsmouth's Godalming station. The Portsmouth Railway was opened with eight stations, and there have been no subsequent closures or openings. Of the eight, two were of a slightly larger 'town type', five belonged to a standard wayside type and one did not quite conform to either pattern. Godalming consisted of two sections with the roof ridges set at right angles to the railway, with a centre section parallel to the railway joining them. The elevation is very asymmetrical, as one of the sections contained the station master's house and was three storeys high, while the other had only one storey. Each of the sections had high-pitched roofs and the gable end of the lower contained a trefoil which was filled in. The higher section had mullioned windows with hood moulds, partly suggestive of a Tudor manor house. Somewhat unusually for the South of England, the buildings were of stone. The Portsmouth's Godalming station had no goods facilities and its signal box was closed in 1939.

Basically, the Portsmouth Railway consisted of two 'gables' with one summit at Haslemere, the second at Buriton tunnel and Petersfield in the trough in between. The climb to Haslemere begins at Godalming, ascending from the valley of the Wey. The Wealden country is very attractive and the residential development sufficiently restrained to be almost unnoticeable from the train. Also inconspicuous are the signs of the Wealden iron industry. However, a feature was the damming-up of streams to provide water power, and some of the resultant ponds have sur-

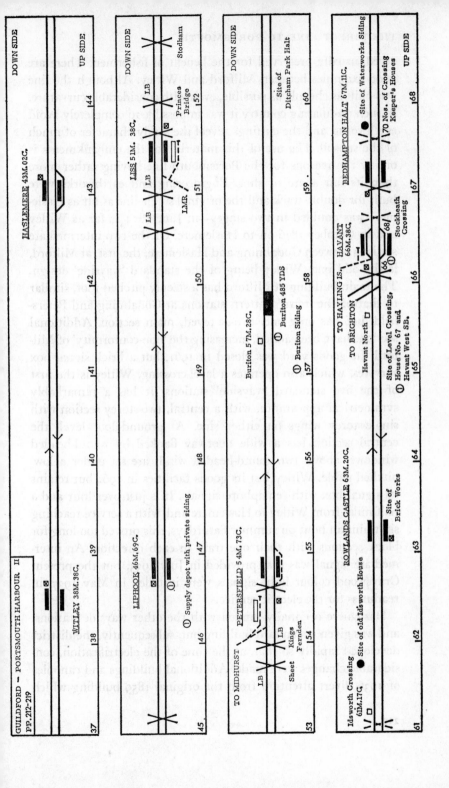

GUILDFORD — PORTSMOUTH HARBOUR II
PP. 212–219

DOWN SIDE

UP SIDE

HASLEMERE 43M.02C.

WITLEY 38M.38C.

LIPHOOK 46M.69C.

① Supply depot with private siding

LISS 51M.38C.

Princes Bridge   Stodham

Site of Ditcham Park Halt

DOWN SIDE

TO MIDHURST

PETERSFIELD 54M.73C.

LB   Sheet   Kings   Fernden

Buriton 57M.28C.

① Buriton Siding

Buriton 485 YDS

ROWLANDS CASTLE 63M.20C.

Idsworth Crossing   ● Site of old Idsworth House
61M.17C.

Site of
Brick Works

BEDHAMPTON HALT 67M.11C.

● Site of Waterworks Siding

70 Nos. of Crossing
Keeper's Houses

HAVANT 66M.38C.

TO HAYLING IS.

TO BRIGHTON

Havant North

① Site of Level Crossing,
House No. 67 and
Havant West SB.

Stockheath
Crossing

UP SIDE

vived, usually preserved for the benefit of fishermen. There are good examples between Milford and Witley. Although the line was built as cheaply as possible, even with considerable curvature, in such undulating country it was impossible to completely avoid earthworks, and the cuttings reveal the sandy character of much of the subsoil. The use of this material for the embankments is one of the reasons for the Portsmouth line having rather more than its fair share of slips. Engineering and earthworks were built for double track and the original single line as far as Haslemere was doubled in two stages—in June 1875 as far as Witley and in October 1876 on to Haslemere. Of the two intermediate stations between Godalming and Haslemere, the first, at Milford, is the odd one, Witley being of the standard 'wayside' design. The main building at Milford has a steeply pitched roof, similar to that of the 'town' pattern stations at Godalming and Petersfield, but has only one, two-storeyed, main section. Additional sections have been added, increasing the 'non-conformity' of Milford. Its goods yard was closed in 1961, but a brick signal box survives, which also operates a level-crossing. Witley is the first of the five standard 'wayside' stations. It has a remarkably symmetrical appearance, with a central, two-storey section with single-storey wings on either side. At ground-floor level, the central section has a wide doorway flanked by round-headed windows; above, two round-headed winds are set under a low-pitched gable. Witley lost its goods facilities in 1962 but retains its signal box with semaphore signals. It is just over four and a half miles from Witley to Haslemere and, with a service reaching six trains an hour on summer Saturdays, this proved too long for block sections with their one train in each direction. An intermediate signal was first provided in July 1933, but the present Grayswood colour light signals were installed in May 1937, in readiness for the electric service.

Haslemere originally ranked with the other wayside stations, and was given a standard building but, subsequently, the district developed rapidly so that, at the time of the electrification, considerable changes were made. Additional buildings and canopies of 1936 divert attention from the original 1859 building which has, however, been retained. The up platform became an island, served by a loop road, to enable the stopping trains to be passed. Most of the signals were changed from semaphores to coloured lights in July 1937. Beyond Haslemere, the descent from the High Wealden country to Petersfield begins, with the line following a stream. This is a tributary of the Wey, which was crossed at Godalming and which, at this point, indicates the boundary first between Sussex and Surrey and then between Sussex and Hampshire. (Nearly three miles of the Portsmouth Railway is in Sussex, between Haslemere and Liphook.) There are considerable military establishments in this area and, before we enter Liphook, on the up side, there is a large military supply depot with an internal railway system. Liphook presents the normal picture for the local stations on the Portsmouth Railway, with a standard wayside station building, a goods depot closed in 1969 and a signal box with semaphore signals. Doubling from Haslemere through Liphook to Liss was completed in 1877, and on through Petersfield to Rowlands Castle in 1878. Liss resembles Liphook except for one special feature: the Longmoor Military Railway in its final form, extended from Bordon, through Longmoor to a terminal at Liss.[8] The single platform was on the up side of the main line station, across the station yard and, especially during the Second World War, carried a very heavy passenger traffic. Freight was exchanged over a connection at the London end of the station. The military railway was closed in 1969, the signals controlling the connection were removed in 1971 but, at present, the track is still in position. The level-crossing at Liss is operated from a typical LSWR signal box but, between this point and the level-crossing at Petersfield, there were no less than four minor crossings. Originally, all of them were looked after by crossing keepers living in houses adjoining the crossings but, with the increase in both road and rail traffic, they were provided with crossing boxes. These were not responsible for regulating traffic; the block section was between Liss and Petersfield boxes and the only function of the crossing boxes was to ensure that the gates were set against road traffic when either Liss or Petersfield indicated that a train was approaching. In some cases, however, signals were provided which could only be cleared when the gates were opened for trains. In geographical order from Liss, the four crossings were given local names as follows: Princes Bridge, Stodham, Sheet and Kings Fernden. In 1966 and 1967 all of them except Stodham had their gates replaced by lifting barriers operated automatically by the trains. The gates remained at Stodham, but the services of the crossing keeper were terminated. Instead, there is a wicket gate for pedestrians who are provided with a telephone connection to Liss signal box, while keys can be issued to anybody authorised to use the crossing for a vehicle.

When the Portsmouth Railway was opened, apart from Godalming, Petersfield was the only town on the route, and this is reflected in its having larger station buildings, virtually identical to those at Godalming. However, the importance of Petersfield for railway operating increased in 1864, when the Petersfield Railway opened its branch to Midhurst.[9] The junction was on the opposite side of the level-crossing to the station and faced Portsmouth. To save branch line trains using the crossing, a separate platform was constructed on the London side. It was built alongside an adjacent commercial building on which the railway arranged to affix a posterboard and two small metal station nameplates of the type mounted on lamp posts. Facilities for passengers consisted of one wooden seat. To allay any doubts, a notice by the wicket gate leading to the road was marked 'To trains for Rogate, Elsted and Midhurst'. It is only fair to say that on the opposite side of the tracks was the signal box and, presumably, the signalmen would have detected any misguided main line passengers who were waiting on the Midhurst platform. The branch closed in 1955 and the site of both rails and platform is only indicated by unoccupied space. At the time of writing, however, the signal box and level-crossing gates still operate on traditional lines, although the number of semaphore signals has been much reduced. Midhurst trains usually started from their own isolated platform, but the up platform on the main line was converted into an island with a loop road at the back. This was intended for local trains on the main line and has now been converted into a terminal siding. The goods yard was closed to all traffic in 1969 and parts of it are now leased to local companies. Petersfield is still a local centre and market town, with a growing residential population, a number of whom travel to Portsmouth or London. In addition, HMS *Mercury*, a naval establishment, has brought in extra traffic during and after the Second World War.

While the scenery between Godalming and Havant is pleasant, that between Petersfield and Havant is among the most beautiful in Southern England. The climb up to Buriton tunnel has a ruling gradient of 1 in 100 and the descent on the far side is at 1 in 80 with a continuous curvature necessitating a permanent speed limit. On the scarp of the South Downs was the large Buriton lime works, with its three quarries, now all overgrown. The company had its internal rail system, with horses for the more level tracks and cable haulage for the inclines. It exchanged traffic with the railway at Buriton sidings.[10] Although these were closed to all traffic in 1962, a siding survives, used by the civil engineers' department and visible on the up side. Buriton tunnel is 485 yards long and constructed through chalk. The line emerges into a steep sided cutting and then passes through about two miles of most beautifully wooded chalk country. This high part of the South Downs is quite sparsely populated, and there are no stations on the six and a half miles between Petersfield and Rowlands Castle. However, at the southern end of the woods, somewhat surprisingly, a solidly built concrete footbridge spans the tracks. This marks the site of Ditcham Park Halt, an obscure establishment which never had a public service. During the Second World War, Ditcham House was made available by Lady Peel as a rest and recreation centre for naval personnel from Portsmouth. Initially, Southdown buses provided transport but, about 1944, a halt was opened near Woodcroft Farm about a mile from the house. Specified trains called to pick up and set down liberty men bound for Ditcham House. After the war, the concrete platforms were removed but the footbridge, which was useful for access to Woodcroft Farm, was left. The six and a half miles from Petersfield to Rowlands Castle were divided into three block sections, with signal boxes at Buriton siding and Idsworth crossing. In 1937 intermediate coloured lights were added near Woodcroft Farm. Both the signal boxes have now gone, and Idsworth crossing no longer carries vehicular traffic. (Alternative road access for Heberdens Farm has been provided via Finchdean.) The crossing house survives and, on the down side, there is a glimpse of an early medieval church surrounded by hummocky ground which was one the site of a village. A quarter of a mile to the south, an avenue of trees on the west side of the line leads up to a walled garden on the east side. The owner of Idsworth House decided that he did not want a railway line adjoining his house and severing its avenue, and used his compensation money to build a new mansion about a mile away. Rowlands Castle is the last of the Portsmouth Railway stations, being a twin of Liss, Liphook, Witley and Haslemere. There was never much industrial traffic on the direct line, but a brick works on the up side at Rowlands Castle for many years received its coal and sent away some of its bricks by rail. Although the works have been closed, at the time of writing its remains are still visible. The avoidance of some parkland on the east side necessitated a curve with a permanent speed restriction. A descent, mostly at 1 in 120 and 1 in 147 down a valley, brings the line to a sharp curve with yet another speed restriction, which leads to the junction with the LBSCR and the site of the 'Battle of Havant'. The temporary platforms at which LSWR passengers joined the replacement bus service in 1859 were just short of the junction.

Havant station was opened in 1847, with the line from Chichester to Portsmouth, and twelve years before the Portsmouth Railway. Havant was a small market town with long established leather and parchment industries, and it was provided with a modest, wayside station. By 1889 traffic had developed to a stage at which the LBSCR determined on rebuilding and, somewhat unusually, this took place on the same site, with the adjoining refreshment room left intact. The station was situated between two level-crossings and, at the time of electrification, it was decided to eliminate the busier crossing at the Portsmouth end and to rebuild the station. On this occasion, the new

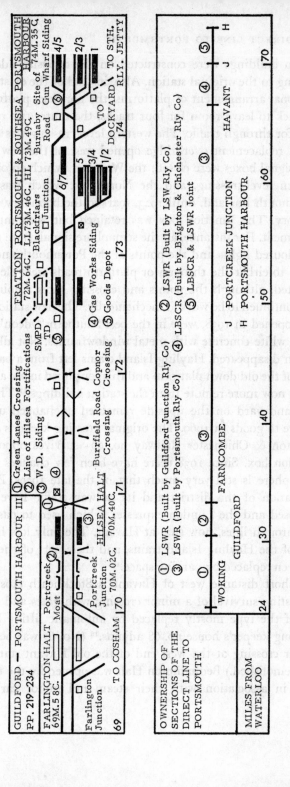

GUILDFORD — PORTSMOUTH HARBOUR III
PP. 219-234

FARLINGTON HALT 69M.5 8C.

FRATTON 72M. 64C. PORTSMOUTH & SOUTHSEA 73M.46C. HL 73M.49C. PORTSMOUTH HARBOUR 74M.35 C

Portcreek Junction LL73M.46C.

① Green Lanes Crossing
② Line of Hilsea Fortifications
③ W.D. Siding
④ Gas Works Siding
⑤ Goods Depot

Blackfriars Junction

Burnaby Road

Site of Gun Wharf Siding

TO DOCKYARD

TO STH. RLY. JETTY

HILSEA HALT 70M.40C.

Farlington Junction

Portcreek Junction

Burrfield Road Crossing

Copnor Crossing

TO COSHAM

OWNERSHIP OF SECTIONS OF THE DIRECT LINE TO PORTSMOUTH

① LSWR (Built by Guildford Junction Rly Co)
③ LSWR (Built by Portsmouth Rly Co)

② LSWR (Built by LSW Rly Co)
④ LBSCR (Built by Brighton & Chichester Rly Co)
⑤ LBSCR & LSWR Joint

J PORTCREEK JUNCTION
H PORTSMOUTH HARBOUR

MILES FROM WATERLOO

WOKING 24

GUILDFORD 30

FARNCOMBE 40

PORTCREEK JUNCTION HAVANT 60

70

station buildings were constructed on the opposite side of the crossing to the original station. Also, instead of the existing conventional arrangement of platforms, the northern platform was set back to leave room for four tracks, the centre two of which were for through traffic. The western level-crossing was stopped, and a replacement overbridge opened west of the new station. Two signal boxes were closed; the West box, which adjoined the western level-crossing, and the North box which was on the Portsmouth line and, until 1923, marked the boundary of LSWR territory. The Junction box was retained but with much new equipment. For instance, all the semaphore signals were replaced by coloured lights and the points at the Portsmouth end giving access to either the through or platform roads were electrically operated, although the points and crossing gates adjoining the box continued to be worked mechanically. The new station buildings, opened in 1938, were in the best Southern 'Odeon' style in clean, white concrete with metal windowframes. Not all the old station disappeared. Hayling Island trains left from a bay at the back of the old down platform and this continued in use although it was now more remote from the station buildings.[11] The goods shed and yard on the up side remained unchanged until the closure to goods in 1969. The original crossing keeper's house— Brighton & Chichester Railway no. 66—survives opposite the Junction box. Since 1938 there have been few changes and the atmosphere is still very much that of the late 1930s. Both the population of the district and its railway traffic have greatly increased and the London expresses, which used to pass by on the through lines, now stop at Havant. The only loss has been that of the Hayling Island trains, and their part of the station has been replaced by parking space.[12]

A short distance west of Havant is Stockheath crossing, an interesting survival of a minor crossing with gates and crossing box of the type mostly replaced by automatic lifting barriers. Crossing keeper's house no. 68 adjoins.[13] (No. 67 was beside the former crossing at the west end of the old Havant station and was demolished.) Bedhampton Halt was opened by the LBSCR in 1906, in association with their steam rail motor car service between Portsmouth and Chichester. The characteristic LBSCR box became a block post in 1929 instead of Bedhampton Mill signal box. Its semaphore signals were replaced by coloured lights at the same time as those at Havant. On the down side, now severed from the main line, but visible in the grass on the far side of the boundary fence, are the rails of the waterworks siding. When steam pumping engines were in use, this carried a regular coal traffic. In contrast with the Portsmouth Railway, this section of the LBSCR follows the coastal plain with no significant curves or gradients.

At Farlington junction, the line from Cosham and Fareham comes in on the up side, facing towards Havant.[14] The connection with the Fareham line is a triangular one, with Cosham junction at the western apex, Farlington junction at the eastern apex and Portcreek junction to the south. Joint LBSCR and LSWR ownership extended from Cosham to Portsmouth so that the western side of the triangle—Cosham to Portcreek—was jointly owned, but the other two sides were LBSCR. The northern side of the triangle makes possible through running between Cosham and Havant and at one time it carried a local service. Subsequently it was used by through expresses between Brighton and Wales and the West. The last survivor was the Brighton to Exeter express and when, in October 1971, this was withdrawn, in order to avoid invoking closure procedure, a once-daily multiple-unit diesel was put on, theoretically to maintain the passenger service over the line. On the eastern arm of the triangle, significant humps mark the site of the only establishment to be closed between Woking and Portsmouth, which was almost a conventional station. Farlington was opened in 1891 to serve a racecourse built on the marshes alongside the line. The premises were decidedly simple, consisting of little more than the two platforms. After a somewhat chequered career, including closure from 1917 until 1922, Farlington achieved a more formal existence in 1928 when it appeared in the public timetables as a halt. Although Cosham, Drayton and Farlington were all growing rapidly at the time, the platforms were badly placed on the edge of the marshes beyond the built-up area and, in view of intensive road competition, it is not surprising that it was finally closed when the electrified service was introduced in 1937. In the apex of Portcreek junction, reached by a footbridge, there is a terrace of distinctive railway housing. The three signal boxes—Cosham, Farlington and Portcreek—were all replaced by the new box in Portsmouth in 1968 and have been demolished.

At Portcreek junction we run on to the joint line, crossing Portcreek and also a moat which formed part of the Hilsea Fortifications. Portcreek connected Portsmouth and Langstone harbours and formed part of the inland waterway route from London to Portsmouth. (This was severed when the Wey and Arun Canal finally went out of use in 1871.) However, the railway bridge is a movable one, although it does not appear to have been moved for many years. (Since 1937, the existence of the live rail would have added to the difficulty of moving it.) Beyond the moat, the line penetrates a curtain wall of the Hilsea Fortifications and then runs south, over the level of Portsea Island, the only obstacles being minor roads. At Hilsea, there are a number of factories and also the City Airport, whose grass runways limit the type of aircraft which it can receive. Hilsea Halt, of typical concrete construction, was opened for war workers in 1941 and is served at peak hours only. One of the two last level-crossings on Portsea Island adjoined Hilsea Halt but has now been closed. The other is at Green Lanes, about half a mile to the south. Here a signal box survives, but is used only for working the gates. In times past, there was a considerable rail traffic to Hilsea gas works, and the gas undertaking operated their own locomotives. (The last of their steam locomotives was recently presented to Portsmouth City Museums.) On the opposite, up side, of the line are extensive WD sidings. The next two level-crossings have both been replaced by overbridges, the one at Burrfield Road since the Second World War, but the one at Copnor many years previously. The evidence for the crossing at Copnor consists of the crossing keeper's house and characteristic kinks in approaches to the overbridge. Also at Copnor is Station Road, but this does not commemorate a closed station, as the proposed Copnor station was never built. Copnor signal box, abolished in April 1935, was near the site of the level-crossing but has gone, virtually without trace.

It was originally intended to construct a triangle of lines at Fratton, so that trains could run directly on to the Southsea branch.[15] Although this scheme was never carried out, the large area of land which was purchased has provided space for an engine shed, an electric train depot and a freight terminal. There has been a long-term tendency to movement from Portsmouth out to Fratton. For instance, the Fratton engine shed replaced that on the north side of the original terminal and, in 1936, this was followed by the goods depot. The locomotive depot included a roundhouse similar in principle but different in detail from that at Guildford. Whereas at Guildford the turntable was in the open, with the shed forming a crescent around it, Fratton had a complete roundhouse which covered the 50-foot turntable. Towards the end of its working life, it housed five locomotives which were earmarked for preservation. In March 1969 the steam shed and the water tower were demolished. A building of 1947 which was demolished at the same time had contained oil pumps used for the fueling of oil-burning steam locomotives. Equipment for fueling diesel traction is still in use and the offices have been retained. The main freight depot for Portsmouth was transferred to Fratton in 1936, releasing the original site in Greatham Street. In addition to trans-shipment facilities for moving freight from road to rail vehicles, a large storage warehouse with a floor area of 13,000 square feet, was provided. At the time, local deliveries were undertaken by Messrs Chaplins, and new offices were provided for them on the site. These are now in use by British Rail and National Carriers. The ample space at Fratton was also used for stabling electric trains. While these developments took place on an adjoining site, Fratton station has undergone no dramatic changes since its opening in 1885. This coincided with the opening of the East Southsea branch. As the junction trailed in on a site where there was no room for building a station, Fratton was constructed short of the junction, with separate platforms on the main line and the East Southsea branch. The main line had a conventional platform on either side, the down platform later having a loop road behind it to convert it to an island platform. The East Southsea platform consisted of an island reached by steps from a footbridge which connected the station platform and was also used as a public footpath, in the same way as the footbridge at St Denys. For many years this was roofed and glazed, but the cost of providing protection from weather on this somewhat lavish scale was considered excessive, and the footbridge is now open. The signalling arrangements at Fratton did not change until the new Portsmouth signal box was opened and there were good examples of LSWR boxes operating semaphore signals at each end of the station until 1968. To complete the negative side of the picture, in addition to the loss of the roof of the bridge and the two signal boxes, the East Southsea platform was demolished between the wars. On the other hand, to accommodate twelve-coach electric trains, both the main line platforms were extended at the London end. A welcome survival is a small refreshment room which also sells newspapers and magazines.

The platforms are on a sharp curve which is of considerable historical significance. Up to this point, in 1847, the railway could be constructed through open country but, beyond Fratton, the line penetrated a built-up area by using the line of the abandoned Portsea Canal. This necessitated a sharp curve from a roughly north and south direction to east and west at Fratton, and the raising of two bridges over the derelict canal to give sufficient clearance for the trains. In order to maintain its level, the canal had run in a cutting and, although the ground was only about 21 feet above sea level, the railway followed the same elevation. Beyond draining the canal and partly filling in the bed, little work was required, and the entry into Portsmouth was highly economical. West of Fratton bridge, which is on the site of the canal bridge, the thoroughfares on the north side are called Sydenham Terrace and, significantly, Canal Walk. Originally, two running lines were provided, with sloping banks on either side. Subsequently these were cut away to make room for additional tracks, the sides being supported by brick retaining walls. A curve in the wall at the west end of Canal Walk indicates the point at which the canal curved away to the north west along the

Main line

The Parish of *Portsea* in the County of *Southampton*

	Description of Property	Name of Owner, or Reputed Owner	Name of Lessee, or Reputed Lessee	Name of Occupier
5	Public roads	Surveyors of Highways for the Parish of Portsea Joseph Craven and others		
6	Cottages and gardens	William Pearce		David Hanbes, John Golding, Thomas Mann, James Hunt, David Honner, Reverend William Mandy Honig, Elorry
7	Garden	Daniel Howards		Henry Hill
8	House, garden and coachhouse	Sarah Mary Tutley Oaby		same
9	Arable land	same		same
0	Garden land	Henry Hill		same
1	Arable land and Plantation	same		
2	Arable land	same		
3	Public roads	Surveyors of Highways for the Parish of Portsea Joseph Craven and others		
4	Garden lands	Henry Hewell		Henry Hill
5	Cottage and garden lands	The Trustees of the late William Oxfulds deceased		Thomas Jolly
7	Garden lands	Jacob Coutis and George Coutis		Henry Hill
8	Private roads	The Mayor, Aldermen and Burgesses of the Borough of Portsmouth		
9	Garden land	John Burell		Francis Sandey
0	same	William Cooper		William Hunt
1	same	John Thomas Ridge and others		same
2	same	William Cooper		Frederick Away
3	same	John Thomas Ridge and others		William Away
4	same	George John Seate		
	30			

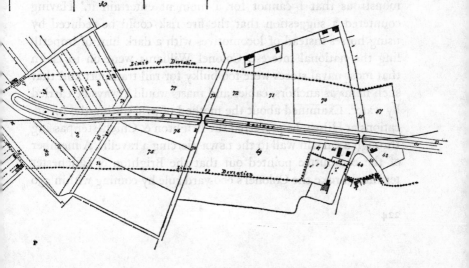

47 (left) A section of the Deposited Plans for the Brighton and Chichester Railway (Portsmouth extension) 1844. This shows the way in which use was made of the abandoned Portsea Canal. The end of the canal had been filled in before the plans were made; the railway filled in the remainder west of Fratton and re-built the two overbridges (the present Fratton and Somers Road Bridges)

48 (below) The numbers on the plan refer to the Book of Reference, a section of which is reproduced. Compulsory purchase powers were restricted to the area inside the limits of deviation. At this time, there were few buildings in the district, but much arable and garden land.

P

255

line of Upper Arundel Street, to its main terminal basin just north of Lower Church Path. (The side is now occupied by the Landport Drapery Bazaar.) Its divergence from the end of the railway left the company with a triangular site which, among other things, left room for an engine shed. In later years it contained a 50-foot turntable of which no visible evidence remains.

Portsmouth & Southsea station was constructed at an appropriate distance from the inner fortifications. In the parliamentary contest, there was no doubt that the Brighton & Chichester (Portsmouth Extension) was advantaged by placing its terminal well clear of the fortifications. For instance, the opposition produced as an expert witness, Colonel Williams, a retired officer who had served in the Engineers for thirty-five years. He felt that the terminus of the line of the LSWR party was far too close to the palisades and thought it would be extremely improper to permit the terminus of either line to approach within a distance of 600 yards of the defences. This suited the Brighton & Chichester case well enough, but Colonel Williams's views on an extension to the dockyard were probably less welcome. He said '. . . I cannot for a moment suppose that the Government would even listen to any such proposal. In the first place, the extreme danger from fire would be so great that I am sure it never could be, for a moment, admitted when we consider the inflammable nature of the stores that are placed in the dockyard—oil, pitch, tar, resin, timber and that sort of thing. The idea of a railroad being brought either into a dockyard or near it appears to me so monstrous that I cannot for a moment entertain it.' Having countered a suggestion that the fire risk could be reduced by using horses instead of locomotives with a dark hint of imperilling the national interest, Colonel Williams went on to claim that most naval stores were too bulky for rail transport and that such items as anchors, cables and masts would always be carried by water. Examined about the method of penetrating the fortifications at Hilsea, he preferred the Brighton & Chichester passing through a curtain wall to the LSWR piercing a ravelin. A member of the committee pointed out that the Brighton & Chichester terminal broke the Colonel's 600-yard rule by coming within 250 yards of the fortifications, to which he replied that the company did not object to being set back 350 yards. He was, however, somewhat deflated by opposing Counsel, who managed to establish that, at Gosport, the railway terminated about 180 yards from the fortifications. There are probably no other lines in England so influenced by considerations of defence as those on Portsea Island. For instance, Section 20 of the B&C Act specified that '. . . whereas it is indispensably necessary that the Fortifications and Defences at or near Portsmouth and Portsea should be preserved from Injury and that the same should be in no respect affected by the said proposed railway; be it therefore enacted that nothing in this Act contained shall authorise the said Company to construct or carry the said Railway across Hilsea Lines or to enter upon or possess or occupy any land or other property belonging to Her Majesty in the Parishes of Widley, Wymering or Portsea, or any or either of them, without the Consent in Writing of the Principal Officers of Her Majesty's Ordance first given to the said Company for the Purpose.' It went on to say that, even if they did agree, the land should be leased and not sold. Other sections permitted the Board of Ordnance to destroy the railway if necessary for the improvement of the fortifications. In fact, although so much was said about the fortifications, they were probably more appropriate to 1810 than 1840, and by the 1860s they were replaced by a new ring of forts on Portsdown Hill and in the waters of Spithead. The Hilsea Lines were retained but the Inner Fortifications were demolished, so that the railway was no longer blocked off from the harbour.

The first station at Portsmouth consisted of a plain building with a single platform. It was replaced by the present building in 1866, constructed at a time of considerable growth, both of the town and of the dockyard. If Southampton is an ideal example of a provincial station of 1840, Portsmouth fulfils a similar role for 1866. It is constructed of brick, using bricks of different colours and also stone to achieve architectural effects. There is an impressive central block, flanked by two wings. The central block projects beyond the wings and has two further features to catch the eye. At road level there is a wide canopy of glass and iron, surmounted by iron rails. (The railings at the front are obscured by a notice proclaiming the identity of the building.) Projecting from the top of the building is a truncated pyramid, which has unfortunately lost the ornamental ironwork which once adorned it. Even without its canopy and 'spire', the central block would still be impressive. At first-floor level there are five large round-headed windows, separated by double columns and accentuated by stone and yellow brick surrounds and keystones. The top of the building is marked by a shallow balustrade with an elaborately mounted clock forming the centrepiece. Although shaded by the centrepiece, the wings are considerable. They have large, round-headed windows on the ground floor and windows with depressed arches at first-floor level. Again, stone and yellow brick is used to stress the composition. The forecourt was separated from the busy Commercial Road by iron railings punctuated with massive brick pillars, capped with stone and surmounted by lamps. (The railings were victims of the salvage drive during the war.) This is, without question, the outstanding railway building of Portsmouth, and is all the more worth attention because its future is uncertain. Inside, the booking hall, with its ten booking positions and its elaborate wooden panelling, is a most valuable period piece. While there have been only changes of detail in the station buildings, there have been a number of changes in the platforms. The terminal platforms are directly behind the buildings and now consist of a side platform and two island platforms serving five terminal tracks. A roof of iron and glass covers the circulating area and there are umbrella-type canopies on the platforms. However, the most important development was the opening of a high-level platform in 1876. As already explained, after the demolition of the inner defences, there was no case for holding back the railway from the harbour, and the Act for the extension line received the Royal Assent in July 1873. The new line had to gain enough height to clear Commercial Road, so Blackfriars junction was made to the east of the terminal station. There was a short, sharp climb at 1 in 61 and then the gradient eased to 1 in 400 beside the island platform. This was reached from the circulating area by a flight of steps and was covered by an overall roof of two spans, the centre being supported by iron columns on the platform. The outer wall was of glass and iron but most of the glass was blown out during the Second World War, and panels of a corrugated synthetic material were substituted. This gave much of the high-level platform a dark, rather cave-like atmosphere. At the time of electrification, when it was decided to operate twelve-coach trains, the platform was extended at the harbour end to reach a total length of 820 feet. With a bridge in position over Commercial Road, there was no case for the retention of the level-crossing for the dockyard branch, and a new junction was made at the harbour end of the high level platform. There was no room to make a double junction, so the up line only was joined by a steeply graded single track which assumed the original alignment near the Edinburgh Road crossing. Because of the steep gradient, the maximum load with one engine was five bogie coaches, and special regulations applied to their working. The junction was controlled by Portsmouth High Level signal box, a wooden box with a slate roof sited in the angle between the converging lines. In 1930, both Portsmouth High Level and Portsmouth East ceased to be block posts, but whereas Portsmouth East was demolished, the High Level box survived, containing a ground frame for operating the junction. The dockyard branch continues to carry freight traffic, but it is many years since a passenger train went down to the private station adjoining the Royal Naval Barracks. (The present writer's last visit was on a Locomotive Club of Great Britain Special Train in November 1963.) Portsmouth & Southsea station was controlled from Portsmouth Yard signal box until 1968, when it was replaced by a new, electric box on the up side. A unique feature of the high-level platform was the device used for starting trains. In modern electric stock, the guard gives the driver the signal to start by means of a bell in the driver's cab, but in the 1930s it was usual to wave a flag and blow a whistle. At night, a hand oil lamp with coloured spectacles was used instead. Visibility along the high-level platform was very restricted and, to surmount this difficulty, in 1937 a bell was installed which could be rung from the opposite end of the platform by the guard. Another development of the same year was the closure of Burnaby Road signal box, between Portsmouth & Southsea and Portsmouth Harbour, and the substitution of coloured light signals for semaphores.

All the new arrangements ran for just over two years, before they were subjected to the strains of war. Portsmouth suffered so heavily from aerial bombardment that the local railwaymen had their own fund, with over 700 members, to give immediate help to those of their number who suffered. The sum of £550 was raised but, by April 1941, this was approaching exhaustion and more money had to be obtained by voluntary contributions from other stations on the Southern Railway. There were not only bombs, but also land mines. On 27 April 1941, Portsmouth & Southsea station was damaged by two of them, with fatal casualties. Sometimes a bomb that failed to explode caused almost as much trouble as one that did. On 26 August 1940 a bomb fell on the up side of the line near Green Lanes signal box and failed to explode. At first, all traffic was suspended but, when it was known that it would take two or three days to remove the bomb, it was decided to place high-sided wagons on the up line as a screen and run essential freight trains on the down line. Train crews were asked to volunteer for this duty and were instructed to lie flat on their stomachs as they passed the site. In this way, twenty-four freight trains, mainly for the dockyard, went through during the four days that the line was closed to passengers.

As it was clearly undesirable to have the platform extending on to the 1 in 61 approach ramp at the London end, it had to be extended on to the bridge over Commercial Road and beyond. A difficulty arose because Section 14 of the Act stipulated a maximum width of 50 feet for the bridge and, within these limits, the up and down tracks and the island platform had to be fitted. Another problem arose from a limit of 3 feet for lowering the roadway under the bridge. (In fact, when electric tram cars were introduced, it was lowered to a greater extent; the present pavements indicate the original level of the road.) Beyond Commercial Road, the railway had three more roads to cross, one existing and two intended—Ordnance Road, Burnaby Road and

Anglesey Road—so that it was built on an embankment with a moderate down gradient, increasing as the line approached the harbour. The area traversed was being developed after the removal of the fortifications, but the first plans show part of them still in position. After crossing Commercial Road, the line swung to south of west over the glacis of the defences and through a corner of the redoubt, to take up the line of an old mill pond. Most of the glacis was to be transformed into Victoria Park, and the Act required part of the railway embankment to be planted with ornamental shrubs and to have 'two arched openings of at least 20 ft. span'. Although allowed for in the plans, Burnaby and Anglesey Roads had not been constructed, but underbridges were provided in anticipation. All the bridges were required by the Act to be constructed with iron spans supported by metal columns and brick abutments. Ordnance Road was crossed on the skew and, despite changing direction to north of west, the line sliced across a corner of the ground attached to the Old Gun Wharf (now part of HMS *Vernon*). At this point, the railway was sandwiched in between the Old Gun Wharf and the road so, to save space, instead of the embankment being continued on the far side of Ordnance Road bridge, it was carried on a brick viaduct, similar to those so much used in South London.

The extension was jointly promoted by the LBSCR and LSWR which, together, absorbed the Albert Pier company. This had been authorised to construct its pier as an alternative to the common hard in 1847. It was used by the Gosport ferries and other vessels, and the railway companies were required to provide an alternative public landing place with a connection to the town. The result was an inverted and distorted Y, with the railway line curving out over the foreshore to join the line of the pier. The public landing place had to consist of a floating landing stage with a frontage of at least 100 feet and a width of at least 30 feet. The approach to both this landing stage and the platforms of the Harbour station was by way of the shoreward end of the Albert Pier, which became the 'Companies' carriage road. The Act describes the way in which the public landing place is to be joined to this 'carriage road' by means of a 'hinged gangway of the width of fifteen feet extending from the floating pontoon which will form the said landing place for a distance of about 100 feet to a fixed gangway of the width of twenty feet and from thence by that fixed gangway for a distance of about one hundred and eighty-five feet to the said Companies carriage road'. The widths were considered sufficient to carry the heavy traffic using the ferries; the length of the gangway was such that, even at low tide, passengers did not have to surmount an unreasonably steep gradient. All these arrangements are still in existence, conforming generally, if not in every respect, to the terms of the Act.

The facilities at the Harbour station were designed to deal with passengers arriving by train or on foot and leaving by steamer, either for Gosport or the Isle of Wight. From 1880, the Isle of Wight steamers were jointly owned by the LSWR and LBSCR companies. Although primarily passenger boats, they also carried mails, parcels and newspaper traffic, and these were all handled at the Harbour station. On the other hand, most freight was carried by cargo boats from the Camber Dock. The railway facilities were not only influenced by the needs of the steamers, as the western half of the extension had to be built in a manner satisfactory to the Admiralty and the War Department. The extension and the Harbour Station did much to improve communications between Portsmouth and the Isle of Wight which previously had depended to a considerable extent on the tramway from the terminal station to the Clarence Pier. It provided formidable competition for the route to the Island via Gosport and Stokes Bay Pier, until this went out of business before the First World War. Always the Harbour station was at its busiest on Saturdays in the summer, when traffic from London and elsewhere to the Isle of Wight was extremely heavy. With electrification, Portsmouth Harbour station was rebuilt on the same concrete 'Odeon' style as Havant. A new brick signal box was constructed, looking very similar to its contemporaries, such as Surbiton and Woking. It was built over the foreshore, in the space between the railway and the Companies carriage road, in a position to allow for the widening of the station if this should become necessary. Platform provision was identical to that at the low-level terminal station, consisting of a side platform and two islands, giving five platform faces. Unfortunately, all this was very short lived, as on the night of 10/11 January 1941 the bombing of the station was followed by fire, which destroyed the two island platforms. It was virtually impossible to fight the blaze as the water main was severed and water could not be pumped from below the station as the tide was out. For the rest of the war, only the side platform, which held nine coaches of a twelve-coach train, was available. After the war, however, holiday traffic to the Isle of Wight revived rapidly and the damaged parts of the station were replaced. When oil-burning vessels were acquired, a siding on the south side was used for storing oil tank wagons.

The extension line had two long sidings. One of these descended by a ramp alongside the railway viaduct to serve the Old and also the New Gun Wharf. It was removed after the Second World War. The second branched off just short of the original Harbour station, crossed the Companies carriage road by a level-crossing and continued across the foreshore on a metal viaduct to reach Watering Island, which became known as the South Railway Jetty. This had been constructed in 1860 and was especially suitable for troopships. Until the opening of the Harbour extension, the only rail access was over the dockyard branch and through the dockyard, so the new connection was a great improvement for soldiers, sailors and the distinguished guests, all of whom used the jetty. While the traffic was significant, it was hardly likely to make the infrequently used viaduct a commercial proposition so that, to ensure that the railways completed it, Section 8 of the Act stated that the main line was not to be opened for traffic until the siding to the South Railway Jetty had been constructed. (Presumably this was complied with, but the line to the jetty was apparently not used until fifteen months after the opening of the Harbour station.) The viaduct cut off Portsmouth hard from the harbour, so, to provide access for masted vessels that could not float under it, an opening span giving a passage of 40 feet was provided near the dockyard end.

231

On the South Railway Jetty itself, an elaborate shelter was constructed under which important visitors might join their train,
and this is still intact. Photographs have survived showing
highly decorated locomotives hauling trains for such very important passengers as the Prince of Wales in 1902 and the Presi-
dent of France in 1913. Between the wars, use of the siding to the
jetty declined, and it was frequently pressed into service for
stabling trains. After the Second World War it was demolished.
However, for those who sought a sign of it, the track on the
level-crossing over the carriage way, although largely covered by
tar, was faintly visible. But in 1968 the carriage way joining both
the station and the landing stage to Portsmouth hard was rebuilt,
and this reminder of the line to the South Railway Jetty was
obliterated.

At present all the London trains, together with the Brighton
trains and the few Bristol and Cardiff trains which survive, run
through to the Harbour station. The Hampshire diesel service to
Southampton, Eastleigh and Salisbury cannot be accommodated
and uses the low-level, terminal platforms at Portsmouth &
Southsea. Although many of the more local passengers are not
for Gosport or the Isle of Wight, it would obviously be preferable
for all trains to use the high-level platform and run on to the
Harbour station. The long-term plan is to extend the Harbour
station so that it can provide terminal facilities for all trains, and
to close the low-level section of Portsmouth & Southsea. This
would absorb a modest amount of foreshore and release a considerable quantity of valuable land in the centre of Portsmouth.
It would also mean the end of a fine Victorian building. However,
although the fate of particular buildings may be uncertain, the
future of the services to London and probably those to Southampton and Brighton would seem to be assured. Unfortunately,
there has been a decline in the number of through services to
Bristol and beyond.

To most passengers, the railway to Portsmouth is the Direct
line, which comes nearest to following the famous Portsmouth
Road. Although used by many people, it must be particularly
associated with holidays and the Royal Navy. I have experienced

journeys on the line, both as the beginning and end of a holiday or, during the war, as part of a serviceman's leave. Although I have made steam journeys over the line—the Stephenson Locomotive Society Special of May 1953 was memorable—these have all been by private trains. They did indicate clearly enough, however, what it was like to toil up from Havant to Buriton tunnel behind a T9 class locomotive and then roar down through Petersfield. But all my recorded journeys by public trains are post-electrification, starting with a holiday journey to the Isle of Wight in the summer of 1939. During the war, I had two periods during which I was a fairly regular traveller—one in early 1943 and another in late 1945. At this time, only the short platform at the Harbour station was intact and the express trains, consisting of three four-coach units (4 COR in Southern jargon) projected well beyond the end of the platform. An early arrival and a determined thrust from the end of the platform invariably secured the required corner seat. At that time, the Portsmouth expresses usually called at Portsmouth & Southsea, Haslemere, Guildford and Woking. Right time arrivals were rare, but not unknown. If the journey were in daylight, observation was no problem although an open notebook could arouse suspicious glances. There were the regular delights, such as the LBSCR Terrier waiting with the Hayling Island train at Havant and, usually, an LSWR M7 class with the Midhurst train at Petersfield. Guildford shed always provided something of interest, as did Wimbledon yard. But, if the journey had to be completed in darkness, the drawing of blinds precluded any possibility of seeing anything, even on a moonlit evening. My down journeys were frequently less pleasurable than the up, and not only because I was returning off leave. Some of the least comfortable were on the 04.00 (Mondays only) train, which was not advertised, but ran non-stop from Waterloo to Portsmouth. Unfortunately it was in the platform for some time and returning liberty men, converging on London, made their way to this train, boarded it, and went to sleep, occupying anything from two to four seats. Londoners, arriving by all-night buses, had the unenviable task of deciding whom to wake up and ask to make room. But, even on this most uncivilised train, there were moments of pleasure if one should be awake, as, shortly after dawn, the South Downs came into view. The Portsmouth line must have been a hard one for the steam locomotive driver, but it has always been most pleasant for the passenger.

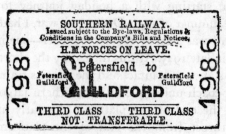

25 August 1945

13 January 1946

8

The Railway to Southampton

As an objective for a railway from London, Southampton had more in common with Dover than with Brighton, for its attraction depended on its role as a port rather than as a final destination. But, in contrast to both the other towns, the initial drive for a railway came from the provincial terminal and not from London. Plans for the line were announced at a public meeting in 1831 and, in 1834, the London & Southampton Railway was authorised by Parliament. This compares with dates of authorising Acts of 1836 for the line to Dover and 1837 for the Brighton line. But being first off the mark did not make the Southampton company correspondingly early in completing their line. A combination of distance, engineering and management problems prevented the completion of the line until 1840, only one year before the Brighton. But, having reached Southampton, the company was as successful as the Brighton in keeping out any competition. There was nothing in LSWR country comparable to the LCDR invasion of the SER territory. All attempts at reaching Southampton, most of which directly or indirectly involved the Great Western Railway, were frustrated, although one rival did get as far as building earthworks in the town.

The early history of the railway to Southampton has been recently told by Mr R. A. Williams in his book *The London & South Western Railway*, Volume One, so the present account will be concentrated on more recent developments. A town the size of Southampton would not itself have generated enough traffic to support a railway with an authorised capital of £1½ million, and this is reflected in the reliance of the promoters on traffic fed on to the line by sea or by land transport from other places. In a speech at Southampton town hall in 1831, Colonel Henderson, who later became the first chairman, enumerated traffics which would reach the railway via the port. He looked forward to freight coming on to the line from many parts of the world, varying from the comparatively local Irish and French traffic to that from North and South America. For passenger and freight traffic from Southampton itself, and from other places linked by road to stations on the line, a considerable catchment area was assumed. Traffic from Weymouth and Portsmouth was expected to reach Southampton by sea or land; that from Andover, Salisbury and the West would use the stations at Micheldever (then Andover Road) or Basingstoke, and that from Guildford would come on at Woking. The list of places where deposits on shares could be paid is of interest in that they are all on or within the catchment area of the line, with the notable exception of Liverpool. At this stage, the title of the company was 'Southampton, London and Branch Railway and Dock Company'. This reflected three aspects of policy. First, realising that seaborne traffic was essential for prosperity, the company intended to construct docks; in the event, this function was delegated to the associated Southampton Dock company. Second, the branch was to connect Basingstoke with Bristol, but Parliament decided that the western seaport would be better served by the Great Western Railway. Thirdly, the placing of Southampton before London indicated the original source of promotion, although by the time construction was under way, meetings were usually held in London.

The economic resemblance of the Dover and Southampton railways, both being lines to ports, has already been noted, but they were also similar in some other respects. For instance, neither of them followed the most direct route. The Dover line, instead of taking the traditional route of the Dover road through North Kent, passed through the Weald and, as explained in Chapter 1, this decision was influenced by the attractions of Brighton. In fact, the two railways did share the same line as far

as Redhill. This situation might have repeated itself, with Southampton and Bristol corresponding to Brighton and Dover. The
first survey for the Southampton line was made in 1830 by a
well-known local engineer, John Doswell Doswell. His London
terminal would have been in the Paddington area. Doswell, however, had no experience of railway construction, and it was
decided to appoint instead Francis Giles. He felt that it was quite
unnecessary to incur the cost of a terminal north of the Thames,
and persuaded the promoters to select a site at Nine Elms,
Battersea, from which London could easily be reached by steam-
boat or road. He surveyed both the traditional route via Guildford, Farnham and Alton and also an alternative line via Basingstoke. The latter was more roundabout but, as explained above,
Basingstoke was a convenient point for a junction for Bristol.
Incidentally, the country between Weybridge and Basingstoke
was familiar to Giles, as he was engineer to the Basingstoke Canal
company. So, just as Palmer was responsible for the original plans
for an indirect route to Dover, so Giles produced the plans for the
route to Southampton via Basingstoke. It will be remembered
that Palmer was incapacitated by illness, and was replaced by
Cubitt as chief engineer of the Dover line before construction
commenced. Deviations in the original line approved by Parliament were authorised for both the Dover and Southampton lines,
these being carried out by Cubitt for the former line and Joseph
Locke for the latter. However, whereas Palmer was prevented
from carrying out his plans by illness, Giles was dismissed. There
was dissatisfaction with almost all the aspects of the construction
work, but especially with the rate of progress. This culminated
in a virtual ultimatum from the Lancashire shareholders and the
replacement of Giles by Locke. Deviations decided on at this
time included a swing to the north west to avoid high ground at
Trinleys Wood near Popham. This was slightly less direct, but
maintained an acceptable gradient while replacing one tunnel,
over a mile long, by three tunnels with a total length of about
three eighths of a mile. The existing contractors between the
river Wey, east of Woking and Basingstoke, continued, as did
McIntosh between Winchester and Southampton. But the crucial

section between Basingstoke and Winchester, which involved a
great deal of earthworks, was awarded to Thomas Brassey, who
was to be so frequently associated with Locke in building railways. Construction proceeded more rapidly, but it was May 1840
before the whole of the line was opened, nearly six years after the
work had started.

Nevertheless, some revenue was earned from May 1838 when
the line was brought into use from Nine Elms as far as Woking,
with a road connection to Guildford. In the following September,
a further fifteen and a half miles were opened to Winchfield,
where the station was less than a mile from one of the main roads
to the south and west (the present A30). Until June 1839, Winchfield enjoyed a period of importance as a railhead with numerous
road coaches waiting to take passengers on to their destinations
but, in that month, another eight miles of line was opened, and
Basingstoke became the terminal. On the same day, the railway
was opened between Winchester and Southampton. However,
pending the settlement of a dispute with the Northam bridge
company, trains stopped at a temporary terminus, north of the
approach road to the river bridge, on the site of the present
Northam junction. The bridge company was finally 'bought off'
by an undertaking to substitute a bridge over the railway for a
level-crossing, and trains first reached the terminal station at
Southampton on 11 May, 1840. On the same day, the eighteen
and three-quarter miles of line from Basingstoke to Winchester
was opened, and the line was complete. The policy for intermediate stations was similar to that prevailing on so many main
lines at the present time—that is, to provide very few, leaving
road transport to feed traffic on to the railway. For instance, there
were only five intermediate stations on the 54¾ miles between
Woking and Southampton, at Farnborough (for Farnham),
Winchfield, Basingstoke, Micheldever (then called Andover
Road) and Winchester. Additional intermediate stations have
been added on most parts of the line except between Basingstoke
and Winchester, where Micheldever remains the only station on
an 18¾-mile section.

As well as new stations, a number of important lines of railway

40 Micheldever in transition. The original station building is on the right; the corrugated iron lamp room and the house on the same side have now been demolished. The original down platform is shown in its new form as an island platform. The down platform and building of 1904 which appears on the left has been removed; the outside loop tracks had gone before this photograph was taken on 10 May 1970

41 Shawford Junction with the Didcot, Newbury and Southampton line coming in on the right. The third down relief track was opened for war-time traffic in 1943. The line to Newbury has now been lifted and the down relief track is now connected to the main line. Rebuilt Merchant Navy class No. 35017 'Belgian Marine' built at Eastleigh in 1945 was passing on a down express on 10 July 1965

42 The erecting shop of Eastleigh Works in steam days. On the left a Southern rebuilt light Pacific, a BR standard 4–6–0 and an unrebuilt Pacific are receiving attention. A BR 2–6–4 tank locomotive is at the end of the shop. Eastleigh was still carrying out heavy repairs when this photograph was taken on 18 April 1964

were built to feed traffic on to the main line. However, the first
major development took place in 1842 when the dock company
opened its Outer Dock, now the Princess Alexandra Dock. The
LSWR extended its line of communication beyond Southampton
by association with the New South Western Steam Packet Company which linked Southampton to Le Havre and with the railway opened from Le Havre to Paris in 1843. At Southampton,
rails were extended across the present Canute Road and boat
trains taken as near as possible to the ships. (The Outer Dock was
one of the first to have railway lines on quays handling passenger
traffic.) Subsequent extensions to the port railway system will be
mentioned later. Another important development of 1842 was
the opening of the branch to Gosport which, until 1847, provided
the only railway route to Portsmouth.[1] In 1845 a branch line to
Guildford was opened. Guildford became a nodal point on the
Reading, Guildford & Reigate line[2] and its branch line became
the first section of the Direct route to Portsmouth.[3] Two important railways were added in 1847. First, the Southampton &
Dorchester Railway was opened from its junction about half a
mile north of the Southampton terminus, through Ringwood
and Wareham. The terminal at Dorchester was sited with a view
to extension to Exeter and the West but, in the event, the limit
was reached in 1857 when trains were extended by means of
running powers over the Great Western to Weymouth. Second,
the LSWR opened a branch to Salisbury from the junction station
at Bishopstoke. (This had been opened to serve the Gosport
branch; it was re-named Eastleigh and Bishopstoke in 1889.) In
1848 the broad gauge Great Western line from Reading reached
Basingstoke. Financial difficulties then checked new construction until, in 1854, a line was opened from Battledown junction,
just over three miles west of Basingstoke, to Andover. This,
rather than the Dorchester route, led the LSWR to the West,
reaching Salisbury in 1857 and Exeter in 1860. An interesting
development of 1865 was the completion of the Mid Hants Railway, filling the gap in the network between Alton, on the end of
a branch from Guildford, and the Southampton main line just
over two miles north of Winchester.[4] While it was necessary to

run via Guildford, this was hardly a reasonable alternative route for London to Southampton trains, but in 1870 a new line was opened, primarily to serve the fast growing military town of Aldershot, direct from the main line at Pirbright junction about a mile and a half west of Brookwood, to Farnham junction on the Guildford to Alton line.[5] This provided a shorter route between London and Southampton than the main line but, as it included steep gradients and single track, apart from the occasional diverted express, only stopping trains used the Mid Hants route. In 1866 a branch was opened from St Denys (then Portswood) to Netley which, in 1889, was extended to Fareham. Over the years, this became increasingly important for cross-country trains.[6]

So far, although three of the lines (the Southampton & Dorchester, the Mid Hants and the Southampton & Netley) had been constructed by independent companies, they had all fallen into the LSWR net. In 1882 the Didcot, Newbury & Southampton Railway was authorised to complete its line to a terminus near the Royal Pier. It connected with the Great Western at Didcot and at Newbury and the way seemed to be open for the Great Western to break the LSWR monopoly of Southampton traffic. But, despite considerable support from the town for a second railway, the LSWR and GWR reached an agreement after which the GWR withdrew its support for the DNSR extension to Southampton. Instead, the DNSR constructed a link between its line which, by 1885, had reached as far south as Winchester, and the LSWR main line at Shawford. By this route, GWR coaches, hauled by LSWR locomotives, first reached Southampton. In 1901, a branch which brought very little traffic to the main line was opened from Basingstoke to Alton.[7] The comparative unimportance of the DNSR and the Basingstoke and Alton lines is indicated by the fact that, unlike the other lines mentioned, they have been closed. (At the present time, the Mid Hants line is threatened.) There have been other short branches from the Southampton railway, but none of them has carried a regular passenger service. As far as the provision of tracks is concerned, the line reached its point of maximum development in 1904, by which time four tracks were provided from London to Worting Junction about two and a quarter miles west of Basingstoke.

Subsequently, the capacity of the line has been increased by signalling improvements and electrification. A most advanced system of semi-automatic control, with both points and sema-phore signals moved by compressed air released by electrically controlled valves, was introduced as far west as Basingstoke when the line was quadrupled. Farther down the line, intermediate signals were introduced to increase the carrying capacity and, although some of the manually operated boxes were closed, these were later replaced by remotely controlled or automatic inter-mediate signals. Since 1966, most of the line between Woking and Southampton has been controlled by the power boxes at Basingstoke and Eastleigh, using electricity to operate both points and coloured light signals.

There has been a great improvement in both the frequency and speed of the passenger services since 1840. In that year, the best train of the day took 3 hours to get from Nine Elms to South-ampton. Dramatic improvements followed and, by 1847, one train was covering the seventy-six miles from Nine Elms to Southampton in 1 hour 45 minutes, at an average speed of 43.4 m.p.h., including a Basingstoke stop. In 1848, the best journey time was extended to 2 hours but this was from Waterloo with stops at Farnborough (for Farnham), Basingstoke, Winchester and Bishopstoke (for Salisbury and Portsmouth). Unfortunately, the passage of time was not accompanied by further improve-ment and, in 1865, the best trains (the 11.00 a.m. and 3.10 p.m. from Waterloo) both took 2 hours 20 minutes. This may not represent so much deterioration as it seems, as there is no cer-tainty that the arrival times promised in 1848 were always achieved. By 1888, the principal Bournemouth expresses were avoiding the Southampton terminus, and the 12.30 p.m. down reached Southampton West in 1 hour 39 minutes and Bourne-mouth East in 2 hours 57 minutes. A 2-hour timing to Bourne-mouth was first achieved in the summer timetable for 1911, but these trains did not stop at Southampton which, nevertheless, could be reached in 1 hour 40 minutes. Speeds were reduced during the First World War but were more than restored by the 1930s. For instance, in 1935, the Bournemouth Limited, which had been introduced in 1929, having left London at 4.30, reached Bournemouth at 6.28. On 5 July 1931, an all-Pullman train named the Bournemouth Belle made its first journey, leaving Waterloo at 10.30 and making a stop at Southampton at 11.58. At first it ran daily only during the period when the summer timetable was in force, its winter runs being confined to the weekends. However, from 1 January 1936, it ran daily throughout the year until the Second World War brought about the withdrawal of Pullman trains. Its restoration in October 1946 was a welcome sign of the return to prewar standards. One prewar feature which was not restored was non-stop journeys to Bournemouth. By the autumn of 1946, schedules were approaching, but had not quite reached, prewar standards. For instance, the train which occupied the prewar Bournemouth Belle's path left Waterloo at 10.30, called at Southampton at 11.59 and reached Bournemouth Central at 12.43, thus taking 1 minute longer to reach Southampton and 5 more to Bournemouth. In 1951, to commemorate the Festival of Britain, an existing service was given the name Royal Wessex. There were minor variations in the timing but, for instance, in May 1961, coaches left Weymouth at 7.34 a.m. and Swanage at 7.38 a.m. to be joined together at Wareham. Calls were made at Poole, Bournemouth, Southampton and Winchester, reaching London at 10.50 a.m. After being taken out to Clapham Junction for cleaning, the stock returned from Waterloo at 4.35 p.m., reaching Southampton at 6.07 p.m., Swanage at 7.53 p.m. and Weymouth at 7.59 p.m. This was not, of course, the fastest train of the day as, by this time, 2-hour timings had been restored to Bournemouth. For instance, the 10.30 a.m. now reached Southampton in 1 hour 21 minutes and Bournemouth in 2 hours. In the early sixties, express steam working was at its zenith. In addition to the Bournemouth and Weymouth trains, Southampton had services to Bristol, Cardiff, Plymouth, Brighton, Manchester and York. Variety was added by the boat trains for the ocean liners and cross channel steamers. (The latter were moved from Southampton to Weymouth in 1964.) Some of the boat trains were named, such as The Cunarder (for Cunard lines), The Springbok (for the Union Castle line) and The Statesman (for United States line).

But the days of steam were drawing to a close and, in 1965, came the first decelerations to allow the work of electrification to Bournemouth to commence. At the same time, much of the track was re-laid and new signalling systems installed. By August 1966, 118 miles out of 209 of continuous welded track had been laid and 139 out of 236 miles of conductor rail. The first charging of conductor rails took place in December and, on the 14th, a trial run with an electric train reached Eastleigh. Public services as far down the line as Basingstoke began on 2 January 1967. Further extensions brought the live rail as far as Lymington Junction on 18 January, to Bournemouth Central on 6 March and, finally, to the carriage sidings near Bournemouth West on 28 March. From 3 April, while the existing timetable remained in force, most of the trains were electrically operated. (The first revenue-earning electric train to reach Southampton was a special from Folkestone Harbour carrying the crew of an Italian ship.) The new electric service began on 10 July 1967 and was far superior in both speed and frequency to anything in the past. On weekdays, eight trains made a non-stop journey to Southampton in 1 hour 10 minutes and reached Bournemouth in 1 hour 40 minutes. This was an 11-minute improvement on the best steam timing to Southampton and a 20-minute improvement to Bournemouth.

This acceleration depended on new trains, a considerable mileage of new electrified track and new signalling. Change of this order tended to erase many features of the steam railway which had served Southampton for the previous 127 years. However, even now much remains for those who care to look closely. When a contract for widening the line was let at the turn of the century, it was divided into three sections—Woking to Frimley, Frimley to Winchfield and Winchfield to Basingstoke. Each section has a distinctive character. Between Working and Frimley, the line climbs to a local summit near Deepcut and then drops into the valley of the Blackwater which separates Frimley

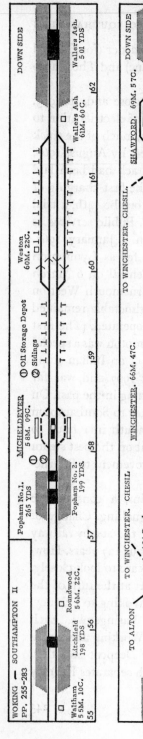
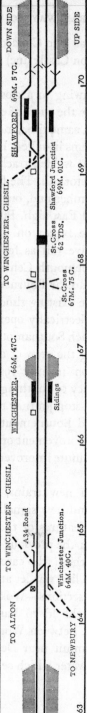

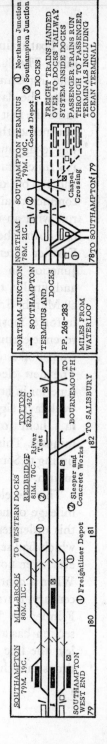

from Farnborough and also Surrey from Hampshire. Much of
the country consists of infertile, sandy heaths with much woodland and few farms. It is an area much used by the Army, Aldershot having grown up only about three miles south of the main
line. The gradient up to Deepcut summit varies between 1 in 298
and 1 in 326 and, to achieve this, considerable earthworks proved
necessary. Shortly after leaving Woking, the line enters Golds-
worth cutting, there is a long embankment past Pirbright and
this is followed by the cutting at Deepcut. Spoil from the two
cuttings provided most of the material for the three and a quarter
miles of Pirbright embankment, both during the original construction and the widening. All the widening was carried out on
the south side—that is, the down side—but, after seventy years,
the vegetation which has grown on each side of the line gives no
indication of difference in age. West of Brookwood, where the
embankment is about 40 feet high, the contractors for the widening found themselves in a quagmire. Spoil from the cuttings did
not provide sufficient filling and chalk was brought from the
LSWR quarry at Micheldever. Another problem was provided by
the Basingstoke Canal. This had been opened throughout in 1794
and the railway, having run to the south of it from Weybridge,
intersected it at Deepcut, where the canal turns sharply south to
follow the east side of the Blackwater valley. As the newcomer,
the railway had to construct a canal aqueduct over its original
double track. On widening to four tracks, a new four-arch brick
aqueduct was constructed, the canal being diverted through a
temporary aqueduct during the construction period.

Woking station was opened as a temporary terminus in 1838,
serving the near-by town of Guildford. Woking itself was a small
village about a mile and a half from the station. At first the 1½-
mile gap was recognised by naming the station Woking Common but, in 1843, it became Woking. In 1845, when the branch
to Guildford was opened, it was re-named Woking Junction,
reverting to plain Woking again in 1913. The present station and
signal box was built by the Southern in 1936 in its best 'Odeon'
style. All the principal junctions on the way down from Waterloo had been made into either flying or burrowing junctions, but

Woking, despite the heavy traffic to and from the Portsmouth line, remained a flat junction. The new station consisted of up and down platforms, each with bays at the ends and a central island platform. The track was removed from the up bay in 1968 and its site has now been walled off from the station. West of the station on the north side of the line are extensive sidings used mainly by the civil engineer's department. In 1885 the LSWR obtained powers to construct what must be one of the longest footbridges on their system, crossing the sidings which were opened at this time, and also the main line. From it there is a good view looking back towards the station and the junction, and showing the way the present down local line diverges from the down through to avoid the old Junction signal box which went out of use in 1936.

Brookwood was opened in 1864 to serve the extensive cemetery opened by the London Necropolis company. It was the junction for two short branches, one to Bisley opened in 1890 and the other into the cemetery, which had been opened in 1854.[8] The original establishment was of a modest character and, about 1890, a new redbrick building was completed on the up side, partly to serve the settlement which had grown up on the opposite side of the line to the cemetery. When the line was quadrupled, as the station was on an embankment, widening was minimised; the original down platform was demolished and the through lines, which were in the centre were not provided with platforms. A new down platform, with shelter and waiting room, was constructed on the down local line. The work was carried out in 1903 and, at the same time, the buildings on the up side were enlarged, being adorned with gables somewhat Dutch in style, but surmounted by pediments. (These were characteristic of the LSWR at the time and are also to be found at Swaythling, Swanwick and other places.) The signal box was contemporary with the new down platform and, after electrically operated signalling was introduced at Woking in 1936, was the eastern limit of electro-pneumatic signalling. Both the branch lines have been demolished and, in 1961, the goods yard, with its capacious weatherboarded shed, was closed. However, being east of Pirbright junction, Brookwood has been served by the electric trains to Aldershot, Farnham and Alton since 1937 and has a good commuting traffic, which compensates for some decline in cemetery visitors.

Pirbright junction is about two miles beyond Brookwood, the flyover being constructed at the time of the widening and brought into use in 1903. There are good views of the Basingstoke Canal on the up side as far as Pirbright junction, beyond which Frimley cutting is entered, 1¾ miles long and reaching a depth of 50 feet. At the time of the widening, local inhabitants were fascinated by the steam navvies which, taking bites of 1¾ cubic yards, lifted the spoil in three stages, from terrace to terrace, to the top of the cutting. Altogether, 420,000 cubic yards was removed, mostly being used on the Pirbright embankment. Near the end of the cutting, the line passes under the Basingstoke Canal aqueduct. There are separate spans for each of the four tracks, all 48 yards in length and, in order to carry the considerable weight of water, of massive construction. During the Second World War, there were fears that a bomb might drop through the canal and penetrate one of the arches, thus emptying the entire contents of the canal from the top lock at Frimley to the next lock at Aldershot on to the railway. To prevent this, stop gates were installed to check the water at each end of the aqueduct.

Half a mile beyond, on the down side of the line, until the Bournemouth electrification, stood Sturt Lane Junction signal box. In addition to being a block post for the main line, Sturt Lane operated the two junctions which led to the Frimley and Ascot branch opened in 1878. East and West curves were provided so that trains could run straight on to the branch from either the up or down directions. In 1879 a single-track link line was constructed from Frimley junction, where the two curves divided, running straight under the main line to join the Pirbright junction to Farnham junction route at Ash Vale. When the Reading route was electrified in 1939, this single line was also electrified, together with the east and west curves and the two local tracks of the main line as far as Sturt Lane junction.

Occasionally use was made of the Frimley east curve by electric trains. The provision of the live rail on the west curve, and on the main line as far as its junction with the west curve, was presumably a precaution in case an electric train was diverted on to the wrong track by the Frimley or Sturt Lane signalman. Both junctions were severed when Sturt Lane box was put out of use, although, in 1971, rusting track survived on both curves. Just beyond the site of the junction with the Western curve, the main line crosses the river Blackwater and trains leave Surrey for Hampshire.

Almost immediately, we cross the Reading, Guildford & Reigate Railway of 1849 which was operated and later owned by the South Eastern. Its directors entertained high hopes of LSWR trains being diverted from its own main line at this point, to run over the RGRR to Reading, and this accounts for the embankment which would have carried trains between the two lines. However, in 1856, the LSWR extended its line from Ascot to join the RGRR at Wokingham, thus reaching Reading with far less use of 'foreign' rails.[9] Although the spur at Farnborough carried a siding for many years, it was never used for the desired service to Reading. Having crossed the valley of the Blackwater, we enter a cutting and, beyond Farnborough station, run out on to an embankment. Geologically the Frimley to Winchfield section is similar to that from Woking to Frimley, consisting of sands, gravels and clays of the Barton and Bracklesham Beds. Scenically, however, it is less undulating and, although there is a great deal of woodland and rough country, the proportion of farmland is slightly greater. For most of this section, the line is level and, although much of it is in cuttings or on embankments, these are shallower or lower than those east of Farnborough. The whole of the section of about six miles was widened on the south side to take four tracks, the work being completed by the summer of 1904. The stations at Farnborough and Fleet both underwent rebuilding. At Farnborough this amounted to the construction of a new station. The old down platform was abandoned and a new platform and buildings constructed on the down local line. Because the old platform was left in position, there was a perceptible curve in the two new lines, which passed behind it, and this is visible at each end of the station. Whereas at Brookwood the buildings on the up side were enlarged, at Farnborough they were demolished and replaced by new shelters and waiting rooms. The only access for passengers was by a footbridge which was provided with a roof. The work was completed by 1904—probably in 1903—by which time Farnborough had developed far beyond its original role of the station for Farnham. It was already a dormitory district for both Aldershot and London and was to acquire increasing importance as its balloon factory developed into the Royal Aircraft Establishment. The RAE has its own power station which was, for many years, coal-fired, and until 1968 the establishment was served by a short branch line.[10] Another special facility at Farnborough was a long and wide platform in the goods yards for use in connection with troop movements. The main station buildings are not quite typical of the LSWR contemporary style. They lack dwarf pediments but include other features such as small dormer windows and a strange, louvred spirelet. A number of minor changes were made at the time of the electrification. The signal box which, like other boxes between Woking and Worting junction, was contemporary with the widening and the electro-pneumatic signalling, was put out of use in November 1966 and subsequently demolished. At the same time, new concrete posts with electric lights replaced the gas lamps with their spiralled columns and prewar station name signs. In 1969 the footbridge lost its roof.

Two and a half miles down the line is an interesting survival consisting of two disused platforms on the up and down local lines. These were opened mainly for the convenience of Bramshot Golf Club and, although, before the rise of the motor car, golf halts were not uncommon, few were situated on main lines. Probably it was acceptable to the operating department as stopping trains there did not impede the express traffic on the through line. The 1934 Appendix to the Working Timetable contains instructions to the Woking station master to ascertain if, on any trains shown to call at Bramshot, there are passengers who wish to alight, otherwise the trains need not stop. The halt

was not officially closed until May 1946, and the continued existence of the platforms presumably indicates that there is no
reason to incur the expense of demolishing them. The station at
Fleet was opened as Fleet Pond in 1847, receiving its present
name in 1869. The railway crosses the pond on a causeway. At
the time of the widening, although part of the pond was filled in,
there were difficulties in expanding the station site so the old
down platform was abolished and the new lines run straight
through as at Brookwood. Fleet signal box did not last until the
resignalling scheme which accompanied electrification, but was
abolished in February 1960. In 1966, instead of receiving a facelift, the 1903 buildings at Fleet were demolished and replaced by
somewhat austere but functional modern buildings. The 1903
footbridge survived, but lost its roof. The goods yard was closed
in 1969. In addition to its station car park, Fleet, in common with
some other stations in the area, had a large cycle shed for the use
of commuters, on the down platform. (The station entrance was
on the down side; it was necessary to ascend to the footbridge to
reach the up platform.) On the up side, a short distance west of
the station, there is evidence of the site of the pump house which
provided air for the electro-pneumatic signal system. Basically,
this consisted of an air line which stretched from Brookwood to
Worting junction, with reservoirs at various intermediate points
to maintain an approximately uniform pressure throughout.
Electrically operated servo mechanisms worked valves which
admitted the air to cylinders, thus operating the signals and
points. The points were all operated from signal boxes, but some
of the signals between stations were operated automatically by
the trains. The original pump was worked by a steam engine and
there were usually a few coal wagons in the small siding which
adjoined the pump house. In the late fifties, the decision was
taken to refurbish the electro-pneumatic system and the steam
engine was replaced by an electric motor. At the same time, considerable lengths of the air line were renewed. The rejuvenated
system only lasted until 1966 when the familiar semaphore
signals which, in a number of cases were still lower quadrant,
were replaced by coloured lights, while remotely controlled

electric motors worked all the points. The new signal box at Basingstoke controlled the line as far as Farnborough, although most of the signals were operated automatically by the trains.

Beyond Fleet, the line passes Railroad Heath which, in the spring, provides a show of rhododendrons which generations of train crews and passengers have enjoyed. A long embankment marks the beginning of an ascent at 1 in 337 to the cutting through Shapley Heath, beyond Winchfield station. As explained above, when the line was under construction Winchfield had a period of importance as a temporary railhead. A small settlement, including the inevitable inn, was based on the station. Until the station at Hook was opened in 1883 and reduced its catchment area, Winchfield drew on a number of places, including the small town of Odiham. When the widening came, the arrangement was similar to that at Farnborough, with the new lines swinging round the back of the old down platform which was abandoned but not demolished until the beginning of 1972. An expanding area like Farnborough was felt to justify a new station, but at Winchfield, the new buildings were confined to the new platform on the down local line. The electrification period brought the usual changes, both the goods yard and the signal box being closed in 1966, although the yard was re-opened temporarily in 1970 for stone deliveries for the M3 motorway. There is little to remind the passenger of the animated scenes of 1838, with the station yard crowded with stage coaches bound for the West Country.

The third section of the widening contract included Winchfield and extended to Basingstoke. Again, the scenery is slightly different from that of either of the two previous sections. London Clay country is entered at Winchfield and, in a cutting near Basing, the first exposure of chalk is visible. (From this point as far as Shawford, south of Winchester, the line traverses chalk country.) Immediately beyond Winchfield station, the line enters a cutting about three quarters of a mile long and of considerable depth. Before the widening, a section towards the western end consisted of a short tunnel crossed by a local road, as an alternative to a high skewed bridge. (A similar short tunnel survives south of Winchester.) However, rather than construct a second bore, at the widening the tunnel was opened out, the road being carried on a skew bridge with a metal span 50 feet above rail level. Beyond the end of the cutting the line runs on an embankment across the valley of the river Whitewater, to Hook station. The embankment was constructed of clay and on 27 December 1960, a slip occurred east of the station which removed much of the original embankment and weakened the earthwork on the south side added for the widening. Fortunately trains were stopped in time, but the main line was closed completely until 3 January 1961 when the down local track was re-opened. Successive restoration then took place, working from south to north —the down through on 24 January, the up through on 8 February and the up local on 13 February.

Hook station was opened in 1883, serving both an adjacent village and also part of the catchment area of Winchfield station. The evolution and devolution of the station buildings, signal box and goods yard at Hook is similar to that at Winchfield. Much of the main line to Southampton passed through rural areas and industrial private sidings were few. One was located on the down side near the end of the cutting beyond Hook, at Newnham. It served a brick yard, the points being operated by a ground frame released from the signal box at Hook. The general upward tendency of the gradient is broken twice, at the crossing of the Lyde and again at the Loddon. These are minor streams passing under the railway embankment in culverts. A long chalk cutting, which has been widened to contain carriage sidings, leads into the important junction of Basingstoke, 47¾ miles from Waterloo. As explained in the historical summary, the GWR broad gauge line reached here in 1848, but there was no physical junction until mixed gauge track was provided in 1856. The Great Western maintained a complete establishment, including a two-platform terminal station, signal box, locomotive shed and goods yard until 1 January 1932. At this time the station was transferred to the Southern, who incorporated the southern of the platforms into their station. From an operating point of view, it became a bay at the back of the up local line platform. The northern GWR

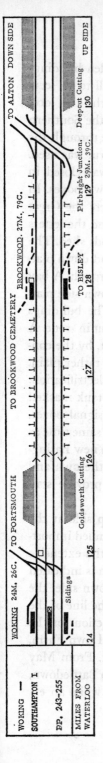
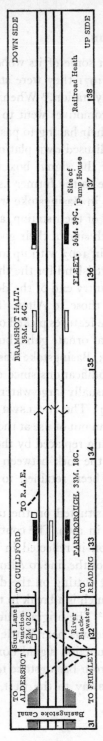
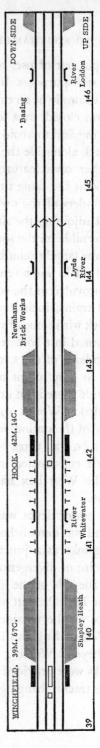
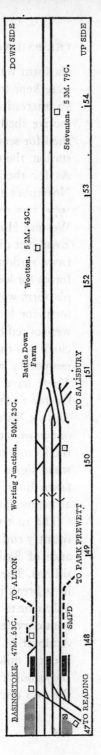

platform was put out of use, but some of its wooden buildings were kept for staff purposes. In 1971 they were still to be seen, an interesting example of an early station.[11] When the GWR locomotive shed was closed, GWR locomotives went to the Southern shed for servicing and to avoid their having to pass through the station, the track alongside the disused GWR platform was used. As for the other GWR features, the signal box was closed in November 1966 at the same time as the former LSWR boxes. In 1971, two reminders of the GWR in Basingstoke were the Great Western Hotel adjoining the site of their station, and the letters 'GWR' just discernible on the south side of their goods shed. The LSWR station was largely rebuilt in 1903 with up and down platforms for local tracks and a centre island for the through. A bay platform was provided at the country end of the down side platform for local trains, including those to Alton. The buildings were of red brick with some of the features picked out in stone. A clock was mounted in a somewhat ornate gable but, by the contemporary standards of the LSWR, Basingstoke was rather plain. There have been only minor modifications since electrification. On the down side there is an unusually large water tank marked 'L&SWR Wimbledon Works, 1904'. The two LSWR signal boxes, one at each end of the station, went out of use at the same time as the former GWR box, all three being replaced by the new Basingstoke signal box constructed in the fork between the GWR and LSWR lines. The West box has been retained to provide staff accommodation.

The motive power depot was situated on the up side at the country end and was demolished in 1969. The continued importance of Basingstoke as a junction is reflected in the extensive sidings. The point of divergence of the line to Alton is indicated by a break in the side of the low cutting on the down side; the only clue to the Park Prewett branch is a break in the line of the boundary fence on the up side.[12] The original junction for the Andover & West of England line was near Battle Down Farm, about a mile beyond Worting Junction signal box. From May 1897, four tracks were provided from Basingstoke to Battledown, the two centre tracks swinging away to the west, while an ex-

43 Southampton Terminus viewed from the Central Bridge about 1901. (This compares with the Ordnance Survey Map of 1910.) The hotel of 1872 and the platforms and train shed are shown before alterations and additions, but the station buildings of 1840 appear on the right in their original form. Details of interest include 4-wheeled oil lit coaches and semaphore signal arms working in slotted posts

44 Southampton Terminus viewed from the Central Bridge in 1957. This shows the station and hotel in their final form. On the left are former Southern Railway coaches in the first BR main line livery of plum and spilt milk. The train on the right is for Newbury and consists of Great Western coaches hauled by No. 3717 'City of Truro' built at Swindon Works in 1903. The vessels in the docks are the *Queen Mary* and the *Mauretania*

45 Looking to the past. Outside porter and ticket collector on the up platform about 1900, before Northam was rebuilt. The outside porter carries his numbered badge, supplied by the company, on his right arm; the ticket collector wears the button hole traditionally worn by ticket collectors. In the background is a semaphore arm marked 'Engine Shed' which refers to the old Northam M.P.D., a semaphore arm in a slotted post with a separate spectacle plate and, under the archway, the old Northam Junction Signal Box

46 Looking to the future. A view from a down train leaving Farnborough showing imminent change. The gas lamps, with their metal posts, are about to be replaced by electricity and concrete. The electro-pneumatic signals with their signal box and gantry are about to be replaced by colour light signals on a concrete bracket. The third rail was in position but not live when this photograph was taken on 27 August 1966

tension of the up local crossed over them on a flyover. High speed crossovers were provided at Worting, so so that the speed limit on Bournemouth expresses changing between the through and local lines was as high as 65 m.p.h. The signal box at Battledown was closed about 1912 but was not finally demolished until 1925. From here to Shawford, beyond Winchester, for most of the way, only two tracks are provided. The extent of the earthworks through the high chalk country, together with four tunnels, would have made widening extremely costly, although at one time, the LSWR contemplated quadruple track right through to Southampton. While this formidably expensive operation failed to materialise, the capacity of the line was increased by the provision of extra signal boxes. This was made more necessary as, in the 18¾ miles from Basingstoke to Winchester, there was only one intermediate station. With block working, there can be only one train on the line between each pair of boxes but, at one time, there were twelve boxes between Basingstoke and Winchester. While some of them, such as that at Micheldever, had normal lever frames associated with fairly complex track layouts, others, such as Steventon, looked like platelayers' huts and controlled only distant and stop semaphore signals on each track. In the economy drive of the early thirties, two of the boxes were abolished—Worthy between Winchester and Winchester junction and Wallers Ash West, in the cutting south of Wallers Ash tunnel, both in June 1932. Faced with a steady climb at 1 in 252 from Winchester up to the summit of the line at Litchfield tunnel, up steam trains were appreciably slower than down and, to get more trains on the up line, automatic colour lights were installed at various points in June 1936, ready for the summer timetable. (At Worthy and Wallers Ash West replacing the intermediate signal boxes, at Warren south of Micheldever and Popham to its north. Winklebury signal box between Worting junction and Basingstoke had been replaced by intermediate signals in March 1932.) All the remaining signal boxes between Winchester junction and Basingstoke were abolished during the electrification period—Steventon and Roundwood in July 1966 and Worting, Wootton, Waltham, Micheldever, Weston and

Wallers Ash in November 1966, the latter group showing a remarkable preponderance of initial letter Ws. Winchester junction
was retained for operating the Mid Hants line.

As indicated by the lack of stations, this high chalk country is
not thickly populated. The alternation of embankments and
cuttings gives views over an ordered but beautiful countryside
interspersed with glimpses of the chalk which lies beneath it.
The angle of slope of the sides of the earthworks gives some indication of variations in the character of the chalk, that at Micheldever being unusually hard. Its strength is reflected in the cutting
sides between the two short tunnels at Popham, north of Micheldever, which are almost vertical. The LSWR purchased land at
Micheldever and a large pit was opened on the down side. This
provided chalk for a number of earthworks, including the widening near Brookwood, but the largest amount going to one place
went for filling for the New Docks in Southampton in the late
1920s and early 1930s. The bottom of the enormous pit has been
used for two main purposes. During the Second World War, part
was used as an oil terminal serving underground storage tanks.
But most of the space was used to relieve pressure from Eastleigh. During the war, freight trains were staged through Micheldever but, in the postwar years, the extensive sidings have been
filled mainly with carriage and wagon stock awaiting transit to
Eastleigh Works for repair or demolition. (As late as 1971, two
coaches from the Bournemouth Belle, withdrawn in 1967, were
still standing in the sidings.) The station itself is one of the most
interesting on the line, being opened as 'Andover Road' in 1840.
It consisted of a plain, flint building, rectangular in plan. Yellow
bricks were used for the corners, windows and doors, with stone
for the sills and keystones of the windows, and a slated roof. It
was surrounded on all four sides by a canopy supported by plain
iron columns. After 1854, Andover acquired its own station and,
in 1856, Andover Road became Micheldever, but for many years
it continued to handle mail traffic. (A sub-Post Office survived on
the premises until 1932.) Nevertheless, there were none of the
dramatic traffic increases which occasioned the rebuilding of such

stations as Woking or Southampton West and the original building of 1840 remains almost unchanged.

However, in 1904, the station underwent an operation very
similar to that carried out to Farnborough, Winchfield and
Hook. The two tracks were replaced by four, a new down platform was opened, and the original down platform became disused. Its surface and brick face was still discernible in the 1920s,
but by the 1950s it resembled little more than a grassy hump. It
is difficult to account for the rebuilding in 1904, except as pre-
paration for quadrupling to Southampton, using a site which had
already been cleared to obtain chalk for the widening to Basingstoke. In April 1966 the loop roads and both the original up
platform and the new down platform were closed, all trains using
the through roads and the old down platform, which had been
restored as an island platform with a simple shelter. Access was
by the subway, constructed at the same time as the loops, and
the usual facilities were retained in the original buildings. At the
end of 1971, work commenced on demolishing the new down
platform whose modest buildings bore a strong resemblance to
those in a similar position at, for instance, Winchfield, and also
the large water tank which was at the top of the cutting on the up
side.

About two miles south of Micheldever, the long embankment
above the hamlet of Weston Colley was widened with chalk,
almost certainly from Micheldever, the work being completed in
1902. While there is no obvious reason for the rebuilding at
Micheldever, the widening from Weston signal box to Wallers
Ash East (later Wallers Ash signal box) provided loops long
enough to contain freight trains, this being the only point at
which they could be overtaken between Eastleigh and Basingstoke. The usefulness of the loops was sufficient to justify their
electrification in 1966. After passing through Wallers Ash tunnel
which, with a length of 501 yards, is the longest on the Southampton line, the next point of interest is Winchester junction.
This somewhat remote spot was selected as the western end of the
Mid Hants Railways when it was opened in 1865.[13] Near by, the
Didcot, Newbury & Southampton line passed obliquely under

the LSWR and, in 1943, a spur was completed, facing Southampton, enabling northbound trains to diverge on to the DNSR at
this point. During the remaining years of the war, traffic was so
heavy as to preclude the use of the main line as far as possible,
but it is possible that, by the early 1950s the spur would have
been brought into general use, thus enabling the DNSR route
through Winchester Chesil to be closed. Instead, the spur was
put out of use in December 1951 and, in August 1964, the DNSR
main line was closed as a through route. Winchester junction
ceased to be a block post in November 1966 but remains open to
control the single line working over the Mid Hants line. As with
some other railway outposts, the company provided cottages for
the staff near the signal box, but these were demolished about
1968. Just south of Winchester junction is the newest underbridge on the line, moved into position in October 1968. It is a
single span of reinforced concrete carrying the line over a new
dual carriage road, linking the A33 to the A34.

When the Southampton line was opened, it was suggested that
its only traffic would be parsons and prawns, the clerical traffic
originating mainly in Winchester. This was a hostile prediction,
although Winchester has always been one of the principal intermediate stations. At this point, the line descends to the Itchen
valley, passing to the west of the city in a deep chalk cutting.
Winchester station was opened in 1839 at a point where the line
emerges from the cutting to cross a tributary valley. The original
building, typical of the design of Sir William Tite, survives on
the down side. Original features, such as the pilasters and stucco
finish, are still discernible, but buildings have been added on
either side and the front is obscured by a canopy surmounted by
a large clock case. From 1949 the station was renamed Winchester City to distinguish it from the slightly obscure former
GWR establishment on the opposite side of the town. However,
this finally closed to passengers in September 1961 and, after a
respectful pause, in 1967 Winchester City became Winchester
again. As with many stations, development has been followed by
retraction. For instance, the goods yard was extended up the side
of the valley at right angles to the main line and even had its

own engine shed. This modest establishment was not much larger than a private motor car garage but, from Monday night to Friday night, it accommodated the small shunting engines which used to come from Eastleigh to act as Winchester pilot. Their main duties were shunting the yard and attaching or detaching the occasional van from a main line train. After a slightly susprising penetration by an SECR P class tank locomotive in 1950, this duty fell exclusively to the LSWR B4 class. Their monopoly was proclaimed by a painted notice on the underbridge leading into the yard, stating that it was to be crossed only by B4 class tank locomotives or—a sign of things to come—a 294 HP diesel. The anticipated event took place in October 1963 and, in December, one of the regular performers, no. 30096, was sold to operate a private siding in Southampton. The diesels lasted until January 1969 when Winchester goods depot was closed; by November 1970 apart from some sidings retained for operating purposes, all the goods lines had been removed. The passenger station, however, has undergone improvements especially on the down side where the booking office is situated and a refreshment room is still provided. The platforms were lengthened in 1965 to take the twelve-car electric trains. A new signal box had been opened in 1960, as the old one was falling down and, although out of use since November 1966, this is retained for staff accommodation.

Virtually the whole route from Woking is either in cutting or embanked, so it is not surprising that, for many years, the first level-crossing to be reached was at St Cross, a southern suburb of Winchester, just over sixty-seven miles from Waterloo. Although only serving a very minor road, its existence brought about the retention of St Cross signal box merely to control the crossing gates, until 1969, when the crossing was replaced by a footbridge. Reference has already been made to St Cross tunnel (62 yards) which is essentially a substitute for a skewed overbridge. Sixty-nine miles from Waterloo is the site of Shawford junction, now marked by a break in the down side of the cutting and the commencement of a down relief track. As explained above, the LSWR were able to stave off the threat of an alternative route to

Southampton by linking the DNSR at Winchester to the LSWR main line at Shawford. The link was short, but included an impressive brick viaduct of twenty-three arches across the Itchen valley. There was little traffic originating on its line, so the only hope for the DNSR was the development of through traffic and, during both wars—but particularly during the Second World War—it carried great quantities. After the war, traffic declined, closure to passengers coming in 1960 and to all traffic in 1964. The southern end as far as Winchester stayed open until 1966.

The next station south of the junction is Shawford, opened in 1882. Most of the original station sites were at transition points between bank and cutting, but the later additions were sited with less regard for structural convenience. The main buildings for Shawford are sited at ground level on the up side of an embankment, the platforms being reached by stairs leading up from a subway. The architectural features include gables, slightly Dutch in style, and rather strange projections from the roof, looking like shrunken dormer windows, but containing louvres. The materials are red brick and tiles and the building is closely related to the other stations of its period, including Brookwood and Swaythling. Wooden shelters and canopies were provided on both platforms but, at the end of 1971, those on the down platform were replaced by a bus-type shelter. The goods yard, which was on the up side at the country end, was closed in July 1960, but the wooden transit shed has survived in non-railway use. The early thirties have already been mentioned as the date of certain economies, and the signal boxes at Shawford station and Otterbourne were both closed in March 1931 and replaced by intermediate signals. At the same time, the line was quadrupled from Eastleigh to a point just south of Shawford station. During the great build-up of traffic on the DNSR before the invasion of Europe, considerable delays were experienced waiting to get on to the main line at Shawford junction. To overcome this, a new track was opened from Shawford junction, passing at the back of the down platform of Shawford station and joining the down relief road just beyond it. There was no access to this new connection from the main line, and its use declined with that of the

DNSR. However, in November 1966, when Shawford Junction
signal box was demolished, this wartime link was made accessible from the main line, and a platform was added at Shawford
so that stopping passenger trains might use it. This was a concrete
erection, linked to the existing platform on the down main line.
Beyond Shawford, the line enters a chalk cutting and then runs
out on to an embankment, with good views of the abandoned
Itchen Navigation on the down side. On the up side, up to the
February of 1969, a private siding supplied the water-pumping
station at Otterbourne with coal. From then, the coal was delivered by road, until, in July 1971, the fires were let down and
the massive steam pumps were stopped for good.

Eastleigh is a challenge to any railway commentator for it
merits a book on its own, and any selection of features is inevitably arbitrary. As mentioned above, Eastleigh became the junction for Gosport in 1841 and for Salisbury in 1847. In addition to
being an operating centre, it became important for manufacturing, the LSWR carriage and wagon works being moved down from
Nine Elms in 1889 and the locomotive works in 1909. In one
sense, places like Woking are creations of the railway, as they
could not exist without a railway service to take their bread-
winners to work in London, but Eastleigh was a railway town in
a more specific sense as, until the 1960s, most of its employed
population worked for the railway. With the running down of
the works and a decline in the number of the operating staff,
accompanied by an expansion of alternative employment, this is
no longer the case, but Eastleigh, even more than Ashford,
retains something of the character of a 'railway' town. While a
considerable amount of land was acquired, the LSWR built few
houses—there is a string of them between the railway and the
main road on the up side. They did, however, open a cheese
market in 1852 when the sale of large cheeses for the London
market was of some importance to Hampshire farmers. (At a
later date, the Great Eastern Railway opened a fruit and vege-
table market at Stratford in East London.) The site of the LSWR
cheese market adjoined the railway and is now occupied by a
BRS parcels depot. The carriage and wagon works of 1889 was

situated to the east of the station and was closed down in 1968. Many of the buildings have now been demolished and the site is being developed for other uses. The locomotive works of 1909 is still active, although no steam locomotives have been built there since 1949. After orders for new construction had ceased, heavy repairs continued to be carried out until October 1966. (No. 34089, a light Pacific, was the last steam locomotive to pass through the erecting shop.) At present, repair work is carried out on electric and diesel-electric locomotives and electric and diesel-electric multiple-unit trains.

In 1903, the engine sheds at Northam in Southampton were closed, and a large new depot was constructed at Eastleigh on the down side of the line, near the locomotive works. This has usually been the largest motive power depot on the Southern Region, and in 1954 had an allocation of 128 steam locomotives. At present, with 93 diesel and electric locomotives, it remains the largest depot, the 'runner-up' being Hither Green with 58 locomotives. Among its features was a large office block surmounted by an enormous water tank. Somewhat surprisingly, this supported a semaphore signal arm which was used for testing the eyesight of engine drivers. The coaling arrangements consisted of a long ramp, at the top of which was a covered shed. Coal wagons, having reached the top, were emptied and the coal was tipped by means of chutes projecting through the wall of the shed, into the tenders of the locomotives down at ground level. This was out of use by 1964, locomotives being coaled by crane. (On the occasion of a visit in May 1964, although a steam crane was available, only a diesel crane was at work.) Eastleigh motive power depot closed with the end of steam, in 1967, and demolition was completed by the end of the year. The site is now used for diesel and electric locomotives and trains.

Primarily, Eastleigh is a junction and operating centre, and this is reflected in the extensive sidings on the down side of the line. Not surprisingly, at one time there were four principal signal boxes—North, South, East and West. The North box was closed in December 1917 as part of the economy measures imposed by war conditions. The East box, which was geographically north of the station, the West box, which was to the south, and the South box which was to the south east, were all replaced by the new box in the fork between the Salisbury and main lines in November 1966. (Following LSWR practice, boxes at the London end of a station were called East, and those at the country end were West.) For many years, Eastleigh was a place where coaches were transferred from one train to another, or passengers changed trains and, while this still happens, the development of the district has resulted in an increase of originating and terminating traffic.

The present passenger station owes most of its buildings to three periods. First, the original building of 1839, though much obscured by later development, survives on the up side. Most of the remainder belongs to the major alterations carried out about 1895. After this, the basic plan of the station consisted of two island platforms separated by four tracks, the centre through tracks having no platforms. As might be expected at this period, the redbrick entrance buildings had the typically LSWR pediment feature, while the footbridge over the tracks was adorned with the same kind of shrunken dormers that were described at Shawford. The station is at ground level but, when the up platform was made into an island, it became necessary to ascend stairs to a booking office at the end of the footbridge, before descending to the platforms. For the benefit of mails and parcels traffic, a swivelling platform can be swung across from the station entrance to the up island platform. This, of course, blocks the track at the back of the platform so that, before it can be used, a locking lever has to be released from the signal box. Rebuilding at the time of electrification was confined to the down side, new buildings being completed in July 1967. At present there are two interesting survivals at Eastleigh. One is the well-known tree growing out of the down platform only just beyond the end of the new buildings. The second is a large notice board, still headed 'Southern Railway' at the country end of the up platform, warning engine drivers against walking along the tracks to the locomotive shed.

Apart from an easing of the gradient through Winchester, the down gradient of 1 in 252 extends from the summit of the line at Litchfield tunnel to Eastleigh. Thereafter it eases, with gradients varying between 1 in 400 to 1 in 562 to St Denys, beyond which the line is level. Speeds of non-stop trains tend to be high through Eastleigh and, for passengers on them, detailed observations are not possible. However, there should be at least a glimpse of the drawing office on the down side at the country end and, beyond the site of the motive power depot, Southampton Airport. After the First World War, emigrants awaiting passage from Southampton were lodged at this point and, to accommodate them, a platform was provided and known as Atlantic Park Hostel Halt. It was still there in 1929, but appears to have been virtually unused. In 1966 new concrete platforms were erected on the same site and, on 1 April, Southampton Airport was opened, being the latest station on the Southern Region. It has no access from the public road and is intended for passengers and staff from the airport. Its opening may well have been inspired by the success of the rail connection to Gatwick Airport. The number of flights from Southampton on a normal day in winter varies between about eight and sixteen and, although in the summer this is considerably increased, especially to the Channel Islands, it is of course modest compared with Gatwick and this applies equally to traffic at the Airport station. Originally, there was a level-crossing at this point, the crossing keeper's house being demolished in the late 1960s. The station buildings at Swaythling were erected in 1883, one year after Shawford, which it strongly resembles. Features of similarity include the gable and the dwarf dormer. Again the redbrick buildings are separated from the wooden shelters on the platforms, in this case not by a flight of steps but by a covered passage way. This arrangement seems to reflect the plan to ultimately quadruple the line, as it would allow for the addition of tracks on the down side without disturbing the station building. The site of the Swaythling goods yard was on the down side at the country end. All the local goods yards in the Southampton area have been closed; Swaythling ceased to handle traffic in July 1959. At the country end of the station there was a public crossing, this being replaced by a footbridge which also linked the two platforms. The signal box was vintage LSWR with ample glazing and small window panes. There was an interesting down starter signal, with repeating arms, one showing above and one beneath the bridge, which both operated in the lower quadrant. In 1966, when the signal box closed and colour light signals were installed, this was removed to Hitchcocks Farm near Braintree in Essex. The built-up area of Southampton extends to Swaythling and from here to the main stations, the scenery is decidedly urban. However, there are some attractive views of the river Itchen, the first being obtainable on the down side as the train emerges on to the embankment which divides the two lengths of cutting between Swaythling and St Denys.

The first Portswood station, which adjoined the overbridge carrying St Denys Road, lasted only for the six years from 1860 to 1866 and, in view of the lack of archaeological evidence, was probably a temporary, wooden construction. When the branch to Netley Hospital was opened, it would have been possible to locate a station north of the junction with platforms on both main line and branch. Something of this kind would have been highly probable if the branch trains had started from the junction, but as they always started from Southampton, no inconvenience arose from their using the platforms of the new station opened in 1866 on the main line. Although the Netley company was nominally independent, its engineering officials were from the LSWR which, presumably, accounts for the new station at Portswood being similar to those at Woolston and Netley.[14] (The name was changed from Portswood to St Denys at the beginning of 1876.) Apart from the addition of a canopy over the platform, the main building has undergone little change, and retains its air of a solid, mid-Victorian residence in a favoured district. Although it belongs to the period when bricks were frequently covered by stucco, here they are exposed, contrasting with the dressed stones of the quoins and windows. Characteristically, the roof is slated. Only seventeen years separates St Denys and Swaythling but, whereas Swaythling would have not looked chronologically out of place in 1900, St Denys, with its classical,

Italianate style, might well have been built in the 1840s. Possibly with the idea of ultimate quadrupling, in 1899 St Denys was altered to a four-track station, but in an important respect, the arrangements differed from those at such places as Farnborough or Micheldever. Here, instead of being put out of use, the down platform became an island and a new side platform was added to the east of the station. The junction with the Netley line which, by this time, had been extended to Fareham, was moved from the London end to the country end of the station so that, in effect, the arrangements for the main line were unchanged but Netley line trains used new platforms on the east side of the station. From an architectural point of view, there was a situation of chronological asymmetry, with the up side buildings belonging to 1866 and the rest to 1899. As at Swaythling, there was a public right of way across the station and, in this case, a covered footbridge combined the functions of linking the platforms and carrying local pedestrian traffic. The junction now at the south end of the station was complicated by the quadrupling of the line between St Denys and Northam junction completed in May 1902. Just beyond the junction, the original line had cut across the side of a meander of the Itchen on a causeway, and subsequently, the section of river bed thus cut off was reclaimed and now provides the site of Bevois Park marshalling yard. While the proximity of Eastleigh diminishes its importance, it still handles a substantial traffic.

At the time of writing, St Denys retains its signal box of 1902 and operates the first semaphore signals encountered by a train coming down from London. There has been an impressive gantry supporting eight signal posts at the country end of the station, probably since 1902, but the present structure was erected in 1955. Of the eight posts, four carry stop signals for the Netley line and four for the main line. In each case, they apply to the following tracks—down local, down through, Bevois Park no. 1 road, Bevois Park no. 2 road. Adjoining the signal box, until 1903, was a level-crossing. Clause 4 of the South Western Railway Act of 1902 authorised the railway company to build a new bridge, with approach roads, to replace the level-crossing, although the footbridge which passed over, and the gas and water mains which passed under the line, were to be retained. There was a *quid pro quo*. The railway reached the docks by crossing Canute Road on the level. At the time, Canute Road carried a horse tramway which the Corporation was proposing to electrify and an electric tram service would have aggravated the difficulties of trains making the crossing. So the railway provided a bridge at St Denys and the Corporation took up the tram track between the South Western Hotel and the floating bridge. Sufficient importance was attached to the bridge to instigate an opening ceremony with the laying of a foundation stone by the Mayor of Southampton. The event took place on 28 October 1902 and the stone can be seen from the railway track, set in the western abutment of the bridge. A single metal span crossed all four tracks. St Denys might have presented the intriguing contrast of gaslit platforms and electric trains, but its gas lamps were replaced by electricity a month before the electric trains started running.

The level-crossing at St Denys was closed in 1903, but its neighbour, Mount Pleasant crossing, is still in use. However, since July 1967 its gates have been replaced by lifting barriers operated from the adjacent signal box. There are more sidings on the down side between Mount Pleasant and Northam junction, where freight traffic is handled. Standing above the sea of wagons which usually fills the yard is the tower of a silo used for bulk cement traffic. Northam locomotive shed was on this site until the removal to Eastleigh. The original junction with the Southampton and Dorchester line faced the terminus and it was ten years later, in 1857, by the time a new spur was opened from Northam junction to enable trains to run straight on to Dorchester without running in and out of the terminal. Even after this, until the opening of the new Southampton West station in 1895, many trains continued to run on to the terminus. Beyond Northam junction the line was reduced to two tracks through the platforms of Northam station. Until January 1970, with appealing conservatism, the line to the terminus was called the main and the *de facto* main line leading direct to Southampton Station was known as the branch. However, at this time, Northam junction was so simplified as to include a short length of single line for trains running on the original line, which then became the branch.

Northam station was an austere two-platform establishment opened in 1872. It was clearly too near the terminus to need its own goods facilities; its passengers descended the steps from the road to Northam Bridge which crossed the railway at this point. The modest buildings were mostly up on the road bridge and when, with the advent of electric trams and increased traffic, in 1908 the bridge was rebuilt, so was the station. The two platforms were provided with simple shelters and the down platform was remarkably longer than the up. This had nothing to do with Northam's traffic, but merely the fact that, before the days of corridor trains and platform barriers, express trains stopped at Northam's down platforms for ticket collectors to pass from compartment to compartment, examining tickets. Northam station was closed in September 1966 and the platforms were demolished in 1969. Southampton junction was at the end of Northam's platforms, with the Dorchester line coming in on the up side and four tracks, two for the docks and two for the terminus station, ran for the rest of the way. (In fact, two goods lines passed round the back of Northam station but, from an operating point of view, there was only double track between Northam and Southampton junctions.) Southampton Junction signal box also controlled a level-crossing which, spanning four tracks, had unusually wide gates suspended from heavy gate posts. British Rail was authorised to close the level-crossing in 1964 and Southampton Junction signal box was closed in October 1966.

Whereas the line from Woking to Northam junction has been modernised, for the rest of the way, beyond the addition of the live rail on the two tracks used by the docks trains, abandonment has been widespread but protracted. For some time the two tracks leading to Southampton Terminus were disused and gathering rust, until they were removed in 1969, together with the tracks and sidings in and around the station. The demise of the level-crossing with Bevois Street, adjoining Southampton junction, has already been described but, originally, there were another three crossings between the junction and the terminus. The roads were unimportant when the railway was opened but, with the rapid development of Northam in the mid-Victorian period, they began to carry a heavy traffic. At the time of writing, only one crossing survives, that with Chapel Road with gates of the traditional type operated from a typical LSWR signal box. The two crossings to the south were with Marsh Lane and its extension, Chantry Road and with Itchen Bridge Road. By 1876 the Corporation was agitating for their replacement by a bridge and the November 1960 issue of *Track Topics* contained details of a survey carried out at this time. It covered six 24-hour days and the results are startling. At Marsh Lane, the number of trains crossing during the six days was given as 2,288 and the number of road vehicles 2,474, and the gates were closed against the road for 3 days, 8 hours, 12 minutes. Bridge Road crossing passed 6,389 trains, 694 road vehicles and was closed for 5 days, 19 hours, 18 minutes. On this basis, the 694 road vehicles had an average of 47 minutes per day during which they could cross the railway. Needless to say, the word 'trains' must have been used to cover shunting movements, which would have been heavy, especially at Itchen Bridge Road which was immediately at the end of the station. The railway's first proposal was to build a bridge to replace Bridge Road crossing which was evidently shut against the road for most of the time, and to close the crossing at Marsh Lane. The Corporation wanted two bridges and the final compromise was for the closing of both crossings and the provision of a new bridge with approach ramps centrally placed between them. The Central bridge was opened in 1882 and, providentially, cast iron plates fixed to the parapet commemorating the event survive at both ends of the bridge. Each plate is letterered as follows:

This bridge was erected by the London & South Western Railway Co. in pursurance of an agreement with the Corporation under the powers of the South Western Railway Act of 1880 and was opened to the public July 1882. The Hon. Ralph

Dutton, Chairman of the Company: William Jacomb, City Engineer: W. H. Davis, Mayor of Southampton: Edward Bance, Chairman of the Corporation Committee. Contractors Messrs Bull & Son and The Horseley Company Ltd, Tipton.

The Horseley company produced the iron spans, while Messrs Bulls constructed the approach ramps of brick and were responsible for other brickwork, such as the parapets. The bridge remains in use and it is hoped that its one hundredth birthday will be marked by a modest celebration.

Beyond the Central bridge, the tracks to the docks divide, forking to the east into the main Southampton goods depot and straight ahead for the docks. The station tracks curve to the west into what was once, next to London, the most important station on the LSWR system. At the time of its closure in 1966, there were three terminal platforms, each with two faces, numbered 1–6 starting on the up side. The original train shed, with its overall roof spanning four tracks, was sited beyond the present no. 5/6 platform. In fact, no. 6 platform face is roughly on the site of the original departure platform and beyond it were two carriage sidings and the arrival platform. The station buildings were situated in Terminus Terrace, unusually remote from the train shed. Because of its relative decline, as more and more trains bypassed the terminal and called at the West station instead, the original buildings, although added to and subjected to minor alterations, were never replaced. Since the closure of the station they are partly disused but, as a Listed Building, demolition cannot be undertaken without consultation with the local authorities. The façade, which is stuccoed and Italianate in style, is unusually handsome. The lowest stage is pierced by five arches, the three in the middle forming entrances and the outer arches containing windows. It projects beyond the two upper storeys and is topped by a balustrade with a clock in the centre. Each successive storey diminishes in depth, this being reflected in the dimensions of the windows. The five sash windows of the second stage are placed over the centres of the arches and surmounted by pediments. The windows of the topmost stage are squat rectangles with no decoration. The principal extension was on the north side and is distinct and separate from Sir William Tite's original building. Because of this, Southampton Terminus provides one of the best examples of major provincial station buildings in the country, and it is much to be hoped that plans of the local authority to retain it as a museum will mature.

All the other parts of the station have undergone change and adaptation. In 1872, the Imperial Hotel was opened between the end of the train shed and the road. It was the first 'Grand' hotel in the town, with elaborate detail in a French Renaissance style. It was re-named the South Western Hotel and, with the transfer of transatlantic liner services to Southampton from Liverpool, became increasingly popular. Originally, in plan, it resembled a letter L with the longer arm on Canute Road, but a major extension after the First World War filled in the space between the arms. In this form, the South Western prospered during the period between the wars, associated with such vessels as the White Star *Majestic* and *Olympic* and Cunard's *Berengaria* and *Aquitania*. During the Second World War, the South Western was requisitioned, and afterwards it was let as office accommodation. As South Western House it still remains in this use, the main tenants being the BBC and, appropriately enough, the Cunard line. Even now, one passes through the main door from the circulating area at the head of the platforms, to enter a foyer with an unmistakable atmosphere of marble and palms, lingering from the heyday of film stars and transatlantic liners. A goods shed on the up side, adjoining the original buildings, was replaced by a much larger building in the LSWR 'Hampton Court' style, opened on the down side. The engine shed on the east side of the station was replaced by the Northam motive power depot and most of this space was taken up by sidings and an expanding fan of tracks crossing Canute Road on the level to give access to different parts of the docks. A major rearrangement of tracks and platforms took place after the First World War, at about the same time as the hotel was enlarged. The original arrival platform on the down side was replaced by a double track giving improved access to the docks, and the overall roof which had spanned the platform roads and sidings was demolished. The departure platform was extended and numbered 5 and 6. The new, long platform which had been added on the west side, was extended up to the Yard signal box, which was sited immediately on the south side of the Central bridge. A third and shorter island platform, numbered 1 and 2, was added on the west side. All the platforms were provided with new umbrella-type canopies and an overall roof covered the cab road which ran between the platform ends and the entrance to the hotel.

The decline of Southampton Terminus was protracted. The first recognition that it was not the only station in Southampton came in 1858 when, to avoid confusion with the through station on the Southampton & Dorchester line, it was re-named Southampton Docks. After the opening of the new Southampton West station, to indicate its more central position, it became Southampton Town and Docks. Finally, in 1923, by which time the 'centre' of the town had moved, it was given the unusual title of Southampton Terminus. At this time, most of its passenger traffic was local, typical destinations being Portsmouth and Andover. When the Hampshire diesel service was introduced in 1957, a half-hourly service ran up the main line to Winchester, with alternate trains running on to Alton. The service over the DNSR to Newbury and Didcot was withdrawn in March 1960. In its heyday, through coaches by this route reached as far north as Glasgow. In the mid-1950s, there was usually a daily run by the restored Great Western Railway record-breaking locomotive, City of Truro, which, with its three GWR coaches, must have been the most photographed train in Hampshire. A second 'foreign' service was that which, beyond Andover, ran over the Midland & South Western Junction line to Cheltenham. Like the DNSR, this route also conveyed through coaches to the Midlands and North. While it never brought anything as exciting as City of Truro to the Terminus station, in the mid-1950s it did provide a daily view of Great Western coaches, usually hauled by a GWR 2-6-0 of the 43XX series. After 1939, no coaches ran beyond Cheltenham Lansdowne, the former Midland Railway station, where there was a reasonable interchange for the Midlands and the North. However, in November 1958, the only daily through train was transferred to the Great Western St James station, a terminal with no interchange facilities. The passenger service over the MSWJR was finally withdrawn in September 1961. One main line service lasted until the end. This was the South Western Travelling Post Office, Waterloo to Weymouth, which every night at about 1.00 a.m. deposited surprised Sotonians, long accustomed to the Central station, at the Terminus. The up and down trains drew in on opposite sides of the main island platform, 3 and 4, and a certain amount of exchange, including that of the Post Office sorters, took place. Briefly, the Terminus became one of the most lively spots in sleeping Southampton. All this ended in September 1966 when, after 126 years, the Terminus was closed and its services transferred to the Central station. Its demise however, was not complete, for at Christmas 1966 and again in 1967 it was re-opened for parcels traffic. (The tracks were not electrified but this was immaterial, as the parcels train were hauled by diesel locomotives.) Its final use was in the spring of 1968 when the facilities for parcels traffic on the down side at Southampton Central were being improved and the last day on which railway traffic was handled in the passenger station was 1 April 1968. The tracks in the station were removed early in 1969 and, by the autumn, only the tracks to the goods depot and the docks remained. The Yard signal box was put out of use in December 1970. Now the signals and station nameboards have gone, grass is beginning to grow where the tracks ran, but nothing else has changed. The platforms are well used, with their canopies providing an unusually shaped car park for staff and visitors to South Western House. The goods depot on the east side remains in use, but the cattle market, with its private platform on the west side, has been disused since the Second World War.

As already mentioned, the tracks fanned out between the goods depot and the passenger station to cross Canute Road. The main line ended on the north side of the road, but the tracks that lay beyond were far more than a modest private siding. The LSWR acquired the Southampton Dock Company, with its railway tracks and locomotives, in 1892, but the dock system was always operated as a separate unit. The first dock basin, formerly the Outer Dock, now the Princess Alexandra Dock, was opened in 1842, and was probably the first dock in which passenger trains ran alongside passenger ships. The single-line level-crossing over Canute Road was on the site of the present no. 3 gate, between the National Westminster Bank and the new Dock House. This continued in use for boat trains until the summer of 1964, when the railway steamer passenger services from the Outer Dock were finally withdrawn. The dock basin now handles more traffic than ever before, but this consists of roll-on, roll-off ferries for road vehicles, and the level-crossing and the lines to what has become the Princess Alexandra Dock were closed in 1966. A second level-crossing, about 50 yards farther west, served the Inner Dock which opened in 1856. The line enters the dock at the opposite end of Dock House to the first crossing and, although its use has declined, still carries a considerable traffic. Since December 1955 it has been controlled by a 24-lever ground frame housed in Canute Road box. There are iron gates which may be closed across the railway, but no gates across the road. All trains cross at walking pace, while flagmen hold up road traffic, freight trains proceeding to the exchange sidings between the site of the former Inner Dock and the Empress Dock of 1890, and passenger trains to the appropriate berth. Since the closure of the Channel Islands Terminal, the most frequent destination for boat trains is the Ocean Terminal, opened in 1950 to serve the two *Queens* and other Atlantic lines.

In 1847, a turntable was constructed on the south side of the road, outside the Dock Company's estate, and this was joined to a track which ran alongside Platform Road to the Town Quay. This was owned by the Harbour Commissioners later the Southampton Harbour Board. The turntable would only take single wagons and the motive power consisted of horses. A better turntable was installed in 1862, but this was still a hindrance to traffic and, in 1871, a curve was constructed obliquely across Canute Road. At the same time the line was extended from the Town Quay to the Royal Pier, in order to carry passenger traffic to the Isle of Wight steamers. Horses continued to provide the motive

power, usually hauling two carriages and a luggage wagon detached from the main line train at the terminus. This unique
example of a horse-drawn boat train continued until 1876, when
the Board of Trade agreed to the use of steam locomotives. In an
article in the May 1970 issue of *Track Topics*, Mr Bert Moody
quoted the regulations, which included a speed limit of 5 m.p.h.
and the provision of condensing apparatus to avoid the emission
of smoke and steam by the locomotives. At this time the horse
trams were running along Canute Road to the floating bridge
and, during the hours of the tram service, trains for the Royal
Pier had to stop before crossing Canute Road.

Both the freight traffic to the Town Quay and the boat trains
to the Royal Pier were operated by the LSWR which kept two locomotives which met the Board of Trade requirements for this
purpose. In 1879 a third locomotive, previously used on a dock
construction contract in Germany, was added. In fact, most of
the London traffic for the Isle of Wight travelled on the Portsmouth to Ryde route, the Southampton steamers drawing traffic
which made little use of the 'boat' trains. By 1914, five trains ran
down to the pier and, somewhat oddly, six returned. At this time,
major repairs were necessary for the part of the pier under the
railway and its station, which consisted of a modest, two-platform wooden establishment. The outbreak of war in August
precipitated a decision to withdraw the service in 1914, this being
the first closure in Southampton occasioned by lack of traffic. The
freight service to the Town Quay was withdrawn in May 1970.
However, when the New Docks, now the Western Docks, were
under construction after 1929, a new line was built beyond the
Town Quay, crossing the landward end of the Royal Pier, to
reach the constructional works. After the completion of the New
Docks, this important link between the two separate parts of the
docks system was retained, and is still in use at the present time.
During the Second World War, railway track was laid down a
ramp between the quay and the pier to enable locomotives and
rolling stock to be shipped to France.

As mentioned above, the LSWR acquired the docks—but not, of
course, the Town Quay or Royal Pier—in 1892 and, until 1948,

railway and docks were under the control of the same board. Under the 1947 Act, partly because of the increasing importance of road transport for dock undertakings, Southampton, with other railway owned dock systems, passed to a docks executive and, later, in 1962, to the British Transport Docks Board. The docks board retained the internal railway system, with its motive power depot in the Old or Eastern Docks and large exchange sidings on both the Western and Eastern systems. However, virtually no main line trains use the link between the two systems, as the Western Docks have independent rail access from the Dorchester line at Millbrook. Motive power for internal movements within the docks was, for over a hundred years, supplied mainly by steam tank locomotives, with a short wheel-base for negotiating the sharp curves leading on to the quays. In 1891 the first of the B4 class locomotives came out from Nine Elms works, and these 0–4–0 side tank locomotives did most of the work in the docks until the tremendous traffic associated with the invasion of Europe. To cope with this, fourteen 0–6–0 side tank locomotives, built in North America, were imported by the US Army. These had a characteristic American appearance, with their stove-pipe chimneys and sand boxes mounted on top of the boiler. After the war, they were purchased by the Southern Railway and continued to work in the docks. Drivers were provided with short-wave radio links, similar to those used in marshalling yards. The Southampton docks locomotives were not purely shunters, being equipped with vacuum brakes and steam heating pipes. This enabled them to move empty passenger trains within the docks and also to heat trains pending the arrival of the main line locomotive. Because of this, they could always be used for passenger work and, at the present time, one of these interesting survivals from the Second World War is at work on the Keighley and Worth Valley Railway. (Others have been preserved elsewhere.)

In the late 1940s, hopes were entertained of the build-up of flying boat services, and a rail-served flying boat terminal was opened in 1948 at Berth 50. After the withdrawal of BOAC from flying operations, Aquila Airways took over until their last flight to Madeira in September 1958, after which the terminal was disused. In 1962 the first diesel locomotive arrived in Southampton docks on a Pickfords lorry and, subsequently, the steam locomotives were displaced. The present tendency is to run down the docks' internal railway system, using the internal road system to carry rail traffic to railheads located at suitable points in or near the dock estate.

While the docks lines were by far the most important extension to the London and Southampton Railway, there were three other lines of appreciable length. Briefly, the siding to the Itchen Wharves left from the northern end of Northam yard and, at present, carries about one train per week; the siding to the coal concentration depot at Dibles Wharf, known as Bull's Run, also leaves from Northam yard and is quite well used; the independently operated Chapel tramway which diverged between Southampton junction and Chapel crossing has been closed and dismantled.

To complete the story of railways in Southampton, further reference must be made to the Southampton & Dorchester Railway. Some independent railways were more independent than others, and the Southampton & Dorchester was one such. Charles Castleman, a Wimborne solicitor, who led the SDR Board, was prepared to join either the Great Western or LSWR parties, depending on the strength of their bids. Unfortunately for the SDR, before it obtained its Act of Parliament, the GWR and LSWR achieved one of their periodic and usually ephemeral agreements under which the Dorchester line was allotted to the LSWR. Accordingly, when it obtained its Act of Parliament in July 1845, the SDR was committed to a lease to the LSWR which was to provide four of its twelve directors. The line could be built with single track, but all the engineering works were to provide for doubling when the gross receipts exceeded £65,000 for three consecutive years. The section between Southampton junction and the river Test followed the line of the abandoned Southampton and Salisbury Canal. This had been constructed from a junction with the Andover Canal at Redbridge, running parallel with the bank of the Test but offering a towpath and sheltered water as an alternative to the difficulties of navigating the estuary of the river. To avoid locks, it crossed the spur between the estuaries of the Test and the Itchen by a tunnel at the east end of which it forked, the main line continuing east to join the Itchen at Northam and a branch following the east side of the old part of the town to a point near the Town Quay. Unfortunately, the supply of money was exhausted before the canal tunnel was completed and, by 1805, the waterway was virtually abandoned. Like the canal, the railway was level apart from its tunnel, where a short hump with 1 in 396 gradients carried it obliquely over the canal tunnel. However, in order to avoid the curves of the waterway, some very shallow cutting and embankment was necessary, cutting off elbows of canal, one of which may still be traced. The line was not unduly long in building and was opened, almost throughout, on 1 June 1847.

A sharp curve from Southampton junction brought it on to the line of the canal, but at a slightly higher level. The canal tunnel was, of course, of no use for a double-track railway, and the new railway tunnel crossed it obliquely. The 1 in 396 gradient of either side of the crossing left the new tunnel only about a foot above the old, which presumably indicated that it could go nearer the surface. In any case, the situation was exacerbated by the contractor making a heading from the new tunnel to the canal tunnel which he proceeded to use as a tip. This upset the drainage, and the saturated subsoil displaced the lining of the new tunnel to such an extent that the main London road over the top of it subsided. Because of this, on 1 June 1847, the line was opened almost throughout, but the tunnel was considered unsafe. The LSWR was faced with the problem of getting locomotives and carriages round it, and these were moved from the terminus through the streets on lorries drawn by numerous horses. Passenger coaches passed through the tunnel unofficially on 29 July, but normal working began on 6 August. For the next 117 years, the tunnel only received routine maintenance. As it is only 528 yards long, no ventilators were provided, making the operation of starting a heavy steam train from the near-by station an extremely unpleasant experience for footplate crews. In 1964 it was observed that the floor, or invert, of the tunnel arch was rising towards the roof, and reconstruction was necessary. This difficult and costly operation was carried out by closing the up and down lines in turn, during the winter of 1964 and early 1965, normal working being resumed in March 1965. It involved the re-opening of the heading to the canal tunnel which had been blocked off at either end for many years. The railway engineers gave Mr Edwin Welch, the author of a book on the canal, the opportunity of exploring the canal tunnel, which he did at the expense of considerable discomfort and damaged clothing. There have been few changes east of the tunnel. The only one of importance was the opening of the spur in 1857 enabling trains from London to run direct on to the Dorchester line instead of reversing in and out of the terminus. Like the original curve, the new one from Northam junction to Tunnel junction was sharp and at present carries a 15 m.p.h. speed restriction. To give the signalman a sufficient view, Tunnel junction was an unusually tall building, brick below and wood above, situated in the fork between the converging lines from Northam and Southampton junctions. It was closed in October 1966 and demolished in September 1969, its functions being taken over by Northam junction. From here to the tunnel mouth the line penetrated a built-up area and, to save space, instead of sloping cutting sides, brick retaining walls were provided.

The terminus was not badly placed for the older parts of the town, but was somewhat remote from the superior property which was going up to the north and north west. With this in mind, Section 33 of the SDR Act required the company to build and adequately serve a station at Blechynden Terrace, mainly for the benefit of the townspeople. There were some problems in implementing this and, until 1850, a temporary wooden station was in use. The permanent station was a modest two-platform establishment, named Blechynden. In 1858, when the new spur made it possible for trains to avoid calling at the terminus, the platforms at Blechynden were extended and it was re-named Southampton West End. Nevertheless, until the direct route via New Milton to Bournemouth was opened in 1888, some trains continued to use the terminus. The need to avoid this time-consuming procedure was clear and, in 1895, a new station, named Southampton West, was opened immediately to the west of Southampton West End, on the opposite side of a level-crossing. It was a substantial building of red brick, with terra cotta embellishments. The main buildings were on the up side which, following the fashion of, for example, King's Cross and Nottingham Victoria, and anticipating the London Transport stations of the 1930s, was ornamented with a tower 100 feet in height. The up platform was 600 feet long and the down, which had a bay road at its country end, was 800 feet. By 1923 it was claimed that this station had the second largest passenger traffic on the LSWR system, being surpassed only by Waterloo. The old station was closed in 1895, but the buildings on the up side were retained as offices for the goods yard.

The next major developments took place in 1934 and 1935. First, in June 1934, the level-crossing, whose gates were operated about 150 times per day, was replaced by an overbridge at the opposite end of the station. The massive reclamation scheme associated with the construction of the new docks made plenty of land available on the south side, so the down platform was converted to an island, and a new side platform, with a bay, constructed on the down side. This was the same kind of procedure as had been followed at, for instance, Micheldever but, in the case of Southampton, the island in the middle was retained, giving four through platforms instead of two. The new buildings on the down side were in concrete, in the characteristic 'Odeon' style favoured by the Southern in the late 1930s. The widening to four tracks necessitated the demolition of the down platform of the original station. To celebrate its development, the station was renamed Southampton Central. In July 1936 it became the first station in Hampshire to be provided with a public address system. During the Second World War, the new buildings on the down side were badly damaged by bombing, and have not been fully restored. The latest changes have been on the up side, on which the 1895 buildings have been replaced by a modern office block with the station offices being housed in part of the ground floor. This was completed in 1967 and so the station continues in the state of chronological asymmetry which it has displayed since 1935—that is, one side newer than the other, except that now the up side is the newer instead of the older.

There is very little left of the station of 1895. However, part of the original platform face survives and, of the footbridge which adjoined the level-crossing, now closed to vehicles, the northern half pre-dates the widening. Wartime bombing removed the up platform of the original station and also most of the buildings of the goods depot. Few changes are directly attributable to electrification, apart from such minor alterations as the removal of the water tank and one of the water columns, and the addition of signs to indicate exact stopping points for trains of various lengths, up to the standard twelve coaches of the London expresses. Traffic is still controlled from the signal box of 1935, with a mixture of electrically and mechanically worked points of signals. The gantry at the country end of the down side is marginally more impressive than that at St Denys, having nine posts with thirteen arms as against eight posts with twelve arms. Originally, apart from shunting movements, the two northern platforms, 1 and 2, were for up trains and 3 and 4 for down, only the bay platform, 5, being reversible. With the closure of Southampton Terminus, more trains have terminated at the through station, and platforms 2, 3 and 4 can now be used in either direction. A final stage in the replacement of the town's first station came in 1967 when Southampton Central assumed its original name of 'Southampton'. On the debit side, the district office, opened in a separate building on the up side about 1911, was closed and finally demolished in 1971. Development of passenger traffic has not been accompanied by that of freight, the bomb damaged yard being closed in 1955. It is now a car park. Two private sidings of interest have both closed.[15] Briefly, that to the Southampton electricity generating station diverged from the down side at the London end of the station, crossing the main road on the level. It was electrified with an overhead wire, and had its own electric locomotive. After some years of disuse, it was severed and the switch removed in the spring of 1964. The

second was operated by the Army from November 1917 until
1919 and ran from a junction near the down bay platform to a
train ferry terminal. Both have disappeared without a trace, apart
from some track in the generating station.

Until the great reclamation scheme for the New Docks, as far
as Millbrook the line ran almost at the water's edge, below a low
cliff, on the style of the Tilbury line between Leigh-on-Sea and
Chalkwell. Foreman ticket collector Arnold was quoted in the
Railway Magazine in 1923 (Vol. 53, p. 337) as follows: '. . . In
times of storm when we had high tides and a south-west wind, I
remember very heavy seas, and the water came into the
station almost sufficient to float a small boat.' Millbrook station
was a modest establishment with up and down platforms, opened
to serve a growing suburb about 1860. When the Central station
was rebuilt, advantage was taken of the docks reclamation
scheme to extend the four running lines to the country end of
Millbrook station. Because they served the most easily accessible
platforms in the Central station, the outside tracks were
designated as the through lines and the centre as local, this being
the reverse of the arrangement between Shawford and Eastleigh.
Millbrook station was rebuilt with a single island platform
between the local lines, reached by a footbridge. (This replaced
a level-crossing which had given access to the no longer existent
foreshore.) Also, in 1935, a new signal box was opened on the
island platform. In May 1966, Millbrook became unstaffed and,
in July 1967, its goods depot, which was on reclaimed land on the
up side, was closed. However, the site was subsequently used for
the Southampton freightliner depot, opened in January 1968.
Under the control of the Millbrook signal box is the junction for
the Western Docks which handle an increasing proportion of the
dock's rail traffic. This is increasing with the extension of the
container berths, and work was started in the autumn of 1971 on
a second container terminal on reclaimed land on the down side
of the line.

Redbridge is the last station to be reached within the city
boundary. It was opened with the line in 1847 to serve what was
then the village of Redbridge. In 1865, when the line from

Southampton to Andover was opened, the junction was located immediately to the west of the station. The station buildings are on the up side and, having been changed little over the years, have the slightly Gothic air characteristic of original Southampton & Dorchester Railway architecture. The line of the Southampton and Salisbury Canal crossed obliquely at the London end of the station and its course is reflected by an indentation running across the allotments behind the up platform. The sleeper and concrete works of the Southern Railway were located on land owned by the railway between Redbridge station and the foreshore. Beyond the junction, the line crosses the Test on the third bridge to have occupied the site, and leaves Southampton.

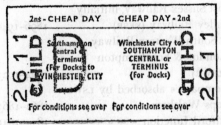

British Rail, 25 February 1963

Appendix 1

Railway Companies of Southern England

All public railway companies in the South, except the RHDR, became parts of British Railways, Southern Region, on 1 January 1948. (See Diagrams 2 and 17.)

A East Kent Light Railways (EKLR)   1911–1948
B Kent & East Sussex Railway, initially
   Rother Valley Railway (KESR)   1896–1948
C London & South Western Railway,
   initially London & Southampton
   Railway (LSWR)   1834–1923
   Railway companies absorbed by LSWR:
   C.1 Bishops Waltham   1862–1863
   C.2 Guildford Junction   1844–1845
   C.3 Lee-on-the-Solent   1890–1923
   C.4 Mid-Hants   1861–1881
   C.5 Petersfield   1860–1863
   C.6 Portsmouth Direct   1853–1859
   C.7 Southampton & Netley   1861–1864
   C.8 Stokes Bay   1855–1875
D London, Brighton & South Coast Railway,
   initially London & Brighton Railway
   (LBSCR)   1837–1923
   Railway companies absorbed by LBSCR:
   D.1 Bognor   1853–1864
   D.2 Brighton & Chichester   1844–1845
   D.3 Brighton & Dyke   1877–1924
   D.4 Brighton, Lewes & Hastings   1844–1846

D.5	East Grinstead, Groombridge & Tunbridge Wells	1862–1864
D.6	Hayling	1860–1923
D.7	Horsham & Guildford Direct	1860–1864
D.8	Lewes & East Grinstead	1877–1878
D.9	Lewes & Uckfield	1857–1859
D.10	Mid-Sussex	1857–1864
D.11	Mid-Sussex & Midhurst	1859–1862
D.12	Oxted & Groombridge	1881–1884
D.13	Tunbridge Wells & Eastbourne	1873–1876
D.14	Uckfield & Tunbridge Wells	1861–1864

E London, Chatham & Dover Railway,
   initially East Kent Railway (LCDR)   1853–1923
   Railway companies absorbed by the LCDR:

E.1	Kent Coast, initially Herne Bay & Faversham, later Margate Railway	1857–1871
E.2	Maidstone & Ashford	1880–1883
E.3	Sevenoaks, Maidstone & Tunbridge	1859–1879
E.4	Sheppey Light Railway	1899–1905
E.5	Sittingbourne & Sheerness	1856–1876

F Romney, Hythe & Dymchurch Railway   1926– still in existence
G South Eastern Railway (SER)   1836–1923
   Railway companies absorbed by the SER:

G.1	Canterbury & Whitstable	1825–1853
G.2	Cranbrook & Paddock Wood	1877–1900
G.3	Crowhurst, Sidley & Bexhill	1897–1906
G.4	Elham Valley	1881–1885
G.5	Gravesend & Rochester	1845–1846
G.6	Hundred of Hoo	1879–1881
G.7	Loose Valley	1877–1881
G.8	Lydd	1881–1895
G.9	Reading, Guildford & Reigate	1846–1852

   South Eastern & Chatham Joint
   Managing Committee (SECR)   1899–1923
   Operated lines of South Eastern & London, Chatham & Dover
   Companies
H Southern Railway (SR)   1923–1948
   The Southern absorbed the principal railway companies in 1923
I West Sussex Railway, initially Selsey &
   Hundred of Manhood   1896–1935

Appendix 2
Opening and Closing of Lines 1830-1969

All the lines included were public railways open to goods traffic, passengers, or both, and situated in Southern England as defined in the Preface. Table 1 indicates the net gain or loss of route mileage in each decade from 1830 to 1969. It will be noted that the biggest increase took place in the 1840s and the greatest decline in the 1960s.

TABLE 1

1830–1839	+41½	1900–1909	+75¼
1840–1849	+294¾	1910–1919	−7
1850–1859	+151¾	1920–1929	+26¾
1860–1869	+194½	1930–1939	−30
1870–1879	+33	1940–1949	−19½
1880–1889	+142	1950–1959	−84¼
1890–1899	+30½	1960–1969	−132¾

TABLE 2

Table 2 shows the greatest route mileage open to traffic in each year from 1830 to 1969. It will be seen that the maximum was reached in the years 1932–1935 and that the 1969 mileage corresponds roughly to that reached in 1879.

1830	6		3	6		6	6		9	41½
1	6		4	6		7	6			
2	6		5	6		8	21			

1840	66¼	2	691¼	4	950¼	7	959½
1	87¼	3	691¼	5	962¾	8	959½
2	130	4	709½	6	962¾	9	953
3	146¼	5	709½	7	962¾	1940	938
4	161¾	6	711½	8	963¼	1	938¾
5	177	7	711½	9	963¼	2	938¾
6	255½	8	711½	1910	963¼	3	938¾
7	303½	9	715½	1	962¼	4	938¾
8	310¾	1880	732	2	972½	5	938¾
9	336¼	1	763	3	972½	6	948¼
		2	792¾	4	970½	7	936¼
1850	336¼	3	796¾	5	968½	8	937½
1	379¾	4	819¾	6	968	9	933½
2	399¾	5	821	7	949½		
3	399¾	6	821	8	950¼	1950	924¾
4	399¾	7	833½	9	956¼	1	910¼
5	399¾	8	842¼			2	902¾
6	411	9	857½	1920	958¾	3	896½
7	411¼			1	959¼	4	888¼
8	438	1890	857½	2	960	5	849¼
9	488	1	860¼	3	959¾	6	866¼
		2	867	4	972¾	7	866¼
1860	518¼	3	872	5	973¼	8	849¼
1	555¼	4	875	6	969¼	9	849¼
2	555¼	5	876½	7	977½	1960	853¾
3	589¼	6	879¼	8	977½	1	825½
4	605½	7	886¾	9	983	2	814¾
5	638¾	8	887¾	1930	983	3	807½
6	663½	9	888	1	981¾	4	801½
7	667½			2	983½	5	777¾
8	681	1900	900	3	983½	6	752¼
9	682½	1	919½	4	983½	7	738½
		2	924	5	973	8	725
1870	690	3	948	6	960	9	716½
1	691¼						

TABLE 3

Table 3 lists the primary main lines described in Volume One of the *Railways of Southern England*. (Lists of secondary lines and branches are given in Volume Two and of independent and light railways in Volume Three.) Against each line is written the year of opening or closure, the operating company at the time, the number of the chapter in which it is described and the route mileage opened or closed. Unless otherwise stated, opening and closure is for both goods and passengers. Where there is an appreciable time gap between the provision or withdrawal of the two types of service, this is shown (P—Passengers; G—Goods).

			Chapter No.	Route Mileage opened	Route Mileage closed
1838	Woking–Winchfield	LSR	8	15	—
1839	Winchfield–Basingstoke	LSWR	8	8	—
	Winchester–Southampton	LSWR	8	12½	—
1840	Basingstoke–Winchester	LSWR	8	18¾	—
	Brighton–Shoreham	LBR	6	6	—
1841	Three Bridges–Brighton	LBR	5	21	—
1842	Edenbridge–Ashford	SER	1	26½	—
1843	Ashford–Folkestone East	SER	1	14¾	—
	Folkestone Harbour branch (to G. only)	SER	1	1½	—
1844	Folkestone East–Dover	SER	1	5½	—
1845	Shoreham–Worthing	LBR	6	4¾	—
	Tonbridge–Tunbridge Wells (Jackwood Springs)	SER	4	4	—
1846	Ashford–Ramsgate	SER	3	30	—
	Ramsgate–Margate	SER	3	3¾	—
	Worthing–Chichester	LBSCR	6	18	—
	Brighton–St Leonards	LBSCR	5	32½	—
	Tunbridge Wells (Jackwood Springs)–Tunbridge Wells	SER	14	¾	—
1847	Chichester–Portcreek junction	LBSCR	6 & 7	12½	—
	Portcreek junction–Portsmouth & Southsea	LBSCR & LSWR Joint	7	3½	—
	Minster–Deal	SER	3	8¾	—

			Chapter No.	Route Mileage opened	Route Mileage closed
	Southampton junction–Blechynden	LSWR	8	1	—
	Keymer junction–Lewes	LBSCR	5	9	—
	Southerham junction–Newhaven Wharf	LBSCR	5	6	—
	Southampton–Southampton Town Quay (to G. only)	LSWR	8	¾	—
1848	Cosham junction–Farlington junction	LBSCR	6	½	—
1849	Folkestone Harbour branch (to P.)	SER	1	—	—
	Polegate–Eastbourne	LBSCR	5	4	—
	Guildford–Godalming (old)	LSWR	7	3¾	—
1851	St Leonards–Bo-peep junction, St Leonards	LBSCR	5	¼	—
	Bo-peep junction, St Leonards–Hastings	SER	4	1½	—
	Tunbridge Wells–Robertsbridge	SER	4	15¼	—
1852	Robertsbridge–Bo-peep junction	SER	4	11¼	—
1857	Tonbridge spur	SER	4	¼	—
1858	Northam spur	LSWR	8	¼	—
	Strood–Faversham	LCDR	2	19	—
1859	Godalming–Havant	LSWR	7	32½	—
	Horsham–Hardham junction	LBSCR	6	13	—
1860	Faversham–Canterbury	LCDR	2	9¾	—
	Faversham–Whitstable	LCDR	3	6½	—
	Meopham–Strood	LCDR	2	7	—
1861	Whitstable–Herne Bay	LCDR	3	4	—
	Canterbury–Dover Harbour	LCDR	2	16	—
1863	St Lawrence spur, Ramsgate	SER	3	½	—
	Hardham junction–Ford	LBSCR	6	9¼	—
	Ford–Littlehampton	LBSCR	6	1¾	—
	Herne Bay–Ramsgate Harbour	LCDR	3	16½	—
1864	Barnham–Bognor	LBSCR	6	3½	—
	Newhaven–Seaford	LBSCR	5	2¼	—

			Chapter No.	Route Mileage opened	Route Mileage closed
	Harbour to Admiralty Pier, Dover	LCDR	2	¼	—
1871	Stone Cross junction–Willingdon junction	LBSCR	5	1	—
	Southampton Town Quay line (to P.)		8	—	—
	Extension to Royal Pier, Southampton	LSWR	8	¼	—
1876	Extension to Portsmouth Harbour	LBSCR & LSWR Joint	7	1	—
1879	Preston Park–Hove (Cliftonville spur)	LBSCR	6	1¼	—
1880	Minster spur	SER	3	¼	—
1881	Buckland junction, Dover–Deal	SER & LCDR Joint	3	8½	—
	Dover Town spur	SER & LCDR Joint	1 & 2	¼	—
	New lines at Polegate	LBSCR	5	1	—
	Old lines at Polegate	LBSCR	5	—	1
1882	Kearsney loop	SER & LCDR Joint	3	¼	—
1887	New lines at Ford	LBSCR	6	¾	—
	Old lines at Ford	LBSCR	6	—	1
1889	Lewes deviation line	LBSCR	5	½	—
1891	Shawford junction–Winchester Chesil	LSWR	8	2	—
1914	Extension to Royal Pier, Southampton		8	—	¼
	Southampton Town Quay line (closed to P. only)		8	—	—
1918	Canterbury spur	SECR	2	¾	—
1920	Canterbury spur	SECR	2	—	¾
	Tonbridge, old spur	SECR	4	—	¼
1926	Thanet loop	SR	3	1½	—
	Spur to Ramsgate Harbour	SR	3	—	1¼
	Ramsgate Town–Margate Sands	SR	3	—	4¼

		Chapter No.	Route Mileage opened	Route Mileage closed
1941	Canterbury spur	SR	2	¾	—
1951	Canterbury spur	BR	2	—	¾
1953	Canterbury spur	BR	2	¾	—
	Canterbury spur	BR	2	—	¾
1960	Shawford junction–Winchester Chesil (closed to P. only)	BR	8	—	—
1966	Shawford junction–Winchester Chesil	BR	8	—	2
	Northam junction–Southampton Terminus (closed to P. only)	BR	8	—	—

Appendix 3

Dates of Opening and Closure of Passenger Stations on Main Lines 1838-1970

The establishments listed define the points at which passengers could join or leave trains on lines described in this book. There is no indication of whether the establishment consisted of substantial buildings and platforms like Basingstoke or a simple wooden platform like Mountfield Halt. There is also no indication of whether the station was served by dozens of trains daily, like Guildford, or a less frequent service, as at Margate East. The criteria for inclusion are that the station appeared regularly in the timetables and was available for use by the general public. The former requirement eliminates such ephemeral establishments as Atlantic Park Halt, near Eastleigh or Ditcham Park Halt on the Portsmouth Direct line. The latter rules out stations for golf clubs such as Bramshot Halt, near Farnborough. No stations have remained unaltered since opening, but the degree of change has varied from complete rebuilding, as at Hastings or Southampton, to very minor modifications, as at Battle.

A problem arises when a station is rebuilt on a slightly different site; is this a rebuilding, which would not be recorded in the list, or the closure of one station and the opening of a different one? The rule applied is that, when the new station was within a quarter of a mile of the old, it is regarded as a rebuilding of the same station, as at Worthing or Tonbridge. This rule is open to objection, as rebuilding can be significant for both operating trains and passenger access. Consequently, some exceptions to the rule have been made, e.g. Southampton and Hastings.

Each entry begins with a number which merely indicates the position of the establishment on Diagrams 1 and 16. Next comes the name, and this is usually the present official name or the name at the time of closure as shown in timetables and on station nameboards. Earlier names are shown in brackets after the last name and are also cross-referenced. Until the 1968/1969 timetable, the Southern Region distinguished between stations and halts and this distinction is retained in the list. It has, however, been dropped in the official timetable as the withdrawal of staff and facilities from many stations has made it obsolete. The county in which the station is to be found is shown as follows: H—Hampshire; K—Kent; Su—Surrey; Sx—Sussex. This is followed by the number of the chapter in which the station appears. Next is the name of the company who provided the train service when the station was opened. The dates given are the first and, where applicable, the last year in which a service was provided—there is, of course, no indication of the proportion of the year or opening or closure during which a station was served. Temporary closures of considerable duration are shown, e.g. St Leonards, Warrior Square. Finally, stations which have been closed for some years are not shown on Ordnance Survey maps. To assist in locating them, for each of the closed stations, the appropriate O. S. sheet number and the grid reference is given. The following list, added to those provided in Volumes Two and Three, covers all passenger stations in Southern England.

1	Adisham	K	2	LCDR	1861
2	Aldrington Halt (Dyke Junction Halt)	Sx	6	LBSCR	1905
3	Amberley	Sx	6	LBSCR	1863
4	Angmering	Sx	6	LBSCR	1846
5	Arundel (New Arundel)	Sx	6	LBSCR	1863
6	Arundel & Littlehampton	Sx	6	LBSCR	1846–1863 (182/028038)
7	Ashford (Kent)	K	1	SER	1842
8	Aylesham Halt	K	2	SR	1928
9	Balcombe	Sx	5	LBR	1841
10	Barnham	Sx	6	LBSCR	1864
11	Basingstoke	H	8	LSR	1839
12	Battle	Sx	4	SER	1852

13	Bedhampton Halt	H	7	LBSCR	1906
14	Bekesbourne	K	2	LCDR	1861
15	Berwick	Sx	5	LBSCR	1846
16	Bexhill (Bexhill Central)	Sx	5	LBSCR	1846
17	Billingshurst	Sx	6	LBSCR	1859
18	Birchington-on-Sea	K	3	LCDR	1863
19	Bishopstone	Sx	5	SR	1938
20	Bishopstone Beach Halt (Bishopstone)	Sx	5	LBSCR	1864–1938, 1939–1941 (183/461004)
	Blechynden (see Southampton, West End)				
21	Bognor Regis	Sx	6	LBSCR	1864
22	Bosham	Sx	6	LBSCR	1847
23	Brighton	Sx	5	LBR	1840
24	Broadstairs	K	3	LCDR	1863
25	Brookwood	Su	8	LSWR	1864
	Bungalow Town Halt (see Shoreham Airport)				
	Bulverhythe (see St Leonards, Bulverhythe)				
26	Burgess Hill	Sx	5	LBR	1841
27	Canterbury East (Canterbury)	K	2	LCDR	1860
28	Canterbury West (Canterbury)	K	3	SER	1846
29	Chartham	K	3	SER	1859
30	Chatham	K	2	LCDR	1858
31	Cheriton Halt	K	1	SECR	1908–1915, 1920–1941, 1946–1947 (173/202366)
32	Chestfield & Swalecliff Halt	K	3	SR	1930
33	Chichester	Sx	6	LBSCR	1846
34	Chilham	K	3	SER	1846
35	Chislet Colliery Halt	K	3	SECR	1920
36	Christs Hospital	Sx	6	LBSCR	1902
37	Collington Halt (West Bexhill Halt)	Sx	5	LBSCR	1905–1906, 1911
38	Cooden Beach (Cooden Golf Halt)	Sx	5	LBSCR	1905
39	Cooksbridge	Sx	5	LBSCR	1848
40	Crowhurst	Sx	4	SECR	1902

41	Deal	K	3	SER	1847
42	Dover, Admiralty Pier	K	2	SER &	1860–1914
				LCDR	(173/323400)
43	Dover Harbour	K	2	LCDR	1861–1927
					(173/317405)
	Dover Marine	K	2	SECR	Replaced Admiralty Pier for general public, 1919
44	Dover Priory	K	2	LCDR	1861
45	Dover Town	K	1	SER	1844–1914
					(173/318403)
46	Drayton	Sx	6	LBSCR	1846–1930
					(181/890043)
47	Dumpton Park	K	3	SR	1926
48	Durrington-on-Sea	Sx	6	SR	1937
	Dyke Junction Halt (see Aldrington Halt)				
49	Eastbourne	Sx	5	LBSCR	1849
50	Eastleigh (Bishopstoke)	H	8	LSR	1839
	East Margate (see Margate East)				
51	East Worthing Halt (Ham Bridge Halt)	Sx	6	LBSCR	1905
52	Ebbsfleet & Cliffsend Halt	K	3	SECR	1908–1933
					(173/338642)
53	Edenbridge	K	1	SER	1842
54	Emsworth	H	6	LBSCR	1847
55	Etchingham	Sx	4	SER	1851
	Ewell (see Kearsney)				
56	Falmer (1st station)	Sx	5	LBSCR	1846–1865
					(183/358089)
57	Falmer (2nd station)	Sx	5	LBSCR	1865
58	Farlington Halt (Farlington Race station)	H	7	LSWR	1904–1917, 1922–1927, 1928–1937 (181/671047)
59	Farnborough	H	8	LSR	1838
60	Farncombe	Su	7	LSWR	1897
61	Faversham	K	2	LCDR	1858

62	Fishbourne Halt	Sx	6	LBSCR	1906
63	Fishersgate Halt	Sx	6	LBSCR	1905
64	Fleet	H	8	LSWR	1847
65	Folkestone (temporary station)	K	1	SER	1843–1843 (173/223363)
66	Folkestone Central (Cheriton Arch, Radnor Park)	K	1	SER	1884
67	Folkestone East (Folkestone Junction)	K	1	SER	1843–1965 (173/234368)
68	Folkestone Harbour (1st station)	K	1	SER	1849–1850 (173/234358)
69	Folkestone Harbour (2nd station)	K	1	SER	1850–1915, 1919
70	Folkestone Warren Halt	K	1	SECR	1908–1915, 1923–1939 (173/249379)
71	Folkestone West (Shorncliffe Camp, Shorncliffe)	K	1	SER	1863
72	Ford (Arundel)	Sx	6	LBSCR	1846
73	Frant	Sx	4	SER	1851
74	Fratton	H	7	LBSCR &	
75	Gillingham (Kent)			LSWR	1885
	(New Brompton)	K	2	LCDR	1858
76	Glynde	Sx	5	LBSCR	1846
77	Glyne Gap Halt	Sx	5	LBSCR	1905–1915 (184/764078)
78	Godalming (Old)	Su	7	LSWR	1849–1897 (182/975445)
79	Godalming	Su	7	LSWR	1859
80	Goring-by-Sea (Goring)	Sx	6	LBSCR	1846
81	Grove Ferry & Upstreet	K	3	SER	1846–1966 (173/235632)
82	Guildford	Su	7	LSWR	1845
	Ham Bridge Halt (see East Worthing Halt)				
83	Hampden Park (Willingdon)	Sx	5	LBSCR	1888
84	Haslemere	Su	7	LSWR	1859
85	Hassocks (Hassocks Gate)	Sx	5	LBR	1841
86	Hastings (1st station)	Sx	4	SER &	
				LBSCR	1851–1931

87	Hastings (2nd station)	Sx	4	SR	1931 (new station on same site)
88	Havant	H	7	LBSCR	1847
89	Havant (Temporary)	H	7	LSWR	1859–1859 (181/724067)
90	Haywards Heath	Sx	5	LBR	1841
91	Headcorn	K	1	SER	1842
92	Herne Bay	K	3	LCDR	1861
93	High Brooms (Southborough)	K	4	SER	1893
94	Hilsea Halt	H	7	SR	1941
95	Holland Road Halt	Sx	6	LBSCR	1905–1956 (182/296053)
96	Hook	H	8	LSWR	1883
97	Horsham (1st station)	Sx	6	LBSCR	1848–1859 (182/180313)
98	Horsham (2nd station)	Sx	6	LBSCR	1859
99	Hove	Sx	6	LBR	1840–1880 (182/298053)
100	Hove (Cliftonville, West Brighton) Jackwood Springs (see Tunbridge Wells, temporary)	Sx	6	LBSCR	1865
101	Kearsney (Ewell)	K	2	LCDR	1862
102	Keymer Junction	Sx	5	LBSCR	1862–1883 (182/319193)
103	Kingston-on-Sea	Sx	6	LBR	1840–1879 (182/228052)
104	Lancing	Sx	6	LBR	1845
105	Leigh Halt (Lyghe Halt)	K	1	SECR	1911
106	Lewes (Friars Walk) (also platform at Pinwell)	Sx	5	LBSCR	1846–1857 (183/419102)
107	Lewes (1st station)	Sx	5	LBSCR	1857–1889
108	Lewes (2nd station)	Sx	5	LBSCR	1889 (new station on adjoining site
109	Liphook	H	7	LSWR	1859
110	Liss	H	7	LSWR	1859

111	Littlehampton	Sx	6	LBSCR	1863
112	London Road, Brighton	Sx	5	LBSCR	1877
	Lyghe Halt (see Leigh Halt)				
113	Lyminster Halt	Sx	6	LBSCR	1907–1914
					(182/028038)
114	Marden	K	1	SER	1842
115	Margate (Buenos Aires, Margate West)	K	3	LCDR	1863
116	Margate East (Ramsgate Road)	K	3	LCDR	1863–1953
					(173/357701)
117	Margate Sands	K	3	SER	1846–1926
					(173/349706)
118	Martin Mill	K	3	SER & LCDR	1881
119	Meopham	K	2	LCDR	1861
120	Micheldever (Andover Road)	H	8	LSR	1840
121	Milford	Su	7	LSWR	1859
122	Minster	K	3	SER	1846
123	Mountfield Halt	Sx	4	SR	1923–1969
					(184/745198)
	New Brompton (see Gillingham)				
124	Newhaven Harbour (Newhaven Wharf)	Sx	5	LBSCR	1847
125	Newhaven Town	Sx	5	LBSCR	1847
126	Newington	K	2	LCDR	1862
127	Normans Bay Halt	Sx	5	LBSCR	1905
128	Northam	H	8	LSWR	1872–1966
					(180/428122)
129	Nutbourne Halt	Sx	6	LBSCR	1906
130	Paddock Wood (Maidstone Road	K	1	SER	1842
131	Penshurst	K	1	SER	1842
132	Petersfield	H	7	LSWR	1859
133	Pevensey & Westham	Sx	5	LBSCR	1846
134	Pevensey Bay Halt	Sx	5	LBSCR	1905
135	Pluckley	K	1	SER	1842
136	Plumpton	Sx	5	LBSCR	1863
137	Polegate (1st station)	Sx	5	LBSCR	1846–1881
					(183/583048)
138	Polegate (2nd station)	Sx	5	LBSCR	1881
139	Portslade & West Hove	Sx	6	LBR	1840

140	Portsmouth & Southsea	H	7	LBSCR	1847
141	Portsmouth Harbour	H	7	LBSCR &	
				LSWR	1876
142	Portswood	H	8	LSWR	1860–1866
	Portswood (see St Denys)				(180/432141)
143	Preston Park	Sx	5	LBSCR	1869
144	Pulborough	Sx	6	LBSCR	1859
	Radnor Park (see Folkestone Central)				
145	Rainham	K	2	LCDR	1858
146	Ramsgate Harbour (Ramsgate)	K	3	LCDR	1863–1926
					(173/386648)
147	Ramsgate Town	K	3	SER	1846–1926
					(173/376657)
148	Ramsgate	K	3	SR	1926
149	Richborough Castle Halt	K	3	SR	1933–1939
					(173/325601)
150	Robertsbridge	Sx	5	SER	1851
151	Rochester	K	2	LCDR	1892
152	Rochester Bridge (Strood)	K	2	LCDR	1860–1916
					(172/740691)
153	Rowlands Castle	H	7	LSWR	1859
154	St Denys (Portswood)	H	8	LSWR	1866
155	St Lawrence	K	3	SER	1864–1916
					(173/371657)
156	St Leonards, Bulverhythe	Sx	5	LBSCR	1846–1846
					(184/784088)
157	St Leonards, Warrior Square	Sx	4	SER	1851–1917,
					1919
158	St Leonards, West Marina	Sx	5	LBSCR	1846–1967
					(184/787089)
159	Sandling for Hythe	K	1	SER	1888
160	Sandwich	K	3	SER	1848
161	Seaford	Sx	5	LBSCR	1864
162	Selling	K	2	LCDR	1860
163	Shawford	H	8	LSWR	1882
164	Shepherds Well	K	2	LCDR	1861
165	Shoreham Airport (Bungalow Town Halt)	Sx	6	LBSCR	1910–1932, 1935–1940 (182/205051)

166	Shoreham-by-Sea	Sx	6	LBR	1840
	Shornecliffe Camp (see Folkestone West)				
167	Sittingbourne (Sittingbourne & Milton Regis)	K	2	LCDR	1858
168	Smeeth	K	1	SER	1852–1954 (172/069384)
169	Snowdon & Nonington Halt	K	2	SECR	1914
170	Sole Street	K	2	LCDR	1861
171	Southampton (temporary)	H	8	LSR	1839–1840 (180/428123)
172	Southampton (Southampton Wes Southampton Central)	H	8	LSWR	1895
173	Southampton Airport	H	8	BR	1966
174	Southampton, Royal Pier	H	8	LSWR	1871–1914 (180/417108)
175	Southampton Terminus (Southampton Town & Docks, Southampton Docks, Southampton)	H	8	LSR	1840–1966 (180/426111)
176	Southampton, West End (Blechynden)	H	8	LSWR	1847–1895 (180/415122)
	Southborough (see High Brooms)				
177	Southbourne Halt	Sx	6	LBSCR	1906
178	Southease & Rodmell Halt	Sx	5	LBSCR	1906
179	Southwick	Sx	6	LBR	1840
180	Staplehurst	K	1	SER	1842
181	Stone Cross Halt	Sx	5	LBSCR	1905–1935 (183/619040)
182	Stonegate (Ticehurst Road, Witherenden)	Sx	4	SER	1851
183	Stonehall & Lyddon Halt	K	2	SECR	1916–1954 (173/269457)
184	Sturry	K	3	SER	1848
185	Swaythling	H	8	LSWR	1883
186	Teynham	K	2	LCDR	1862
187	Three Bridges	Sx	5	LBR	1841
	Ticehurst Road (see Stonegate)				
188	Tonbridge (Tunbridge)	K	1	SER	1842

189	Tunbridge Wells (Jackwood Springs)	K	4	SER	1845–1846 (171/587403)
190	Tunbridge Wells Central (Tunbridge Wells)	K	4	SER	1846
191	Wedhurst	K	4	SER	1851
192	Walmer	K	3	SER & LCDR	1881
193	Warblington Halt (Denville Halt)	H	6	LBSCR	1907
194	Westenhanger	K	1	SER	1844
195	Westgate-on-Sea	K	3	LCDR	1871
196	West St Leonards	Sx	4	SER	1887
197	West Worthing	Sx	6	LBSCR	1889
198	Whitstable Town	K	3	LCDR	1860–1914 (173/109661)
199	Whitstable & Tankerton	K	3	SECR	1915
	Willingdon (see Hampden Park)				
200	Winchester Chesil	H	8	GWR	1885–1960 (168/488292)
201	Winchester (Winchester City)	H	8	LSR	1839
202	Winchfield	H	8	LSR	1838
203	Witley	Su	7	LSWR	1859
204	Wivelsfield (Keymer junction)	Sx	5	LBSCR	1886
205	Woking	Su	8	LSR	1838
206	Woodgate (Bognor)	Sx	6	LBSCR	1846–1864 (181/938043)
207	Worthing (Worthing Central)	Sx	6	LBSCR	1845
208	Wye	K	3	SER	1846
209	Yapton	Sx	6	LBSCR	1846–1847, 1849–1864 (182/981044)

Appendix 4

Electrification 1933-1967

Between 1933 and 1967 all the main lines in Southern England were electrified, except for the route from Tonbridge to St Leonards. This would have been electrified but for the loading gauge restrictions which made it impossible to use standard electric trains. In addition, the section of the original Dover main line between Redhill and Tonbridge still lacks the live rail.

The third rail, low tension, DC system favoured by the Southern is cheaper to install but, because of the impossibility of providing continuous electrical contact, is not suitable for separate electric locomotives. There is also a safety problem in sidings. Initially, the Southern met these problems by working all freight trains and passenger trains from non-electrified lines with steam locomotives. (The multiple-unit passenger trains had their contact shoes sufficiently widely spaced along the length of the train to ensure that they never lost contact with the live rail.) Subsequently, specially designed electric locomotives were developed with a device enabling them to keep moving provided they were not out of contact with the live rail for too long. (Basically this was a fly wheel device which could generate enough electricity to move a locomotive which had been 'gapped'.) The electrification to Dover included some large freight yards, and the problems of both discontinuity of the third rail and of safety, were met by the provision of overhead wires. In addition to collector shoes for the live rail, electric locomotives were provided with pantographs, so that current could be collected either from overhead wires or from the track. However, by the time of the Bournemouth electrification, there were two developments. First, motive power for express passenger trains was provided by four-coach power units which hauled or propelled another four or eight coaches between Waterloo and Bournemouth. The non-powered coaches could be taken on to Weymouth by diesel-electric loco-motives. Second, electro-diesel locomotives were designed which normally ran as electric locomotives, but had a diesel generating set with sufficient power to move them at reduced speeds if they were 'gapped' or for running in sidings or other non-electrified lines. They were particularly useful for hauling boat trains over the non-electri-fied dock lines. There are hopes of completing the electrification of the SER route to Hastings, the line from Southampton to Portsmouth and possibly Reading, Redhill and Tonbridge in the not too distant future.

In the following table, the mileages are approximate.

		Route mileage electrified
1933	Three Bridges–Brighton	$21\frac{1}{4}$
	Brighton–West Worthing	$11\frac{1}{2}$
	Preston Park–Hove	$1\frac{1}{2}$
1935	Keymer Junction–Lewes	9
	Brighton–Ore	$35\frac{1}{2}$
	Polegate–Eastbourne	$4\frac{3}{4}$
	Southerham junction–Seaford	8
1937	Guildford–Portsmouth Harbour	44
1938	Horsham–Havant	$40\frac{3}{4}$
	West Worthing–Ford	$8\frac{1}{4}$
	Littlehampton and Bognor lines	$5\frac{1}{4}$
1939	Meopham–Gillingham	10
1959	Gillingham–Ramsgate	$44\frac{1}{2}$
	Faversham–Dover	$26\frac{1}{2}$
1961	Buckland junction–Ramsgate	$21\frac{1}{2}$
	Tonbridge–Dover	47
	Ashford–Minster	$25\frac{3}{4}$
1967	Woking–Southampton (and on to Bournemouth)	$55\frac{3}{4}$

Appendix 5

Lines in Southern England in Receipt of Grant in Accordance with Transport Act 1968

Amounts payable for the year 1970

THREE YEAR GRANTS (1970, 1971, 1972)
  Reading–Guildford–Redhill–Tonbridge (£459,000)
TWO YEAR GRANTS (1970, 1971)
  Portsmouth–Southampton–Salisbury/Fareham–Eastleigh

(£690,000)

In addition, a sum of £15,000,000 for London Commuter services which operate on all the lines in Southern England except those mentioned above. The following lines are included:

SOUTHERN REGION, SOUTH WESTERN DIVISION
  From Waterloo to Portsmouth; Alton; Basingstoke and Southampton.
SOUTHERN REGION, CENTRAL DIVISION
  From Victoria to Uckfield via Oxted and Ashurst; Portsmouth via Horsham and Arundel; Bognor via Dorking and via Redhill; Littlehampton via Dorking and via Hove; Brighton; Ore via Lewes and Eastbourne; Portsmouth and Bognor via Redhill.
  Lewes to Seaford; Brighton to Eastbourne; Tonbridge to Eridge via Tunbridge Wells.

SOUTHERN REGION, SOUTH EASTERN DIVISION

From Charing Cross/Cannon Street to Ashford, Dover, Deal, Canterbury, Ramsgate; Ramsgate via Strood and Herne Bay; Hastings.

From Victoria to Margate via Maidstone, Ashford and Canterbury; Sheerness; Ramsgate and Dover via Faversham.

Paddock Wood–Maidstone West–Strood; Sittingbourne–Sheerness.

NOTES

In these notes the current volume is designated 'Volume One'. The companion volumes on *Secondary & Branch Lines* (Batsford, 1974) and *Independent Railways* (projected for 1975) are referred to as 'Volumes Two and Three'.

Chapter 1

1 Neither idea was impossible. The 'pannier' idea materialised on the Listowel & Ballybunion Railway in Ireland, while sail propulsion was used on the Spurn Head Railway and—unofficially —on the Thames Haven branch of the London, Tilbury & Southend Railway and on a private line at Cliffe in Kent. (See Volume Three, Chapter 6.)

2 'Are you the first person who has found out this chalk rock is valuable for cement; did you discover it? Last year I did.' Minutes of evidence before parliamentary committee, SER Bill, 24 March 1836.

3 See Chapter 4.

4 See Volume Two, Chapter 5.

5 As late as 1952, 4,442 hop pickers and 23,000 friends were conveyed by special trains to Paddock Wood.

6 See Volume Three, Chapter 3.

7 See Chapters 3 and 4.

8 See Volume Two, Chapter 2.

9 SER 0–6–0 no. 65, built at Ashford in 1896 and SECR 0–4–4 no. 263, built at Ashford in 1905.

10 See Volume Two, Chapter 5.

11 See Volume Two, Chapter 5.

12 See Volume Three, Chapter 4.

13 A link span is due to open in 1972.

Chapter 2

1 The three crossings had been closed by the end of 1971.

2 See Volume Two, Chapter 5.

3 See Volume Three, Chapter 4.

4 See Volume One, Chapter 3.

Chapter 3

1 See Volume Two, Chapter 1.
2 See Volume Three, Chapter 6.
3 See Volume Two, Chapter 1.
4 See Volume Three, Chapter 6.
5 See Volume Three, Chapter 6.
6 See Volume Three, Chapter 5.

Chapter 4

1 The contractor appears to have reduced the brick lining by one course of bricks. When this was discovered, the extra lining had to be inserted, thus reducing clearances still further.
2 Electrification was proposed in 1938, but it was finally decided to give priority to the Otford junction to Maidstone East line.
3 See Volume Three, Chapter 6.
4 See Volume Two, Chapter 6.

Chapter 5

1 See Chapter 4.
2 See Volume Two, Chapter 3.
3 See Volume Two, Chapter 3.
4 See Volume Two, Chapter 3.
5 See Volume Two, Chapter 6.
6 It has been suggested that the present building is the result of reconstruction in 1890. (Wikeley and Middleton: *Railway Stations, Southern Region*).
7 See Volume Two, Chapter 3.
8 See Volume Two, Chapter 3.
9 See Chapter 4.
10 See Volume Two, Chapter 3.
11 See Volume Three, Chapter 6.

Chapter 6

1 See Volume Two, Chapter 6.
2 See Volume Two, Chapter 3.

3 See Volume Two, Chapter 6.
4 See Volume Two, Chapter 6.
5 See Volume Three, Chapter 3.
6 See Volume Two, Chapter 3.
7 I am indebted to Mr J. Bagley for information on Shoreham and other airports on the Sussex coastal plain.
8 See Volume Three, Chapter 3.
9 See Volume Two, Chapter 6.
10 See Volume Two, Chapter 6.
11 See Volume Two, Chapter 6.
12 The Arundel to Littlehampton local service was withdrawn on and from 1 May 1972.

Chapter 7

1 See Volume Two, Chapter 2.
2 See Volume Three, Chapter 2.
3 See Volume Two, Chapter 6.
4 See Volume Two, Chapter 6.
5 See Volume Two, Chapter 7.
6 See Volume Two, Chapter 2.
7 See Volume Two, Chapter 6.
8 See Volume Three, Chapter 6.
9 See Volume Two, Chapter 6.
10 See Volume Three, Chapter 6.
11 See Volume Two, Chapter 7.
12 In 1972 the Hayling Island platform and the goods shed were demolished.
13 Stockheath crossing was closed by 1972.
14 See Volume Two, Chapter 3.
15 See Volume Two, Chapter 7.

Chapter 8

1 See Volume Two, Chapter 7.
2 See Volume Two, Chapter 2.
3 See Chapter 7.
4 See Volume Two, Chapter 7.
5 See Volume Two, Chapter 7.
6 See Volume Two, Chapter 3.

7   See Volume Three, Chapter 2.
8   See Volume Three, Chapter 6.
9   See Volume Two, Chapter 2.
10 See Volume Three, Chapter 6.
11 Unfortunately, they were demolished in 1972.
12 See Volume Three, Chapters 2 and 6.
13 See Volume Two, Chapter 7.
14 See Volume Two, Chapter 3.
15 See Volume Three, Chapter 6.

Index